Essays in Life Writing

This book showcases a unique, innovative form for contemporary life narrative scholarship. Life Narrative is a dynamic and interdisciplinary field defined through attention to diverse styles of personal and auto/biographical narration and to subjectivity and ethics in acts of self-representation. The essay is a uniquely sympathetic mode for such scholarship, responsive to diverse methods, genres, and concepts and enabling a flexible, hybrid critical and creative approach. Many of the essays curated for this volume are by the authors of creative works of life writing who are seeking to reflect critically on disciplinary issues connected to practice, ethics, audience, or genre. Others show academics from a variety of disciplinary backgrounds engaged in creative critical self-reflection, using methods of cultural analysis, ethnography, or embodied scholarship to address foundational and emerging issues and concepts in relation to identity, experience, or subjectivity.

Essays in Life Writing positions the essay as a unique nexus of creative and critical practice, available to academics publishing peer-reviewed scholarly work from a variety of disciplinary backgrounds, and a form of scholarship that is contributing in exciting and vigorous ways to the development of new knowledge in Life Narrative as a field.

The chapters in this book were originally published as a special issue of the journal *Life Writing*.

Kylie Cardell is Senior Lecturer in English at Flinders University, South Australia. She is the author of *Dear World: Contemporary Uses of the Diary*, and editor (with Kate Douglas) of *Telling Tales: Autobiographies of Childhood and Youth*. Kylie is an executive member for the International Auto/Biography Association (IABA) Asia-Pacific and co-directs the Flinders Life Narrative Research Group (Flinders University). She is the Essays editor for the scholarly Australian journal *Life Writing*.

Life Writing
Academic Editor: **Maureen Perkins**, *Macquarie University, Australia*

Life Writing, founded in 2004 by Mary Besemeres and Maureen Perkins, is one of the leading journals in the field of biography and autobiography.

Its title indicates that it reaches beyond traditional interpretations of biography and autobiography as genres belonging solely in the study of literature. It welcomes work from any discipline that discusses the nature of the self and self-expression and how these interact with the process of recording a life. Life writing is about expanding the ways in which we understand how lives are represented.

The journal has a special, though not exclusive, interest in cross-cultural experience. It also has the unique and unusual policy of carrying both scholarly articles and critically informed personal narrative. It is published four times a year and its editorial board comprises leaders in the field of life writing practice.

Trauma Texts
Edited by Gillian Whitlock and Kate Douglas

Poetry and Autobiography
Edited by Jo Gill and Melanie Waters

International Life Writing
Memory and Identity in Global Context
Edited by Paul Longley Arthur

Dissenting Lives
Edited by Anne Collett and Tony Simoes da Silva

Border Crossings
Essays in Identity and Belonging
Edited by Paul Longley Arthur and Leena Kurvet-Käosaar

The Selfless Ego
Configurations of Identity in Tibetan Life Writing
Edited by Lucia Galli and Franz Xaver Erhard

Essays in Life Writing
Edited by Kylie Cardell

For more information about this series, please visit:
www.routledge.com/Life-Writing/book-series/LFWR

Essays in Life Writing

Edited by
Kylie Cardell

LONDON AND NEW YORK

First published 2022
by Routledge
2 Park Square, Milton Park, Abingdon, Oxon OX14 4RN

and by Routledge
605 Third Avenue, New York, NY 10158

Routledge is an imprint of the Taylor & Francis Group, an informa business

Introduction, Chapters 1–10, 12 and 13 © 2022 Taylor & Francis or SOCIETY
Chapter 11 © 2019 Linus Hagström. Originally published as Open Access.

With the exception of Chapter 11, no part of this book may be reprinted or reproduced or utilised in any form or by any electronic, mechanical, or other means, now known or hereafter invented, including photocopying and recording, or in any information storage or retrieval system, without permission in writing from the publishers. For details on the rights for Chapter 11, please see the chapter's Open Access footnote.

Trademark notice: Product or corporate names may be trademarks or registered trademarks, and are used only for identification and explanation without intent to infringe.

British Library Cataloguing in Publication Data
A catalogue record for this book is available from the British Library

ISBN: 978-1-032-10739-4 (hbk)
ISBN: 978-1-032-10742-4 (pbk)
ISBN: 978-1-003-21682-7 (ebk)

DOI: 10.4324/9781003216827

Typeset in Minion Pro
by Newgen Publishing UK

Publisher's Note
The publisher accepts responsibility for any inconsistencies that may have arisen during the conversion of this book from journal articles to book chapters, namely the inclusion of journal terminology.

Disclaimer
Every effort has been made to contact copyright holders for their permission to reprint material in this book. The publishers would be grateful to hear from any copyright holder who is not here acknowledged and will undertake to rectify any errors or omissions in future editions of this book.

Contents

Citation Information		vii
Notes on Contributors		ix
	Introduction	1
	Kylie Cardell	
1	Writing (from) the Rubble: Reflections on the August 4, 2020 Explosion in Beirut, Lebanon	7
	Sleiman El Hajj	
2	Will the Real Subject Please Stand Up? Autobiographical Voices in Biography	24
	Karen Lamb	
3	Speculative Biography and Countering Archival Absences of Women Clowns in the Circus	30
	Katerina Bryant	
4	'A Man of Violent and Ungovernable Temper': Can Fiction Fill Silences in the Archives?	44
	Katherine E Collins	
5	Killing the Silent Witness: The Benefits of an Authorial Stance as Interpreter in Future-focused Natural Biography	51
	Sarah Pye	
6	How to be a Fan in the Age of Problematic Faves	64
	Matt Bucher and Grace Chipperfield	
7	Letter Writing and Space for Women's Self-expression in Janet Frame's *Owls Do Cry* and Jane Campion's *An Angel at My Table*	76
	Hannah Matthews	
8	In Parallel With My Actual Diary: On Re-writing an Exile	92
	Chris Campanioni	

9 Metaphor and Neonatal Death: How Stories Can Help
When a Baby Dies at Birth 109
Tamarin Norwood

10 Three Wheels on My Wagon: An Account of an Attempt to Use Life Writing
to Access Shared Family Narratives After Bereavement 121
Jane Hughes

11 Becoming a Traitor 130
Linus Hagström

12 My Obscure Career as an Aspiring Poet 139
Eugene Stelzig

13 Archive of the (Mostly) Unspoken: A Queer Project of Caring for the Dead 149
Margot Francis

Index 163

Citation Information

The chapters in this book were originally published in the journal *Life Writing*, volume 18, issue 1 (2021). When citing this material, please use the original page numbering for each article, as follows:

Introduction
Kylie Cardell
Life Writing, volume 18, issue 1 (2021), pp. 1–6

Chapter 1
Writing (from) the Rubble: Reflections on the August 4, 2020 Explosion in Beirut, Lebanon
Sleiman El Hajj
Life Writing, volume 18, issue 1 (2021), pp. 7–23

Chapter 2
Will the Real Subject Please Stand Up? Autobiographical Voices in Biography
Karen Lamb
Life Writing, volume 18, issue 1 (2021), pp. 25–30

Chapter 3
Speculative Biography and Countering Archival Absences of Women Clowns in the Circus
Katerina Bryant
Life Writing, volume 18, issue 1 (2021), pp. 31–44

Chapter 4
'A Man of Violent and Ungovernable Temper': Can Fiction Fill Silences in the Archives?
Katherine E Collins
Life Writing, volume 18, issue 1 (2021), pp. 45–51

Chapter 5
Killing the Silent Witness: The Benefits of an Authorial Stance as Interpreter in Future-focused Natural Biography
Sarah Pye
Life Writing, volume 18, issue 1 (2021), pp. 53–65

Chapter 6

How to be a Fan in the Age of Problematic Faves
Matt Bucher and Grace Chipperfield
Life Writing, volume 18, issue 1 (2021), pp. 67–78

Chapter 7

Letter Writing and Space for Women's Self-expression in Janet Frame's Owls Do Cry *and Jane Campion's* An Angel at My Table
Hannah Matthews
Life Writing, volume 18, issue 1 (2021), pp. 79–94

Chapter 8

In Parallel With My Actual Diary: On Re-writing an Exile
Chris Campanioni
Life Writing, volume 18, issue 1 (2021), pp. 95–111

Chapter 9

Metaphor and Neonatal Death: How Stories Can Help When a Baby Dies at Birth
Tamarin Norwood
Life Writing, volume 18, issue 1 (2021), pp. 113–124

Chapter 10

Three Wheels on My Wagon: An Account of an Attempt to Use Life Writing to Access Shared Family Narratives After Bereavement
Jane Hughes
Life Writing, volume 18, issue 1 (2021), pp. 125–133

Chapter 11

Becoming a Traitor
Linus Hagström
Life Writing, volume 18, issue 1 (2021), pp. 135–143

Chapter 12

My Obscure Career as an Aspiring Poet
Eugene Stelzig
Life Writing, volume 18, issue 1 (2021), pp. 145–154

Chapter 13

Archive of the (Mostly) Unspoken: A Queer Project of Caring for the Dead
Margot Francis
Life Writing, volume 18, issue 1 (2021), pp. 155–168

For any permission-related enquiries please visit:
www.tandfonline.com/page/help/permissions

Notes on Contributors

Katerina Bryant is South Australian-based writer and PhD student at Flinders University. Her work has appeared in Griffith Review, The Guardian and Island magazine, amongst others. Katerina's first book is *Hysteria: A Memoir of Illness Strength and Women's Stories Throughout History*.

Matt Bucher is independent scholar and the managing editor of the Journal of David Foster Wallace Studies. He also co-hosts a podcast devoted to Wallace (The Great Concavity) and serves as the administrator of wallace-l, the David Foster Wallace listserv. His writing has appeared in Publishers Weekly, Dublin Review of Books, Electric Literature, and other places. He lives in Austin, Texas.

Chris Campanioni is the author of seven books, including *A and B and Also Nothing* (Otis Books | Seismicity Editions, 2020), a re-writing of Henry James's *The American* and Gertrude Stein's 'Americans' which merges theory, fiction, and autobiography. He teaches at Pace University and Baruch College, and is a Provost Fellow at The Graduate Center/CUNY, where he works on the convergence between migration and media studies.

Kylie Cardell is Senior Lecturer in English at Flinders University, South Australia. She is the author of *Dear World: Contemporary Uses of the Diary* (2014), and editor (with Kate Douglas) of *Telling Tales: Autobiographies of Childhood and Youth* (2015). Kylie is an executive member for the International Auto/Biography Association (IABA) Asia-Pacific and co-directs the Flinders Life Narrative Research Group (Flinders University). She is the Essays editor of the scholarly Australian journal Life Writing.

Grace Chipperfield is Fulbright Scholar and tutor in English and Creative Writing at Flinders University, South Australia. She recently completed her PhD in Creative Writing, a collection of essays on David Foster Wallace and his fans. She is on the board of the International David Foster Wallace Society and an associate editor for The Journal of David Foster Wallace Studies.

Katherine E Collins has held research posts at UWE and Goldsmiths College and is currently working on the Andrew W. Mellon-funded Humanities & Identities project at TORCH. Her research interests include the creative and critical practices involved in the writing of marginalized and activist lives, issues like the politics and poetics of life-writing, testimonial cultures and witnessing, and autobiographies of resistance.

Sleiman El Hajj is Assistant Professor of Creative and Journalistic Writing in the departments of English and Communication Arts at the Lebanese American University. He was appointed Visiting Research Fellow at the Department of International Development, University of Oxford, in 2019. His research interests include creative nonfiction, gender studies, narrative constructions of home, queer theory, and Middle Eastern literature.

Margot Francis is Associate Professor in Women's and Gender Studies, cross appointed to the Department of Sociology at Brock University.

Linus Hagström is professor of political science at the Swedish Defence University. He analyses East Asian security from power and identity perspectives. Recent publications appeared in Cambridge Review of International Affairs, International Studies Review, Journal of Japanese Studies, Survival and European Journal of International Relations. Hagström is also a senior research fellow at the Swedish Institute of International Affairs.

Jane Hughes is studying for a PhD in Creative Writing, exploring creative uses of memoir in the twenty-first century. She is a psychotherapist in private practice in Manchester, UK.

Karen Lamb is author of *Thea Astley: Inventing Her Own Weather* (2015), shortlisted for five national literary awards, and winner of the prestigious Prime Minister's Award for Non-Fiction for 2016. She has edited a book of Australian short stories, and published book chapters and articles on Australian authors, including a book on Peter Carey. She lives in Sydney and teaches literature at the Australian Catholic University.

Hannah Matthews is Early Career academic at Cardiff University. She has a particular interest in the varying forms of women's creative work and how these forms illuminate contemporary social roles. She explores the nature of letter writing as an entry point to academic exploration, with a consideration of how this form may contend within the canonisation of writing by women through the passage of time. Her work is feminist in its approach, but critically analytic of the evolving nature of feminism.

Tamarin Norwood gained her doctorate in Fine Art as a Clarendon scholar at the University of Oxford in 2018 and is now postdoctoral research fellow at the Drawing Research Group, Loughborough University, writing a book on metaphor and neonatal loss. Tamarin's scholarly publications focus on representation and loss in drawing; her related prose fiction, poetry and artwork have been published and shown widely including with the BBC World Service, Art on the Underground, ICA Philadelphia, MOCCA Toronto and Tate Britain.

Sarah Pye is Doctor of Creative Arts candidate at the University of the Sunshine Coast (USC), Queensland. Her creative non-fiction artefact, Saving Sun Bears, focuses on the life of Founder and Director of the Bornean Sun Bear Conservation Centre (BSBCC), Dr Wong Siew Te. Pye's previous publication, a guidebook called *Kids Welcome to Queensland* (2009) led to her award as 2010 Sunshine Coast Small Business Woman of the Year.

Eugene Stelzig works at Department of English, State University of New York [SUNY], Geneseo, NY, USA.

Introduction

Kylie Cardell

In *Essayism*, his 2017 critical lyrical essay (inevitably) on the essay as genre, Brian Dillon opens with a kind of textual performance: a teeming list of examples, oblique references to unnamed essayists, a litany of topics and a profusion of content, discursive, paratactic and contradictory. This performs, Dillon observes, something of the effect that the term 'essay' denotes: 'Imagine a type of writing so hard to define that its very name should be something like: an effort, an attempt, a trial' (2017, 12). Essays can be partial and contingent, doubtful or incomplete and these qualities are values. 'What holds these tendencies together? Classically, we say it is the writing "I" ' (Dillon 2017, 18).

As I have discussed elsewhere, the essay is a flexible scholarly mode that allows for fragmentation, disparity, doubt and openness and that strategically privileges a personal subjective point of view (Cardell 2019). As such, the essay is a way of speaking and a mode of epistemology that hasn't always seemed to fit comfortably into academia, and specifically academic institutional frameworks, even in disciplinary traditions where 'essays' are well-established as a mode of scholarly discourse. Here's the feminist philosopher Jane Tompkins in 1987, getting to the point:

> I say to hell with it. The reason I feel embarrassed at my own attempts to speak personally in a professional context is that I have been conditioned to feel that way. That's all there is to it. I think people are scared to talk about themselves, that they haven't got the guts to do it. I think readers want to know about each other. Sometimes, when a writer introduces some personal bit of story into an essay, I can hardly contain my pleasure. I love writers who write about their own experience. I feel I'm being nourished by them, that I'm being allowed to enter into a personal relationship with them, that I can match my own experience with theirs, feel cousin to them, and say, yes, that's how it is. (Tompkins 1987, 169–170)

Tompkins is arguing for a shift away from objectivity as a dominant narrative position and she uses an arresting image, one that reminds us that genre too is a form of power. Tompkins has found herself in a state of opposing tension, as though two beings: 'one writes for professional journals; the other in diaries, late at night' (2017, 169). It is, of course, a 'false dichotomy' and Tompkins refuses to be cleaved. The personal is in the professional; the diary is a form of knowledge: 'You can't get behind the thing that casts the shadow. You cast the shadow. As soon as you turn, the shadow falls in another place. Is still your shadow' (Tompkins 1987, 174). Essays are wonderfully full of shadows.

The kind of work that is published in *Life Writing* as Essays, and collected here for this special issue, might best be described as part of a continuum. Like other peer-reviewed academic nonfiction (or what *Life Writing* distinguishes as Articles), essays in general mobilise evidence-based and verifiable information about a topic or experience but, unlike most academic writing, they may also juxtapose this to an overtly personal or subjective point of view. Essays can function (and this is crucial) as both scholarship and literature: seeking to entertain, to build empathy and to craft a satisfying plot or meaningful arc. The essay, as Dillon observes, often has a pleasure-function – a characteristic that has tended to elevate or reduce the genre's value, depending on your point of view (22).

As this collection demonstrates, *Life Writing* essays cover a diverse field of topics and present scholars in various degrees of self-reflexivity and self-consciousness, exploring various issues from both personal and disciplinary perspectives, harnessing the essay's ability to tell a story at the same time as to make a larger argument or point. Rachel Robertson and Paul Hetherington have argued that essays may encourage readers to question themselves in self-reflexive ways, rather than simply act as passive recipients (2016). For some scholars, their use of the essay within a context of scholarship might also be seen as a form of activism. Certainly, many of the essays collected here seek to raise issues of systemic injustice or to reveal more about broader socio-cultural or historical contexts that are also connected to individual experience. Others explore issues of method and ethics, and a notable feature of the essays collected here are examples of exegetical work that explore and reflect on acts of life writing from the point of view of the life writer.

This issue opens with an essay that is seeking not only to explain, drawing on disciplinary knowledge from trauma theory and cultural studies, but also to witness a recent experience of trauma that is yet ongoing. In 'Writing (from) the Rubble: Reflections on the August 4, 2020 Explosion in Beirut, Lebanon', Sleijman El Hajj uses diary, a life-writing form associated with temporality and liveness, to structure a discursive account of the aftermath and legacy of a shocking explosion in Beirut. El Hajj's essay is a breaking account, narrated over the course of a week. For citizens of Beirut, this event is not only new; it brings with it echoes of historical trauma that El Hajj contextualises to political and cultural life in Lebanon. 'It has happened again,' sobs El Hajj's friend Kirsty, 'they tried to kill us again'. Kirsty has lived in Beirut for twenty years; her apartment is 'a warren of ornate woodwork and damask tapestries', full of carefully curated curiosities, beloved antiques and precious art, now 'smashed to the floor: I notice these for they orientate me'. El Hajj's essay facilitates a complex act of witnessing and mourning; testimony and scholarship, reason and feeling are inextricably intertwined and powerfully mobilised.

Contributors to *Life Writing* essays are often authors of published works of nonfiction and seeking to reflect on and think through disciplinary questions in relation to form, genre, ethics that have been encountered through the act of creating a life-writing text. Donna Lee Brien and Quinn Eades have noted recently that contemporary life writing is increasingly a genre in which those '*doing*' life writing are also those '*thinking about*' life writing (2018, 3) and 'Essays' is a particularly lively and resonant space for such work. Notably, several essayists in this collection are also the authors of published biographies. In 'Will the real subject please stand up? Autobiographical Voices in Biography', Karen Lamb tackles one of the key issues in biographical writing, one that, in the 'afterlife' of publication, she now sees in a different light. Lamb's musing essay makes a case for more nuanced approaches to the biographer's art. 'Autobiography in the biography' is inevitable, but Lamb here draws attention to the need for complexity in thinking about the biographical 'I' and she illustrates some of the richness such attention might produce.

The biographical 'I' is also of interest to Katerina Bryant, who is currently navigating the writing of a biography. In 'Speculative Biography and Countering Archival Absences of Women Clowns in the Circus', Bryant is 'looking for Loretta', the first female clown in America and a ground-breaking performer of whom little has been left by way of archival records or documentation. As she reflects on her creative process, part of which involves 'combining' archival records of circus performers contemporaneous to Loretta, Bryant negotiates with foundational issues for life writers and academics. 'Countering' gaps in the archive is a project that must negotiate with both limits and possibilities in relation to biographical speculation and Bryant turns careful attention to the politics and ethics of such work.

Katherine Collins' essay, ' "A Man of Violent and Ungovernable Temper": Can Fiction Fill Silences in the Archives?' also reflects on biographical writing in connection to archival research, specifically, on the use of 'biofiction'. Where Bryant uses 'researching around' to speculate about aspects of life and character for her biographical subject, while still retaining a status as biographical nonfiction, Collins works towards creating an experimental piece that shows life writing self-consciously transformed into 'something more like fiction'. Braiding creative and critical reflection, Collins' vivid and original exploration of creative methodology engages with key scholarly issues of ethics and the politics of genre negotiating the 'silences' in the archives and it performs this for the reader through the presentation of creative examples that illustrate and usefully compound the points being made.

In her essay, Sarah Pye reflects on authoring a biography on the Malaysian naturalist-environmentalist Dr Wong Siew Te, whose important scientific work on the Malayan sun bear led to a decades long personal campaign. Amidst the significance of a range of political issues to do with conservation and environmentalism in South East Asia in particular, Pye details the narrative, authorial choices that this biography needed to negotiate with. Pye discusses the established idea of the biographer as 'silent witness' but argues for a subjective interpretive stance. This is not a new idea, but Pye's discussion of why such a stance might be particularly relevant in a biographical story seeking to contribute positively to environmental outcomes is fresh and important.

While many of the essays for this special issue reflect on creative process and life writing, some directly use creative forms that interrogate generic boundaries of scholarly or creative, revealing the essay as a vibrantly cross-discursive mode. In 'How to be a Fan' Matt Bucher and Grace Chipperfield use the form of letter, and a role as correspondents, to work through a problem of 'moral responsibility': both are fans of David Foster Wallace and both are troubled by various revelations made about his personal life, and that continue to surface. One of the key contexts for Bucher and Chipperfield's correspondence is the digital landscape of social media, through which Wallace's reputation has both flourished or been 'cancelled', sometimes in equal parts. Of course, the letter is also the classic mode of the fan; the letter is a devotional mode and a genre of romance. In time-honoured epistolary fashion, Bucher and Chipperfield are fans who write to each other about their 'problematic fave', addressing and elaborating thoughts and drawing on a range of ideas and references from literary theory, for example, Rita Felski's work on postcritique, through to popular culture.

Letters also feature in Hannah Matthews' essay, 'Letter Writing and Space for Women's Self-expression in Janet Frame's *Owls Do Cry* and Jane Campion's *An Angel at My Table*'. Here, the letter is addressed to a correspondent who cannot reply. These letters might be considered 'unsent' but they are no less full of desire for response or connection: 'I am searching for you, Miss Frame', writes Matthews (1). A genre of writing often associated with the domestic, seen as private and emotional – used for the fostering of friendship, the fanning of romance, as much as for imparting information or communication – letters remain, as Matthews observes, a way of expressing knowledge that yet seems counter to the 'fixed form for writing intellectually' that 'is prescribed as the precursor to academic success' (3).

Issues of form and prestige that Matthews alludes to in her essay are also significant for Chris Campanioni in 'In Parallel with my Actual Diary: On Re-Writing an Exile'. Through creative repurposing and collage of archival letters, Campanioni retells the seven-year exile of German philosopher and writer Walter Benjamin. In doing so, Campanioni reclaims a personal, autobiographical story of migration and exile that also seeks to draw attention to the ongoing story of displaced persons that continues today. Does scholarship adequately account for the body, for the life of the academic who writes? Campanioni was a child 'born to two exiles', whose trajectory as writer, instructor, researcher has been crucially informed by lived experience: 'who could only theorise a migratory text by looking first and my own life, where so much of the personal has been deferred or dislocated through the institutionalised agenda of objectivity and distance […] Everything I wish to theorise goes through the body first' (1-2).

For many academics, even when their scholarship is connected deeply to personal interest or lived experience, an emphasis on theoretical knowledge as an intellectual, professional hallmark has seemed to presuppose the expression and incorporation of either feeling or experience. It is notable that several essays included in this special issue centre, as Campanioni does, on 'the body – inextricable and intimate' within the context of professional academic and scholarly work. The essay thus reveals itself as distinctive form through which an academic can make visible personal intersections in relation to the work of scholarship, something powerfully explored in Tamsin Norwood's essay, 'Metaphor and Neonatal Death: How Stories Can Help When a Baby Dies at Birth'. Norwood's story of neo-natal infant loss is personal; it is a bodily, emotional experience and an event that affects all within her family. Her story is both unique and, in crucial ways, all too common. Yet, as Norwood explains: the story of parent bereavement is 'uniquely under-served by the stories and cultural scripts we usually depend upon to make sense of death' (1). Norwood finds herself in an 'unexpected' position: 'the neonatal loss of our son and [my] research specialism in metaphors of liminality' present an opportunity to intervene in and explore the story of parent bereavement from a dual perspective. Here, the personal is a catalyst for academic enquiry but it is also part of that enquiry, functioning as illustration and evidence in a powerful and affective mode.

In 'Three Wheels on my Wagon: An Account of an Attempt to Use Life Writing to Access Shared Family Narratives After Bereavement', Jane Hughes offers a corollary discussion that might be read usefully alongside Norwood's account. Hughes' essay recounts the loss of the author's mother and explores an experience of using life writing as part of a communal grieving process for the family. Hughes offers here a rich qualitative discussion, she includes long excerpts of narrative from the members of her family who participated in the life writing exercise and these excerpts are instructive. Like life writing, grief and bereavement are relational. When Hughes reflects on the different accounts produced by family members, she finds unexpected pain but also healing and reconciliation. 'The wheels are coming off', says Hughes (8). The journey is worth the ride.

The issue ends with work that sites more towards autoethnography, essays that, while employing a self-reflexive 'I', are less interested in overtly theorising or interrogating genre. In 'Becoming a Traitor', Linus Hagstrom uses the mode of confession to document (and talk back to) a dislocating experience of social and professional shame. After his opinion piece criticising the NATO transatlantic military alliance is printed in Sweden's main daily newspaper, Hagström finds himself stigmatised by colleagues at his military-aligned University as well as by friends and in public. Hagström's autobiographical essay witnesses to the personal struggle and cost that the author experienced in the aftermath of an unpopular commentary on a highly political topic. Eugene Stelzig similarly uses the essay as mode to narrate and think personally about a professional challenge. In his thoughtful, wry essay 'My Obscure Career as an Aspiring Poet', Stelzig narrates a side-career spent 'aspiring' to publish poetry but acquiring mostly rejection slips. While 'My Obscure Career' details its author's lack of success in achieving publication, it also reveals the immensely difficult landscape of small, literary (and so almost by default, poetry) publishing and the arcane workings of literary prestige and reputation that can also trace (or obscure) a career in writing. Both Stelzig and Hagström articulate a sense of personal grief in relation to public contexts for loss or shame. In 'Archive of the Mostly Unspoken: A Queer Project of Caring for the Dead' Margot Francis explores 'family silence' and a corollary public and private context for the family archive: 'How does one make sense of an archive of the unspoken, interrupted by rare and traumatic speech? How does one interpret a familial heritage founded on deeply contradictory evidence?' Francis' beautifully composed essay is a deeply felt and meticulously theorised autoethnography that offers a personal story of witnessing, recognition and 'condolence' within a framework of queer history and politics.

This collection curates a selection of recent examples by scholars reflecting on experiences connected to their professional identity, personal aspirations – their work and life – and who are deploying the flexibility of the essay as a form for both *doing* and *thinking, about* life writing and related disciplinary issues. While *Life Writing* also publishes 'articles', which are then distinct to 'essays', it is clear that these forms are in fact entwined modes for publishing scholarly research and analysis. Essays contribute to disciplinary knowledge and literacy in important and creative ways, and the flourishing state of examples in this genre shows that readers and writers continue to be invested in these as forms of knowledge that make visible the 'shadow' as well as the subject.

Disclosure statement

No potential conflict of interest was reported by the author(s).

References

Brien, Donna Lee, and Quinn Eades, eds. 2018. *Offshoot. Contemporary Life Writing Methodologies and Practice.* Perth: UWAP.

Cardell, Kylie. 2019. "The Essay as Life Writing: The Year in Australia." *Biography* 42 (1): 1–8.

Dillon, Brian. 2017. *Essayism.* Fizcaraldo Editions.

Robertson, Rachel, and Paul Hetherington. 2016. "A Mosaic Patterning: Space, Time and the Lyric Essay." *New Writing: The International Journal for the Practice and Theory of Creative Writing* 14 (1): 36–46.

Tompkins, Jane. 1987. "Me and My Shadow." *New Literary History* 19 (1): 169–178.

Writing (from) the Rubble: Reflections on the August 4, 2020 Explosion in Beirut, Lebanon

Sleiman El Hajj [iD]

ABSTRACT
This reflexive piece integrates its author's experience of Beirut's August 4, 2020 port explosion with those of other Lebanese citizens writing on the heels of the calamity. The overall narrative approximates a collective biography that apprises and appraises the emergent fears, concerns, and anxieties roiling the country at present. I explore a lived, critically informed, spectrum of post-traumatic behaviours and responses to the widespread destruction and its implications – whether that be the loss of limb, home, or the physical loci of emotional memories, including cultural and heritage sites. The narrative also makes a connection between the recent explosion and earlier iterations of warfare and/or terrorism to show how the long-standing inability to functionally articulate and process pain is now translating into retributive calls for violent justice in a country still recovering from civil war.

August 4, 2020

I am barely parked on the street outside Kristy's[1] apartment block when I'm thrown off my feet and slammed against the trunk of a neem tree on the other side of the road; the dense foliage provides cover from the various windows that continue raining glass for at least two minutes after I regain consciousness, get back on my feet, and start running toward the building entrance.

Frantic thoughts course through my head. What has just happened? Can it be another bomb? Is Kristy hurt? For nearly twenty years, Kristy has been a trusted mentor and friend. I often refer to her as my literary mother – the researcher, artist, and author who has helped launch my career, and always carves time to listen when personal demons get loud. This is our first get-together in months, a once-weekly rendezvous that Coronavirus has halted.

There is no need to buzz me in. The main door to the building is lying shattered, along with its frame, in the middle of the road. I see no porters and there is no electricity. I sprint up the six floors to her apartment. The same scene repeats itself on every landing. There is debris and destruction, and unhinged doors, and broken glass. I hear people screaming and frightened dogs howling; maids in blood-sullied uniforms are speaking frantically on their phones; there are groans, cursing, and exhortations. An elderly man is scrambling down the stairs in his underwear; there are a few more unhinged doors, including, finally, Kristy's.

I walk in, unannounced, into Kristy's home, a warren of ornate woodwork and damask tapestries, most rooms crowded to her content, and to her parents' before her, with furniture and *objets d'art*. Her antique chests, carefully collected over the years, are now dangling, open on their hinges, their contents of chinaware, cloisonné boxes, and other curiosities smashed to the floor: I notice these, for they orientate me. And there sits Kristy, dazed, surrounded by debris, playing the piano from memory. I collapse on the divan next to her.

'You are here,' she says. 'You're bleeding.'

She fetches a first-aid kit, and does her best to clean the scratches, bruises, and blood on my face. 'You will need to go to ER, but it will be the apocalypse there.'

Our long experience with catastrophe has taught us the basics of emergency relief, and that when needed to help, to do so stoically. But then Kristy breaks down, crying softly at first and then louder, keeling over.

'It has happened again,' she says in between sobs. 'It has happened again. They tried to kill us again.'

Indeed, this is not the first time in our history that our state tries to kill us, and looking back, Kristy's reaction does not surprise me. After all, despite our age difference, we have both lived through the Lebanese Civil War (1975–1990), experienced numerous Israeli insurgencies, were almost killed in the terrorist bombing that burned our prime minister alive in 2005, and lost loved ones in the July 2006 war. We were reading in a café by the 'Corniche,' Beirut's famed seaside promontory, when one politician was assassinated nearby in 2006, and were lucky to remain unscathed in the car bomb in Ashrafieh that killed the country's head of intelligence in 2012.[2]

At first we aren't told why or how the explosion happened. Surmises, all believable, are cranked out with aplomb. The port and/or its immediate vicinity is the common denominator: A covert cache of Hezbollah weapons has been blasted by Israeli rockets, explosive material has been substituted for innocuous fireworks, former Prime Minister Saad Hariri has been car bombed, or a set of petrol stations have been set aflame in yet another incident of suspected terrorism.

The truth, which unravels over the course of the long and harrowing night, is debilitating. None of the speculation is true. The explosion at the heart of the capital turns out to be 2,750 tons of ammonium nitrate, confiscated from a vessel headed to Mozambique in 2014. The chemicals were stored at the port, without adequate safety measures, and with the full knowledge of Lebanese officialdom across its various cross-sections.

August 6, 2020

Warfare, terror attacks, assassinations, and the cutthroat censorship of dissident voices have long been part of Lebanon's body politic. In other words, violence perpetuates across and threads through generations to form one continuous narrative that pervades (and purloins) Lebanese lives and livelihoods.

Sara El-Yafi, a public policy consultant, explains that people here 'constantly have to guess who wants to kill them, and they never truly find out, because they live in a world where so many hostile actors benefit from killing them.' Lebanese life writing in the aftermath of the blast – whether in the form of diary entries, short memoirs, opinion articles, blogs, or social media posts – attests to the derailing impact of this violence on people's lives (El Amine 2020; Ghattas 2020). As Yasmine Khayat and Rola Khayat (2020), sisters and assistant professors, put it, 'to be attuned to the seasonality of war in this country means that the end of summer is often the 'preferred' timing for elective bombings.' But never before have we undergone anything like this.

Seismic shock waves spawned by the explosion have not only ravaged swathes of Beirut and its suburbs but also rattled windows in Nicosia, a coastal city on the Mediterranean island of Cyprus, almost 100 miles (160 kilometres) away from Beirut. According to Roland Alford, an expert in the disposal of explosives, 'this is probably up there among the biggest non-nuclear explosions of all time.' The size of the blast is said to be the equivalent of 200–300 tons of high explosives (Hernandez and Scarr 2020). Colleagues and friends are sending me videos of returning home to scenes of thorough devastation. The extent of destruction is without precedent in the country's history.

Damages are worse, and happened faster and more pervasively, than anything we lived through in the Civil War whose ordnance did not create as many fatalities and injuries in less than two minutes. Georges Ghanem (2020), a cardiologist and the chief medical officer at the Lebanese American University Medical Center, writes that 'The scale of severe injuries is something I have never witnessed before, not even in field hospitals on the frontlines where I worked during the war.' Similarly, the War did not create as much homelessness. Buildings at the time suffered various levels of damage at different time intervals, but many at least remained inhabitable.

New footage from August 4 is being released. Companies and offices, private households, hospital wards, shopping malls, hotels, restaurants, gyms, supermarkets, schools and universities, museums, bookshops, and even places of worship are starting to share their stories of destruction. I slowly process the magnitude. Videos have surfaced of the exact moment the port exploded: a nurse in a destroyed hospital is carrying three newborn babies as she calls for help. A migrant worker vacuuming on a glass-paneled balcony saves the life of the girl in her care, scooping her away from the raining shards. A bewildered father reaches for his son as they shelter beneath their dining room table. Another migrant worker leads her employer's children to safety after their nursery's window collapses. An elderly priest celebrating mass dodges falling debris from the ceiling, and a bride rushes for cover in the midst of her wedding day photoshoot.

More poignant are the images of bloodshed: the gaping wounds, the dead strewn along the sidewalks, the carnage at (and outside) the hospitals. We see too a rescue worker's funeral transformed into a postmortem wedding celebration; we hear the chanting, the supplications, the ululations, as her coffin is draped in the Lebanese flag and carried on the shoulders of the men massing alongside her fiancé, marching toward the cemetery. Coming after a protracted economic crisis that saw the Lebanese lira lose over 80% of its value in under a year, banks exerting capital control, and a global pandemic, the explosion, reportedly the third most powerful after Hiroshima and Nagazaki, feels crushing.

'We're in hell,' Kristy says in a voice message. 'If this were a film script, its writer would be asked to tone it down.'

Many remain under the rubble. Somewhere in Beirut tonight, a mother is on her way home, maddened by the anguish of not yet finding her child. The platoon of firefighters sent to extinguish the fire at the port are still missing as well; they weren't aware of the tons of explosives there. We don't know if any are alive.

August 8, 2020

In the late Maroun Baghdadi's documentary film *Hamasat (Whispers)*, the Lebanese poet Nadia Tueini (1935–1983), a wordsmith par excellence, returns to Beirut in 1980 and tries to make sense of the destruction of the first five years of the Civil War, assuming, incorrectly, that it has ended. As the camera pans over a ruined neighbourhood, Tueini, losing words, says, 'I will never get accustomed to this' (qtd. in Baghdadi 1980). I share that sentiment. For those of us who have lived wars and repeated destruction of our cities and people, failing to get back to business as usual is a way of refusing to normalise, and resisting to accept, the blast as yet another manifestation of what choosing to live in Lebanon entails.

Since the explosion I have been numb, finding solace in the flow of messages and phone calls from friends and colleagues around the world, almost as soon as the port exploded. I am astounded by how fast the news has reached all corners of the globe, more proof, if any were needed, of the size of the tragedy (Mounzer 2020; Wright 2020). A friend in New York tells me she was home on maternity leave when the blast happened, and all her Lebanese friends there checked on her as though the explosion had happened in central Brooklyn. These phantom geographies, which conflate Beirut with everywhere else, are embedded in our psyches as Lebanese.

Growing up in Lebanon, Lina Mounzer (2020) suggests, teaches us 'that an explosion resonates across time, that the shock reverberates forward into your life, and the pressure reconfigures the landscape of the mind.' Whenever anything happens in Beirut, our bodies automatically revert to phantom geography, to war mode. Insofar as our initial reactions to tragedy are shaped by inherited trauma, it doesn't matter if we didn't fully experience the brunt of the Lebanese Civil War, or if today's bombs detonate in cities not our own.

Inherited trauma means that we all have our familial rituals that we perform in the immediate aftermath of violence – what the Lebanese poet Zeina Hashem Beck (2020) calls 'traumatic peculiarities,' passed from one generation to another. Sharing her brother-in-law Rami's near-death experience, Hashem Beck writes:

> amid the fear, right before the blast, his mind was ordering him to close the balcony glass so the apartment wouldn't get dusty, and at the same time to stay away from the glass so he wouldn't get hurt. 'It was like I had my mother and my aunt's voices inside my head. One was worried about the dust, and the other was warning me about the glass.'

As a child, I vividly recall my parents screaming at me to avoid windows whenever they heard fireworks; they would stack emergency bags within arm's reach should we run to our basement bomb shelter. I have seen them react to the murder of Prime Minister Rafic Hariri in 2005, the Hezbollah-Israel war in 2006, and the numerous high-profile assassinations and multiple car explosions that, throughout the 1990s and the 2000s, marked my formative and young adult years. Time and again, the clock pauses, notions of setting collapse, and reasoning doesn't cohere with breaking news. You start calling your closest and dearest regardless of location; phantom geographies set in as speculation on what happened is gradually replaced by hope that the local media will be allowed to provide the facts.

In the aftermath of the blast, the government has deployed national security rhetoric to push for implementing military emergency rule – in many ways an attempt to curb non-state media's ability to sway public opinion by covering the rebirth of the October 2019 revolution.[3] This uprising, forced to take a backseat during Coronavirus lockdown, is unquestionably back, both online and on the streets. Despite the continuing backlash against online activism (El Hajj 2020), many Lebanese have, since August 4, taken to social media, to blogging and writing personal narratives and opinion articles reflecting on their experiences of the explosion.

In yoking the criminal negligence of storing 2,750 tons of explosive material in close vicinity to residential neighbourhoods, and without alerting the public to their existence, to the rampant corruption characteristic of the ruling elite, the life narratives shared by angry citizens reveal unprecedented calls for retaliation against the political class whose leaders were symbolically hanged, one dummy next to another, in downtown Beirut today. Rabih Alameddine, a Lebanese novelist, and Sara El-Yafi, a public policy consultant, write along these lines:

> It's not bad apples, it's the whole orchard, all the orchards. It's a systemic failure of governance. For years, every faction in the country blamed the other for any disaster. [...] But enough, enough! This government must go. All of them. The government, the president, the prime minister, Hezbollah, the Hariris, the Lebanese Forces, the Aouns, the Jumblatts, the Berris, the Gemayels, every one of them. Enough. Get out. We need to plant anew. (Alameddine 2020)

> But what is not a matter of investigation is the absolute guilt of the entire political class. Every single political party has a parasitic representative in the Port of Beirut, who answers to one of their parasitic, incompetent ministers, who answers to the oligarchs. And every single one must be brought forward and tried in an international court of justice. Justice can only be found in the destruction of this wretched political system, and retribution must be served on the platter of the annihilation of each of its henchmen's massacring politics. (El-Yafi 2020)

Even as a bloodthirsty narrative is being proposed by the state's detractors, what I am describing here is but a bare-bones portrayal of lives, and lives lost. Desperation suicides in the weeks before the explosion were on the rise, one man leaving a note saying, 'I am not a heretic, but hunger is heresy.' The government threw a televised concert afterwards without addressing either the suicides or their undergirding call for economic reform, and yet remained focused enough to replace a few (potentially subversive) lines from one of the concert's songs – 'A revolution is born from the womb of sorrows' – with more vapid lyrics. Indeed, the Lebanese people have been living under psychological, economic, and physical duress akin to state-sponsored terrorism. As Ayah Bdeir, an entrepreneur, aptly puts it, this is a hostage situation, not a country:

> As I write, we are being held hostage by a ruling class that refuses to leave. In the meantime, we had one of the biggest forest fires in our history, the economy collapsed, our buildings crumbled, we are being detained and beaten by police. Fifty percent of the population is in poverty, the currency lost 80% of its value, our life savings are wiped, we are not allowed to withdraw more than 1,000$ a month if we are lucky. The lucky ones are those of us that emigrated to any country that would take us. Our elderly are begging for food. All the while, there is a global pandemic and recession going on. (Bdeir 2020)

Because of the general mistrust in the state's ability to manage the crisis, there are fears that politicians will try to line their pockets with the incoming relief funds while leaving their people to suffer and die. Therefore, most donations from foreign governments to date have been handed directly to NGO and civil society groups, thus sidelining the official bureaucracy. As I write, citizens and activists who have been cleaning the city over the past three days are back on the street, calling for international support and for toppling the regime. The three-year-old Alexandra Najjar, the blast's youngest victim, is centre-stage in the protesters' chants (Aboueish 2020). And the clouds of tear gas, close-range rubber bullets, live shootings, and beatings are back too.[4] Nina, a feminist activist partaking in the August 8 protests, four days after the explosion, reflects on this experience:

> We have been in a state of abandonment for 30 years. We have been shattered and broken for too long. And now we have nothing left to lose. Now we march toward blasting this system to the ground. The effort exerted in quelling the protestors today, shooting them with live bullets, targeting them to kill and maim, is a clear indication of priorities: saving the system to the last bone. Our sight remains focused, no matter how many of our eyes you poke out with rubber bullets. And yours will be plucked out, one by one. (email communication, August 8, 2020)

Teargassing protesters in the middle of a global respiratory pandemic comes with the full knowledge that the August 4 explosion also eviscerated medical reserves, which were already lacking, and compromised if not outright destroyed several medical care facilities. Alaa Bou-Ghannam (2020), an ophthalmologist at the American University of Beirut Medical Center shares that, on August 8, 'the number of eye injuries due to police/army brutality requiring surgeries today at AUBMC, matched and exceeded the number of similar cases presented to AUBMC the day of the explosion.' Writing for *Literary Hub*, Farah Aridi, a writer and researcher, describes the ongoing situation in Lebanon as a state-engineered 'urbicide':

> This is premeditated urbicide. Following the blast, a state of emergency was announced. But neither you nor your people were the emergency, Beirut. Instead of picking you up, instead of clearing the rubble, of pulling people from under your wreckage, they watched our misery at a distance, patrolling the streets, and harassing the volunteers, before teargassing us. The fumes of your blast were not enough. (Aridi 2020)

The term 'urbicide' is apposite. The number of dead has risen to 158, to date, the injured to 6000, and the homeless to 300,000 (Uras and Najjar 2020).[5] Two of Kristy's friends, both retired, have fled their utterly collapsing house and moved in with her. What few intact belongings they had were pillaged by the needy and greedy under cover of night. Houses in Beirut no longer have doors. Anyone can walk in.

'They even stole what remained of their undergarments,' Kristy says, overwhelmed. 'The thieves will probably sell them at one of the flea markets. Many have lost everything in the rubble.'

Under the rubble too remain the unaccounted for in the emerging official records. Unmentioned as well have been the Coronavirus patients dying of suffocation in their beds due to the power cuts on the evening of the explosion. Amid the still unfolding catastrophe, new COVID-19 cases have skyrocketed in the past few days. According to the local English newspaper, *The Daily Star* (2020), just the weekend after the blast registered 309 new infections, amidst concerns about dwindling PCR testing and skewed official figures. Since we have been pushed to such extreme unlivable conditions, and with

7,121 infections to date, contagion now means we will either be excluded for weeks from lending out a hand to the hundreds of thousands who have lost their homes, or that we'll have no safe space to quarantine.

Should we require hospitalisation, we will not be able to find available rooms because torn limbs trump restricted breath and Beirut's hospitals already teeming with patients are now mostly destroyed; survivors have been transferred to medical centres in the north and south of the country. Healthcare providers themselves are now traumatised, having to navigate their own pain with that of the wounded in their care. Rana Asmar (2020), an internal medicine resident, describes suturing a 24-year-old who started having seizures and had to be transferred to radiology for a brain scan: 'In the elevator, he kept on asking me if I was his sister. I said 'yes,' because I needed him to stay stable, and kept on talking to him as if I really was. This was very traumatic to me, and I will never forget his name.'

Tarek Kosaifi, a wound-care expert at the Saint George Hospital, writes that, in this hospital alone, the blast killed twelve patients in their beds and four nurses on duty. The injured had to be treated in the surrounding parking lots since the hospital itself was no longer operative:

> We had no hospital, barely any resources, and no lights, so we used phone torches (with almost dead batteries) as we sutured our colleagues and casualties without anesthesia; seeing them in pain was still better than losing them altogether. The worst was yet to come. When the corpses started to arrive, some I recognised as my colleagues. (Kosaifi 2020)

I am brought back to Elaine Scarry's words, now more timely than ever. She cautions that the inability to verbalise pain may collude with a political design to downplay the impact of wartime or regime-related atrocities (Scarry 1985, 12). The physical pains inflicted by the port explosion have been followed by today's police brutality and teargassing, and by the psychological distress thereafter somatised, physically, under different forms of post-traumatic behaviour (that I ponder later in detail). Trauma here is long-standing and omnipresent, transcends the personal, and aligns oppression along similar lines of experience. It is as though the storylines in our diaries are not only contiguous, but also progress through a process of mimesis in which swathes of tragedy self-replicate. Such episodes are 'archived' thereafter in our psyches but are not sufficiently processed to achieve a semblance of closure or reconciliation, conducive to healing.

This learned helplessness – the expectation of the recurrence of trauma(s) – means that the spectrum of pain Kosaifi reports, that of the country's wounded and of those tending to them, is 'monolithically consistent in its assault on language' (Scarry 13). Thus, our perpetual inability as Lebanese to functionally articulate the silos of pain, to which new chapters keep getting added, pushes it, understandably, into the realm of anger and impassioned calls, like Nina's and El-Yafi's above, for retributive, even violent, justice against the country's ruling junta. Rima Rantisi, lecturer and activist, writes:

> Today, all of the clichés of beauty that have defined the country – the joie de vivre, the resilience, the hospitality, the food, the harmony of east and west – have no weight. The ugliness outweighs the beauty, and it outweighs any semblance of the identity that has buoyed this festering place of corruption all of these years. Today, Beirut city is the site of a mass murder. The blast did not only destroy our city, it destroyed any previous delusions that we could get

it back without bloodshed. To get our country back, our city back, they said we need blood. But it's our blood that was lost. Now we need theirs. (Rantisi 2020)

In his poem 'To Those Who Follow in Our Wake,' Bertolt Brecht (1939) describes the emotional, even ethical brunt of fighting political regimes notorious for their acts of thuggery and brutishness. He famously writes: 'And yet we knew: / Even the hatred of squalor / Distorts one's features. / Even anger against injustice / Makes the voice grow hoarse. We / Who wished to lay the foundations of kindness / Could not ourselves be kind' (lines 66–72). If the uprising starting October 17, 2019 foregrounds the need for a new system of governance that supersedes sectarian divisions and partisan loyalties, the August 4 explosion has laid bare the extent of our losses, should the necrotic status quo in Lebanese politics persist. As shifting (and shifty) state security protocols and COVID-19 quarantine policies suggest that imposing lockdown is a measure to curb civil unrest, rather than flatten the viral curve, Zeead Yaghi (2020), a Lebanese graduate student, writes that 'To pick up the rubble and bury the dead is to realise that this is now a zero-sum game. It is either us or the regime; we cannot coexist.'

Away from the incendiary rhetoric, my friend Tarek Zeidan's more conciliatory words alleviate, in part, my anguish about the recrudescence of civil war, this time between the rebels on the street seeking reforms and the stooges who still idolise their political and/or sectarian leaders. Tarek directs Helem, the first and oldest LGBTQI organisation in Lebanon's history, and he had returned to Beirut after a successful career at Harvard, specifically to take up this job. Although the building that houses Helem is now, like Beirut, a gutted husk, he takes strength from our friends' and colleagues', and the queer community's, willingness to come together to help rebuild a city that resembles our embattled aspirations for a less violent future.[6] At the end of a grueling week, Tarek writes:

> I don't know if I deserve the human beings I work with. I don't know if we, the people, don't deserve Beirut, or if she doesn't deserve the people rebuilding her as we speak. I cannot explain what it feels like to be lifted when you buckle at the knees by the very same people you feel responsible for lifting. There can be no going back or away anymore; the land is just land were it not for the people that sculpt its spirit. The people I share my life's work with are the reason why now I have the strength and the sense of self-worth to even write this. There is struggle to be waged after we grieve and bury our dead. There is restoration to be planned. There are people to be with, and work to be done. I am sad and burdened and grateful to be alive. (personal communication, August 8, 2020)

August 9, 2020

Five days after the Port Blast, I am finally able to return to Beirut. I can't control my emotions as I walk through the Mar Mikhael and Gemmayzeh neighbourhoods, two of the worst hit. I try to offer as much help as I am capable of before breaking down. I did not mean to break down. Unlike so many who lost limbs in the explosion, I, like Tarek, am grateful to remain able-bodied despite the bruises and stitches, but seeing Beirut in ruins in the light of day is too brutal to carry. The images are more poignant than what TV cameras capture.

The places that held our versions of ourselves, our dreams, our memories are in smithereens. Beirut even sounds different, a cacophony of despair connecting the angry shouts of people, the pleading voices of the now-homeless elderly, the timid attempts at scotching the damage, the bangs of metal and hammering, and the grating din of glass being swept away by civilians' broomsticks and dustpans that, due to hyper-inflation, cost close to the national minimum wage.

Among the crowd carrying brooms are migrant workers, Filipinas and Ethiopians on their day off. Although they are the most underpaid in this economy, they are clearing the rubble of our corrupt state, volunteering to help the broken, even as they are most vulnerable themselves. One of them tells me her cousin is in hospital: 'She was bathing her disabled madam when the blast happened, and a piece of glass from the mirror pierced her eye.' We are all grieving.

Beirut is churning with an energy that I don't recognise. The streets now home the rubble which in turn bears blood and dust and body parts. Bones, hair, plasma. This is the site of so many coming-of-age, and coming-out, experiences, played out against the backdrop of the city's historic centre, a nucleus of bars, restaurants, cafes, shops, community centres, art galleries, and convenience stores I have known, one by one. In the different haunts of the young that dot these streets, many a story of heartbreak and healing, discord and reconciliation, and of the gumption and irreverence of youth, first dates and loves, have unfolded, and some of these have entered the storylines in my own fiction and research. Here is where Kristy and I have spent every birthday. Here is the table, now covered in debris, we have sat at to celebrate my Ph.D. graduation.

Art catalogues with splashes of blood are scattered in the rubble. This is the gallery where Kristy has twice exhibited her mixed media tapestries. There lies the café that hosted our last play reading before the lockdown, and next to it is the pub where a close friend came out to me three years ago. Here is the restaurant where I took my mother out for her first outing after her father died. This is where we have had countless happy moments before the exuberance of youth was dulled by the sobering realities of this fractious country. A chunk of my past has been obliterated.

Writing in the wake of the explosion, the Lebanese novelist Rawi Hage describes a similar void premised, in his case, on the irrevocable decimation of childhood home, a reflection that suggests that physical pain, as a predicament for which language becomes impotent (Scarry 1985, 5), may align in terms of its inexpressibility with emotional pain, perhaps especially so when calamity is collective.

> The devastated area is my childhood neighborhood. Now its streets are carpeted with fragments of glass that once gave some dignity and shelter to its inhabitants. It is also a setting for many of my novels. Down the French stairs of Gemmayzeh district, what remains of old Beirut with its distinct Lebanese architecture, a fusion between Ottoman and Venetian styles, is all destroyed. [...] My brother sent me a video of our devastated home. He was silent; there was nothing to say. It seems that when the tragedy is omnipresent and touches everyone, even to breathe, or to complain, is a shameful indulgence. (Hage 2020)

Amputee journalist May Chidiac, herself a victim of a terrorist attack on 25 September 2005 (Smith 2006), has expressed similar feelings of spatial and temporal disjunction, and the pain of realising that even the emotional narratives of the past are now lost. To date, no culprits have been apprehended in connection with her case, and the state's expressions of sympathy, akin to corporate courtesy emails, have been scant consolation. In a televised interview on a local channel yesterday, Chidiac challenged the official script starting to emerge that Tuesday's disaster, like her own, may have been terrorism-related:

> The negligence in storing the chemicals for so many years colludes with whatever scenario the government may want to postulate. [...] When they blew off my limbs 15 years ago, they ripped away my present and my future. Now that my childhood home has been wiped out, they have also stolen my past. (Chidiac 2020)

Other than homes and the loci of our memories, the loss of the past comes in different forms that will take time to grieve, and possibly may never be restored or recovered. For the time being, the pain is more immediate and pressing, more physical than cultural. Fractured skulls versus charred books. And yet the time for grieving the loss of culture, our museums, our history will come. All the art galleries, libraries, nineteenth-century stately homes, Ottoman structures, and French mandate neighbourhoods over a radius of 10 kilometres have been destroyed (Proctor 2020; Singh-Bartlett 2020). The restored wall-length stained glass windows of several historic churches – sights of hieratic beauty that were the labour of several decades of artwork after the Civil War – have been pulverised afresh. As I walk back to my car, more than one artist in Gemmayzeh are gazing at their imploded installations, splattered along the sidewalks.

Among the heritage sites brought to their knees is the recently renovated Sursock Museum, which a few months before the lockdown, had hosted a Pablo Picasso exhibit, featuring the rare artwork inspired by his childhood. Kristy and I had been thrilled to attend the opening, a remarkably opulent affair akin to a fictional party thrown by Scott Fitzgerald's Gatsby, but what comes to mind now more than the quaint endearing depictions from Picasso's past is what we did not see at the exhibit: the notorious *Guernica* (1937) whose gory images of destruction resonate most fittingly with our present.

Already, for Sursock Museum, as for many of the city's crumbling historic edifices, the clock is ticking. Hage (2020) warns that the 'unique façade that tells of the rich historicity, complexity and multiplicity of the place is now defenseless against the pariahs, the corrupt developers and the governmental officials, who are wetting their lips and sharpening their curved swords to tear down the last glimpses of past history.' Realtors and developers keen on replacing, not rebuilding, these storied landmarks are already approaching the beleaguered owners for buyouts, even as our dead are still unburied.

Later, among the reams of photographs taking stock of the destruction on social media, I am drawn to one in particular: The Grand Diwan (Hall) at Sursock Palace, a mainstay of Beirut's heyday cultural itinerary, where only a Christmas past Kristy and I were invited to lunch with Yvonne, the Dowager Lady Cochrane, the Irish-Lebanese doyenne of this nineteenth-century historic house. Speaking over the phone, Kristy wants to make sure I made it home safe after my day's walk through the carnage. She shares that Yvonne, who turned 98 this year, has suffered cuts in the blast.[7]

At the far end of the 'diwan,' in the corner where the colonnaded arcades open upon the garden, Kristy and I had sat drinking coffee with the Dowager last December, regaled by feisty after-lunch anecdotes from a past I hadn't lived, and by a discussion of literature and history, and of our art and writing and research. A heap of shattered china and glass shards, and of splintered woodwork and shredded tapestries, has now taken our seats, and for a moment, I imagine us under the debris, collateral damage in this once-enriching space.

Destroyed interior of Sursock Palace
(Courtesy of 'Live Love Beirut' organisation: https://www.facebook.com/LiveLoveBeirut/photos/a.451878981519422/4462384533802160/?type=3&theater)

August 10, 2020

If Chidiac and others are suspicious of officials' suggestion that the port blast was engineered by an external party, it is because the story has been largely speculative, and keeps changing. There is a growing feeling that writing the rubble, so to speak, is the citizens' first step toward reclaiming a modicum of agency and providing impetus afresh to the October 2019 revolution. Rami El Ali, a university professor, states:

> I have to write because, if I don't, I will be accepting this tragedy's recurrence. Assume any context you want: that Lebanon was attacked, had a normal but devastating case of human error, or is being subjected to a world conspiracy backed by the devil itself. Not one of these detracts from this government's responsibility. (El Ali 2020)

An accidental spark caused by fireworks, officials first said, triggered the initial fire and thick mushroom clouds, an infernal display that eyewitnesses recorded on their phones before the hangar exploded and the shock wave knocked them, and the city, off their feet. 'Fireworks are apparition,' Adorno (1997) tells us: 'They appear empirically yet are liberated from the burden of the empirical, which is the obligation of duration' (81). The reality of the explosion, however, is very much laden with 'empirical being' in that each of us embodies its trauma – a personal as well as collective narrative of losing lives and livelihoods in a haphazard moment of apparitional smoke. As Adorno suggests, this type of narrative may not, in the near future, be 'read for its meaning' (81).

Ever fond of numbers, a friend who is an economist has linked the 2,750 tons of explosives to the size of 14 blue whales – the planet's largest animal since the dinosaurs – each weighing 200 tons (Choucair 2020). This image too haunts my slumber: 14 hapless whales filled with ammonium nitrate ready to explode anywhere, anytime. I try listening to ocean sounds to relax, but every time I close my eyes I imagine that the waves are the sound of all the glass getting swept off the streets. Since the explosion, I have only been able to collect a couple of hours of sleep at a time. I keep awakening from sundry nightmares of bloodshed and flailing limbs, tear gas and suffocation, only to reemerge into the real inferno, which is what happened to Beirut last Tuesday.

Ziad Itani, a cinematographer, describes checking on his neighbour, an 85-year-old woman called Thérèse, whose clap of hands once punctuated the day, signalling the return of the sparse state-generated electricity, rationed at four hours daily before the explosion. 'I was still dazed myself, and then I saw an elderly woman descending the stairs, groaning,' Itani told a reporter. 'Her face was covered in blood, and I only recognised her when she said my name. By the time we made it to hospital, she had slipped away. Now I hear Thérèse calling out to me every time I sleep' (Itani 2020). I am reminded of Dante's famous verse, as Virgil, the Roman poet, gives him a foray into the punishments of hell:

> That thou mayst follow me; and I, thy guide,
> Will lead thee hence through an eternal space,
> Where thou shalt hear despairing shrieks, and see
> Spirits of old tormented, who invoke
> A second death
> Inferno, Canto I, *The Divine Comedy*, lines 110–114 (Alighieri 1321)

The psychological aftermath of a nuclear-like explosion approximates Dante's notion of a 'second death' in the form of reliving the trauma daily. Given that tragedy hit at 6.08p.m. around dinner time, many were in their houses after a day's work – getting their meals ready and/or grocery shopping – so that the trauma is being retriggered by the mundane sounds of otherwise innocuous, even comforting, activities related to cooking and food preparation. The somatic manifestations of Post-Traumatic Stress Disorder (PTSD), as experienced in the excerpts that follow, are outlined by Cathy Caruth (1995, 4) as 'repeated, intrusive hallucinations, dreams, thoughts or behaviours stemming from the event, along with numbing that may have begun during or after the experience, and possibly also increased arousal to (and avoidance of) stimuli recalling the event':

Every time I hear the hint of a sound, however familiar, such as doors opening or closing my neck tilts itself with my hands above it, to protect my head from the next blast. Yesterday I was getting groceries and the electricity went off for three minutes, putting us in total darkness, and then the kickoff of the lights and the corresponding ignition of the central air-conditioning systems sent me cowering under the meat fridges. (Samer, social worker; email communication, August 8, 2020)

During the Civil War in Lebanon, my mom was preparing us grilled cheese sandwiches for breakfast, and the moment she gave me one, a huge explosion took place on the street where we live – a failed assassination attempt against one of the country's warlords. Five days ago, I was preparing a grilled cheese sandwich for Yasmina, our daughter, when another huge explosion rocked Beirut – an assassination attempt against the people by the same warlords still in power. When the port exploded, I was not a mother comforting her four-year-old daughter in what was left of our kitchen. I was a little girl, again, hugging her little girl. (Mireille Hammal 2020, Reiki practitioner)

I follow several food blogs, more for visual relief after work than for cooking instructions. Watching food being made relaxes me. It elevates my brain cells into instant ephemeral visual pleasure. But this time even that tenuous 'foodgasm' has been severely altered. Every time I try opening a food blog or video, my mind crashes as the moment of the explosion repeats itself. (Nermine, student; email communication, August 9, 2020)

You know you're damaged when you come across a photograph of swirls and swirls of glazed cinnamon rolls stacked atop each other, drizzling with caramel and crushed nuts, and think for a moment that it's another image of the disastrous crumbling of yet another building from Tuesday's cold-blooded massacre. (Anwar Azzi, photographer; email communication, August 10, 2020)

I used to love hearing the sound of sizzling pans. Of fuming casseroles. Of a kettle on the boil. Of vegetables being chopped. These once-satisfying sounds are now terrifying. (Tracy, pianist; email communication, August 10, 2020)

Research on the immediate aftermath of disaster and trauma has cobbled the term 'surge capacity' to describe a litany of coping mechanisms, mental and physical, that may facilitate short-term survival in periods of acute adversity (Masten 2015). People here have been opening their houses to the newly homeless, as Kristy has; they are setting up donation drives, raising hundreds of thousands of dollars through GoFundMe campaigns, and organising the volunteer cleanup crews I joined for some time yesterday. In other words, we have been operating on surge capacity, but it neither stretches out indefinitely, nor does it, as we have seen, assuage the individual or collective impact of shell shock. As more pain and trauma narratives emerge, an already exhausted population will gradually lose this important resource.

Coupled with the country's cadaverous political grid, freefalling economy, and moribund state services, as well as civilians' inability to verbalise or neutralise pain due to its sheer abundance and continuity, the inevitable gradual depletion of our surge capacity rekindles my fears of the possibility that violent episodes will follow. As expected, the government's bumbling resignation fails to bear any palliative effect; the calls to uproot the regime continue. Meanwhile, the platoon of firefighters first called to the site of the explosion are all confirmed dead.

A colleague tells me her children are waking up at night, recalling the moment they found her unconscious under the rubble of her collapsed teleworking desk in their living room. I hear about the flashbacks, the hallucinatory explosions other colleagues and their partners are having as they shut their eyes, their knee-jerk reactions when a car alarm goes off, a door bangs, or a child starts crying (Caruth 1996).[8] And it hits me, again and again: the rage, coupled with the rawness of pain and of despair. I wonder if any of us will be able to sleep once more.

August 11, 2020

Fashionably late, the insurance people start to arrive in teams in suits and ties, almost a week into the catastrophe. Their usual stern and glum complexions are further darkened by the enormity of the disaster, and by the hefty cost home insurance is expected to levy. Each flat in Kristy's building is inspected.

The lead officer, a pontificating man dubbed Mister Rodge, is thorough in his task. Copious notes and multiple photographs are taken, and he spends a day to canvas the property, including the underground garage, staff elevators, and concierge quarters. Kristy tells him that the battered antiques in her atelier should not be listed in his inventory: She has volunteered to fix these for a charity auction. Mister Rodge repeats his disclaimer; insurers shall not cover damages, should the rumours linking the explosion to an Israeli attack, or to any act of warmongering, prove true (Meuse 2020).

Finally, he asks Kristy if anything else remains.

'Only my memories,' she answers. 'And only a few.'

Notes

1. In the following order of appearance in-text, the names of Kristy, Nina, Samer, Nermine, and Tracy have been changed for reasons of privacy.
2. The temporality and implications of war are so prominent in Kristy's academic and artistic practices, as well as mine, I have coined the term 'post-postwar' in a life writing study to designate a time frame following the latest full-on war in Lebanon, that of 2006 between Israel and Hezbollah (El Hajj 2018).
3. In the post-Civil-War years, cultural outputs, such as documentaries, movies, novels, television shows, or even newspaper articles that went beyond nugatory or idle distractions, were perceived as a breach of the status quo and a threat to the Lebanese state's imaginary of national security, and were therefore censored (Seigneurie 2011, 100, 215; Traboulsi 2007).
4. 728 protesters were wounded on August 8, by either live ammunition or rubber bullets (Uras and Najjar 2020).
5. By the time this memoir was peer reviewed, the number of dead had risen to 180. See United Nations Office for the Coordination of Humanitarian Affairs (OCHA 2020) report.
6. For a discussion of the strategies used by LGBTQI people in Lebanon to navigate a spectrum of everyday violence in a precarious setup, see Ghassan Moussawi's *Disruptive Situations: Fractal Orientalism and Queer Situations in Beirut* (2020).
7. Lady Cochrane subsequently died of her injuries on September 31, 2020.
8. Caruth describes Post-Traumatic Stress Disorder (PTSD) as 'basically biphasic, that is, consisting of alternating flashbacks and numbing,' adding that this description of the experience has stayed the same over time 'both in clinical and theoretical accounts and in survivor stories.' See Caruth, *Unclaimed Experience*, 130.

Disclosure statement

No potential conflict of interest was reported by the author(s).

ORCID

Sleiman El Hajj http://orcid.org/0000-0001-8827-6981

References

Aboueish, Tamara. 2020. "Beirut Explosion: Three-Year-Old Succumbs to Injuries After Surviving Port Blasts." *Al Arabiya English*, August 8. Accessed 9 August 2020. https://english.alarabiya.net/en/News/middle-east/2020/08/08/Beirut-explosion-Three-year-old-succumbs-to-injuries-after-surviving-port-blast.

Adorno, Theodor W. 1997. *Aesthetic Theory*, translated by Robert Hullot Kentor. Minneapolis: University of Minnesota Press.

Alameddine, Rabih. 2020. "As Beirut Mourns, Our Failed Leadership Looks for Someone to Punish. I Say They Must All Go." *The Washington Post*, August 5. Accessed 6 August 2020. https://www.washingtonpost.com/opinions/2020/08/05/beirut-mourns-our-failed-leadership-looks-someone-punish-i-say-they-must-all-go/.

Alighieri, Dante. 1321. "Inferno, Canto I," *The Divine Comedy*. Accessed 7 August 2020. https://www.bartleby.com/20/101.html.

Aridi, Farah. 2020. "Letter from Beirut: After Grief There Is Rage." *Literary Hub*, August 17. Accessed 17 August 2020. https://lithub.com/letter-from-beirut-after-grief-there-is-rage/.

Asmar, Rana. 2020. "I Will Never Forget the Patient's Name." *LAU Now*, September 3. Accessed 3 September 2020. https://www.lau.edu.lb/lau-now/voices/dr-rana-asmar-third-year-internal-medicine-resident.php.

Baghdadi, Maroun. 1980. *Hamasat (Whispers)*. Beirut: Farid Chehab Productions.

Bdeir, Ayah. 2020. "Help, we are being held hostage." Instagram, August 10. Accessed 10 August 2020. https://www.instagram.com/p/CDgByT2pHRH/.

Bou-Ghannam, Alaa. 2020. "The number of eye injuries due to police/army brutality." Facebook, August 9. Accessed 9 August 2020. https://www.facebook.com/alaa.boughannam.

Brecht, Bertolt. 1939. "*An die Nachgeborenen* (To Those Who Follow in Our Wake)." Translated by Scott Horton, January 15, 2008. *Harpers*. Accessed 8 August 2020. https://harpers.org/2008/01/brecht-to-those-who-follow-in-our-wake/.

Caruth, Cathy. 1995. "Trauma and Experience: Introduction." In *Trauma: Explorations in Memory*, edited by Cathy Caruth, 3–12. Baltimore and London: John Hopkins University Press.

Caruth, Cathy. 1996. *Unclaimed Experience: Trauma, Narrative, and History*. Baltimore and London: John Hopkins University Press.

Chidiac, May. 2020. Al Jadid News: Special Episode, Presented by George Salibi, August 8. Accessed 10 August 2020. https://youtube/Ec48la5jmt4.

Choucair, Farah. 2020. "Beirut Explosion: A Weapon of Mass Corruption." *Middle East Eye*, August 10. Accessed 10 August 2020. https://www.middleeasteye.net/opinion/beirut-explosion-lebanon-corruption-destruction.

The Daily Star. 2020. "Record 309 New COVID-19 Cases, Seven Deaths." August 11. Accessed 11 August 2020. http://www.dailystar.com.lb/News/Lebanon-News/2020/Aug-11/510184-record-309-new-covid-19-cases-seven-deaths.ashx.

El-Yafi, Sara. 2020. "Interview with CNN Connect's Becky Anderson." Facebook, August 6. Accessed 6 August 2020. https://www.facebook.com/watch/?v=283759149595279.

El Ali, Rami. 2020. "I have to write because, if I don't, I will be accepting this tragedy's recurrence." Facebook, August 7. Accessed 7 August 2020. https://www.facebook.com/rami.elali.10/posts/2913497702091845.

El Amine, Loubna. 2020. "Clearing the Rubble." *London Review of Books*, August 7. Accessed 8 August 2020. https://www.lrb.co.uk/blog/2020/august/clearing-the-rubble.

El Hajj, Sleiman. 2018. "Rewriting Home: A Life Writing Study in Post-Postwar Lebanon." *Life Writing* 15 (2): 255–272. doi:10.1080/14484528.2017.1396525.

El Hajj, Sleiman. 2020. "Voices Against Disavowal, Obscurantism, and Exclusion: The Year in Lebanon." *Biography: An Interdisciplinary Quarterly* 43 (1): 121–129. doi:10.1353/bio.2020.0019.

Ghanem, Georges. 2020. "We Rolled Out the Disaster Plan." *LAU Now*, September 3. Accessed 3 September 2020. https://www.lau.edu.lb/lau-now/voices/georges-ghanem-cardiologist-and-chief-medical-officer.php.

Ghattas, Kim. 2020. "Beirut Is No Stranger to Disaster, But This Is Like Nothing We've Seen." *The Guardian*, August 6. Accessed 6 August 2020. https://www.theguardian.com/commentisfree/2020/aug/06/invasions-and-economic-collapse-didnt-make-lebanons-people-as-angry-as-they-are-now.

Hage, Rawi. 2020. "In Beirut, A Nightmare Comes to Life." *The Globe and Mail*, August 6. Accessed 7 August 2020. https://www.theglobeandmail.com/opinion/article-in-beirut-a-nightmare-comes-to-life.

Hammal, Mireille. 2020. "During the Civil War in Lebanon, my mom was preparing us grilled cheese sandwiches for breakfast." Facebook, August 9. Accessed 9 August 2020. https://www.facebook.com/mireillee.hammal/posts/10165237490250725.

Hashem Beck, Zeina. 2020. "When the Healing Place Exploded." *The Rumpus*, September 1. Accessed 2 September 2020. https://therumpus.net/2020/09/when-the-healing-place-exploded/.

Hernandez, Marco, and Simon Scarr. 2020. "How Powerful Was the Beirut Blast?" *Reuters Graphics*, August 14. Accessed 14 August 2020. https://graphics.reuters.com/LEBANON-SECURITY/BLAST/yzdpxnmqbpx/.

Itani, Ziad. 2020. "Sar El Wa'et [It's About Time]," presented by Marcel Ghanem, August 9. https://www.youtube.com/watch?v=HbS16gZGRa0.

Khayat, Yasmine, and Rola Khayat. 2020. "Ruminating Over Ruins in Beirut." *Jadaliyya*, August 6. Accessed 6 August 2020. https://www.jadaliyya.com/Details/41537/Photo-Series-on-the-Continuity-of-Trauma.

Kosaifi, Tarek. 2020. "We had no hospital, barely any resources, and no lights, so we used phone torches (with almost dead batteries) as we sutured our colleagues and casualties without anesthesia." Facebook, August 11. Accessed 11 August 2020. https://www.facebook.com/tarek.kosaifi/posts/10164356730810624.

Masten, Ann S. 2015. *Ordinary Magic: Resilience in Development*. New York: Guilford Publications.

Meuse, Alison Tahmizian. 2020. "Trump May Be Right About Beirut 'Attack'." *Asia Times*, August 8. Accessed 8 August 2020. https://asiatimes.com/2020/08/trump-may-be-right-about-beirut-attack/.

Mounzer, Lina. 2020. "It Sounded Like the World Itself Was Breaking Open." *New York Times*, August 5. Accessed 5 August 2020. https://www.nytimes.com/2020/08/05/opinion/beirut-port-explosions.html.

Moussawi, Ghassan. 2020. *Disruptive Situations: Fractal Orientalism and Queer Situations in Beirut*. Philadelphia: Temple University Press.

OCHA (United Nations Office for the Coordination of Humanitarian Affairs). 2020. "Lebanon: Beirut Port Explosions Situation Report No. 5." August 19. Accessed 23 September 2020. https://reliefweb.int/report/lebanon/lebanon-beirut-port-explosions-situation-report-no-5-17-august-2020-enar.

Proctor, Rebecca Anne. 2020. "Huge Explosion in Beirut Decimates City and Leaves Art Scene in Disarray." *The Art Newspaper*, August 5. Accessed 10 August 2020. https://www.theartnewspaper.com/news/beirut-explosion.

Rantisi, Rima. 2020. "Losing Beirut: On Life in a Shattered City." *Literary Hub*, August 11. Accessed 11 August 2020. https://lithub.com/losing-beirut-on-life-in-a-shattered-city/.

Scarry, Elaine. 1985. *The Body in Pain: The Making and Unmaking of the World*. Oxford: Oxford University Press.

Seigneurie, Ken. 2011. *Standing by the Ruins: Elegiac Humanism in Wartime and Postwar Lebanon*. New York: Fordham University Press.

Singh-Bartlett, Warren. 2020. "What Happens Next to Beirut's Bomb-Damaged Buildings?" *Architectural Digest*, August 6. Accessed 7 August 2020. https://www.architecturaldigest.com/story/what-happens-next-beiruts-bomb-damaged-buildings?

Smith, Craig S. 2006. "Critic of Syria Loses a Hand and a Foot, but Not Heart." *New York Times*, April 15. Accessed 8 August 2020. https://www.nytimes.com/2006/04/15/world/middleeast/critic-of-syria-loses-a-hand-and-a-foot-but-not-heart.html.

Traboulsi, Fawaz. 2007. *A History of Modern Lebanon*. London: Pluto Press.

Uras, Umut, and Farah Najjar. 2020. "Clashes in Beirut as Anger Swells Over Port Blast: Live Updates." *Al Jazeera*, August 8. Accessed 8 August 2020. https://www.aljazeera.com/news/2020/08/60-missing-beirut-mega-blast-live-updates-200808061240497.html.

Wright, Robin. 2020. "After Twin Explosions, An Apocalypse in Lebanon." *The New Yorker*, August 5. Accessed 6 August 2020. https://www.newyorker.com/news/our-columnists/after-twin-blasts-an-apocalypse-in-lebanon.

Yaghi, Zeead. 2020. "Lights Out, Beirut." *The Point Magazine*, August 24. Accessed 25 August 2020. https://thepointmag.com/examined-life/lights-out-beirut/.

Will the Real Subject Please Stand Up? Autobiographical Voices in Biography

Karen Lamb

ABSTRACT

Biographers exist in a tight partnership with their chosen subject and there is often during the research and writing an equivalent reflective personal journey for the biographer. This is generally obscured, buried among an overwhelming magnitude of sources while the biographer is simultaneously developing the all-important 'relationship' required to sustain the narrative journey ahead. Questions and selections beset the biographer, usually about access to, or veracity of, sources but perhaps there are more personal questions that could be put to the biographer. The many works on the craft of biography or collections about the life-writing journey tell only some of this tale. It is not often enough, however, that we acknowledge how biography can be unusually 'double-voiced' in communicating a strong sense of the teller in the tale: the biographer's own life experience usually does lead them to the biography, but also influences the shaping of the work. These are still 'tales of craft' in one sense, but autobiographical reflections in another. Perhaps this very personal insight can only be attempted in the 'afterlife' of biography; the quiet moments and years that follow such consuming works. In this article, I reflect on this unusually emotional form of life writing.

When the 'Editing the "I"' session at the Modern Languages Association in Seattle, USA called for papers, I noticed this comment:

> There also is the recent trend for scholars of life writing to author or edit their own life stories for presentation. For a host of human reasons—some subconscious, perhaps—might they edit accounts of their own lives to fit a genre or political reality?

Biographers wanting to tell us about their writing journey is not new, as we know from the many works about the journey and craft of biography, but this statement appears to herald something more distinctly personal. Yet even though biography as a form presumes to 'edit' a life for 'presentation', that does not mean that a biographer is not at the same time—even subconsciously—editing their own life as part of the writing of a biography. Interestingly, in life writing, we tend to acknowledge the voice possibilities of memoir, as it delivers multiple versions of 'I', yet we don't necessarily think of biography in this way. Perhaps we should.

Discussing memoir—those of Salman Rushdie and Paul Auster—Suzanne Guillette in her article on memoir (2019) conjures a description that just as aptly fits the writing of biography, detailing the virtues of 'stepping out of first person' and the 'dreamlike state' that allows an 'intersection of present consciousness with past events'. It is certainly not the way we usually view the form.

Because it is four years after the publication of my biography of Australian novelist Thea Astley, *Inventing Her Own Weather* , I have entered the reflective 'afterlife' of a biographer, one that has also connected me to moments in the work that in many respects parallels years of my own life story. If the biography itself is series of narratives over time—Thea Astley, her career as a novelist (15 works of fiction and multiple major awards), 50 years of Australian publishing—then one of those narratives must also be mine. A biographer's own life story necessarily plays into the creation of biography. In other words, there is 'autobiography in biography' and that too encompasses other voices from the biographer's own life history, that is, other lives. It would be a very crowded stage, were if not for the fact that biographers intentionally shape works which are vividly about one life. Traces of the person writing the biography may come to the reader in words and phrases, framed by critics with terms as vague as 'style' or 'voice'.

In the 'afterlife' of biography, however, some aspects of the biographer's experience that may have been buried—subconsciously or otherwise—can be resumed. These are the biographer's stories we know of: the long years of research, sometimes intimate meetings with famous folk, frustrations with estates and the joys of an unexpected discovery or outcome. They make fascinating reading, *Lives for Sale: Biographer's Tales* by Mark Bostridge being a prime example. It see-saws through the triumphs and sometimes bitter times of the biographer experience.

Even as they reveal the feelings of the biographer at the time of writing, the essays in Bostridge's collection are controlled narratives, written after-the-event. The honesty can be refreshing. Acclaimed biographer Claire Tomalin describes approaching her biography of Samuel Pepys, as 'stepping into a new century and trying to inhabit it' with 'terrific enthusiasm' while the writing of it also plunged her into a state of 'absolute despondency'

.

Sometimes, a biographer sees a quality or an achievement in their subject that is particularly affecting, and which sustains the biographer—well after writing—as in the case of Miranda Seymour who wrote about the 1930s Chaplin film star, Virginia Cherrill. She longed to have actually met 'this sexy, unpretentious, funny woman' but reconciled this desire with the thought that 'writing her life [had] been the next best thing' to that. (Seymour in Boyt) But it is Tomalin, again, who underscores the sensitive emotional relationship between biographer and subject:

> Also, I felt deeply depressed when Pepys died. I had grown up so close to him, despite his defects of character. I think the older you get as a biographer, the less you are prepared to tick anyone off for their failings. You have lived your own life and you are somehow more accepting of other people's flaws.

This captures the biographer's enduring struggle with the question of how close the emotional attachment can be before it raises issues of interpretation, dangers of over-identification or bias. One answer to this is the now reasonably commonplace disclaimer and other inventive forms of the biographer's 'I' that appear in biography, self-conscious markers of the biographer's presence. I am thinking here of Ian Hamilton's confessions of failure in his 'search' for J.D. Salinger (d. 2010), or Brian Matthews' invented alter-ego biographer 'Owen Stevens', who speaks directly to the reader of his hapless quest: he must tell the story of Louisa Lawson, in the biography *Louisa* (1987), about whom there is precious little primary source material and who is better known as the wife of the famous nineteenth century Australian author Henry Lawson.

This only demonstrates how intriguing is the construction of works that are born of a certain kind of intimacy, whether your intention as the biographer is to remain detached, or you muster some tricks to 'fess up' to your part in the story. For long after a biography is published there are biographers who admit to a nascent presence of the work-they-would-one-day-write in their life. This is often in the serendipitous events that can, with hindsight, be seen as having originally called them to their subject. Viewed this way, biography has a 'before', as well as a 'during', and 'afterlife'.

The 'before' might not be all that mystical after all. For in the main, who would want to spend years writing the life of someone who did not attract their interest or whose field of achievement did not appeal? Often as not a literary biographer falls in love with the creative work first; the interest in biography often emerges from a literary sensibility or training. Or does it? Reflections on my biography of novelist Thea Astley has made me wonder whether I am as much the subject of my literary biography as the noted author herself.

For it is surely true that if we seek affirmation and solace in literature, then our preferences are likely a reflection of something deeply personal, emotional and intellectual. Australian writer Michael McGirr's recent *Books that Saved My Life: Reading for Wisdom, Solace and Pleasure* rather underscores this point. Part commentary, part memoir, this is a witty and heartfelt story of the relationship between knocking about in life—and in your mind—and the writers we discover along the way who make that a less lonely experience.

If relationships can be formed in imagination in such a way, then perhaps it is not so odd to think of biography as a form autobiography. It encompasses that 'intermingling of present consciousness and past events' Guillette wrote about which must be pivotal to the original interest of a biographer but also to the eventual shape of the biography: in my own case, there is little of my life that has not found its echo in Astley's writing. At every point in twenty or more years of involvement with her novels and stories, and later in the writing of *Inventing Her Own Weather*, it seems a counterpoint can be found in my own story.

It all began so long ago, this synchronicity, that it almost seems natural. The name 'Thea Astley' meant little to me when I was residing in Brisbane, Astley's own home town in Queensland. It was the late-1980s and I first encountered Astley's mid-career novel *It's Raining in Mango* [3] about colonial Queensland when it arrived for review. This family heritage novel is loosely based on Astley's own family but told from a matriarchal point of view—a picaresque sweep of the generations of migration, disgruntlement, folly, and madness that made up 200 years of Australia's history.

What I saw in the novel was the same, but in reverse: my own family's English migration to sub-tropical Brisbane in the mid-1960s, an absurd choice for my parents, since the broader family was in the civilised cooler Victoria. The novel took me back to that moment of arrival, a pale-faced English child getting off the plane; the exotic appeal of this sub-tropical town—not yet a city—with timber houses on stilts. Reading

Astley's novel, I was remembering that topsy turvy experience of migration and wondering what kind of strangers my parents were.

Migrants certainly know about re-invention. From the vantage point of a melting corrugated iron Nissan hut (where new arrivals housed back then), I learned that Brisbane did not match the migrant brochures in any respect but the sunshine (humidity carefully edited out). Not even Astley's literary talents would have been a match for the disillusionment of my mother at that time, nor her dissatisfaction with my father for landing us there. 'My subject is self-delusion and the pity of self-delusion ... the point ... of all my books', Astley once said. No wonder I was drawn to her work.

My next Astley encounter was post-Brisbane. I had 'escaped', but not for an island or a cyclone as Astley characters so often do, rather for cooler climes, literally and emotionally. The years in Brisbane and an unsuccessful relationship were still viewable at a distance but with decreasing acrimony. Just as 'Inventing the weather' was both a reality and a metaphor for Thea Astley, I too was 'inventing my own weather', independent and unattached for the first time, researching and writing on this novelist whose characterisation of women's choices and lives were well-attuned to my own. I was particularly well primed for Astley's acerbic confrontations with romantic love which were a feature of her early novels, particularly the first Miles Franklin Award-winning *The Well-Dressed Explorer* .

This is perhaps Astley's most brutal picture of male insensitivity, and she wastes no sentiment in the novel's bleakly comic moments. I recall one such scene, where the philandering journalist George Brewster holds up a blouse (a present for his wife) seeking the opinion of—none other than his current mistress. A later novella, 'Inventing the Weather' in *Vanishing Points* (1992) reverses this: here a marital split is neatly resolved when the about-to-be-deserted wife proposes that the newly-in-love husband and mistress take on the full care and responsibility of the children of the marriage.

It is easy to see how the themes of Astley's fiction appealed to a wide variety of women over many generations (Astley's writing career spanned more than five decades), including me, though I suspect that the same scenes would not appeal to me in the same way now. Astley's novels and stories drew on her awareness of human foibles and what she gleaned from 'flummery gossip'—as she termed the chit-chat she would encounter at writers' festivals and other literary gatherings. I know from writing Astley's biography that her renditions of dismal relationships in the novels did not have a particularly strong biographical parallel in her life. Astley's own marriage, despite its volatile episodes, survived more than 50 years. She never lived separately from her husband, nor it seems, even when she was miserable, did she particularly wish to.

As I continued to read and write about Astley's life and work, I was still looking for signs of my own life on the page. It was as if the novels were charting me—even the later works. These are full of caricatures of untrammelled avarice, including 'The Big Developer' structure she invented to mimic the larger-than-life plastic monuments (like the Big Pineapple) that dot the north coast of Australia. She had lived there for some years near Cairns and was angry about the large tracts of rainforest being subdivided into small plots. I, too, had once briefly encountered big business close-up: I recognised that peculiarly Australian strain of what might be called 'entrepreneurial decease', where certain folk seem compelled to build blocks of flats in place of peaceful vistas.

As the biography was written so many years after my original research on Astley, it was commonplace for me to drift between Astley's fiction and events and memories of my own life. The autobiographical elements in biography are nevertheless more nuanced and likely to be buried because they are at their core emotional, the entanglements of the biographer-subject relationship so complex. I have begun to look for this in the 'absences' in the biography so that I can trace sensitivities that were related to Astley in some way, but which are also shared by me; part of an unexpressed intimacy between subject and biographer that continues to exist even after the work is complete.

Let me share a few examples: my father and my mother died a year apart when I was 27. Less than ten years after this I had my first meeting with Astley. I would have thought then that that there had been time enough for grief, but I think my sixty-something author knew otherwise. A few well-chosen questions from her and I suspect she saw how emotionally raw from those deaths I still was. It helped that she and my father were born in the same year, 1925, which Astley made much of—and they were both teachers of languages and English. Astley's son was one year older than me. The famous novelist was, to be frank, being motherly.

It was me, I reflect now, who would have found this emotional gesture on her part a bit too close for comfort. I may have felt awkward, without being able to articulate why, about attracting too personal an interest. I note with interest that I do not see anything of this early meeting recorded in the biography: no vignette of Astley singing Gabriel Faure's 'Pavane' as she did on this occasion—a lovely moment—so that I had the melody right (she was a gifted pianist). There is no mention either of *The Diary of a Nobody* , that late nineteenth century work of English whimsy we both remembered with affection, since it belonged to the English heritage we shared.

Circumspection can be a form of self-censorship. I can speculate from this vantage point that grief may well have been a strong force behind the writing of *Inventing Her Own Weather* and it therefore interests me to see that it is this intimate first meeting with Astley that yields the most unconscious self-editing in the published biography. Clearly, that was the moment of the most intense emotional connection with my author as a person responding personally to me. Again, it was experience of deep loss that led me to write at furious speed, albeit in tears, the first draft of the Epilogue covering Astley's death, as seen through the eyes of her son.

Doubtless these very personal aspects of biography do influence interpretation and inclusion or exclusion of material, albeit in subtle ways, but not necessarily to the detriment of the work. Perhaps one might lean a bit too much towards being 'accepting of other people's flaws', to use Tomalin's wording. I know that when I came to appreciate that Astley was a passionately devoted mother of a single child, much as I was, to the point where the intensity of her attachment concerned others, I tended to frame any judgement in quoted remarks from other people, slightly shifting the onus of interpretation away from me.

The final untold small anecdote is perhaps the most revealing example of how emotionally driven biography can be. I had been told a story about a keepsake, the kind a mother might cherish, that was found in Astley's bedside table drawer after her death. What was it? Sorry, even now I find this too heartrending to reveal. There are certain intimacies in life that cannot and perhaps should not be exposed to public view in the way that silence can be the most important part of the song.

Disclosure statement

No potential conflict of interest was reported by the author.

References

Astley, Thea. 1962. *The Well-Dressed Explorer*. Sydney: Angus and Roberston.
Astley, Thea. 1981. "Writing in North Queensland." *LINQ* 9 (1).
Astley, Thea. 1987. *It's Raining in Mango*. New York, USA: Putnam's.
Bostridge, Mark. 2004. *Lives for Sale: Biographers' Tales*. London, UK: Continuum.
Editing the 'I'". 2020. Conference Session at MLA (3/15/2019; 1/ 9-12/2020) Seattle, USA.
Grossmith, George, and Weedon Grossmith. 1999. *Diary of a Nobody*. London, UK: Penguin Classics.
Guillette, Suzanne. 2009. "This Happened to Me: Musings on the Perspective and Memoir-worthy Bar." Accessed January 17, 2019. https://tinhouse.com/this-happened-to-me-musings-on-perspective-and-the-memoir-worthy-bar/.
Lamb, Karen. 2015. *Thea Astley: Inventing Her Own Weather*. Queensland: University of Queensland Press.
Matthews, Brian. 1987. *Louisa*. Melbourne: McPhee Gribble.
McGirr, Michael. 2018. *Books That Saved My Life: Reading for Wisdom, Solace and Pleasure*. Melbourne: Text.
Tomalin, Claire. 2004. "Starting Over." Chap. 14 in *Lives for Sale: Biographers' Tales*, edited by Mark Bostridge. London, NY: Continuum.

Speculative Biography and Countering Archival Absences of Women Clowns in the Circus

Katerina Bryant

ABSTRACT

My biographical research on Loretta La Pearl, the first woman clown in America, is a case study of responding to the incomplete and biased nature of archives for women. Through my lens as a creative practitioner, I use the methodology of speculative biography as a means of countering the official archival gaps in Loretta's story by re-deploying self-made archives of other circus women. I discuss the challenges of fragmentary records, speculation, authorial sympathy and intersectionality. In drawing on these creative methodologies, I am countering the incompleteness of circus archives and making visible the otherwise largely erased life of the first woman clown.

One would have thought that the very rarity of women clowns would have been an attraction rather than the reverse, but there seems to be an idea among the circus world that no woman can be as "clown funny" as a male.

- Chronicle, 1939.

Introduction

It's 2016 and I find Loretta in an archive at the Oregon Historical Society. But I do not know this is her name. I find an image of her, filed under 'circus'. She is the only woman dressed in baggy clown silks rather than the more alluring acrobatic costumes with their revealing cuts and adornment in sequins. Beneath the image, there is a caption, 'Mrs Harry La Pearl', with no additional information and lacking any reference to her first name. It takes another few days of researching her husband, Harry, before I learn that she is *Loretta*. It is this image that is the first of the few archival traces I find of her; her husband and his family are much easier to find. And so, despite living a life that I find was subversive and politically important, Loretta remains unknown and few of her circus achievements documented. The brief text under her photo is representative of the minimal archival material available on her life before or after clowning. In short, she is only clearly documented for the duration of her marriage with Harry La Pearl (estimated 1919 or 1920–1946). Her story is at risk perhaps of what philosopher Hannah Arendt called the 'danger of oblivion' (Kristeva 2001, 17; Tamboukou 2010, 174). At least, for now.

ESSAYS IN LIFE WRITING 31

Archives are imperfect. Arlette Farge observes, 'the archives are not a stockpile that can be drawn from at one's convenience' and she quotes Michel de Certeau's definition of knowledge, '"that which endlessly modifies itself by its unforgettable incompleteness"' (2004, 54). The knowledge stored in the archive is partial and socially constructed. Cassie Findlay writes in *Archives and Manuscripts* that:

> the myth of archival impartiality has been thoroughly dismantled. Archivists/recordkeepers know that every recordkeeping act—record creation, destruction, access—occurs in and is influenced by its layers of context, from the systems and people that are directly associated with the act, to the motivations of the organisation that funded it, to the expectations and norms of the wider society in which it occurs. (2016, 155)

The lack of impartiality and the extension of this idea, presence of systemic bias, is because archives are 'social constructs' (Schwartz and Cook 2002, 3). Historian Joan M. Schwartz and archivist Terry Cook elaborate on this idea, for example, discussing how archives have systematically discriminated against women:

> The gendered nature of the archival enterprise over time is a stark example that archives are not (and, indeed, never have been) neutral, objective institutions in society. Archives, since their very origins in the ancient world, have systemically excluded records about or by women from their holdings and, as institutions, have been willing agents in the creation of patriarchy by supporting those in power against the marginalized. (2002, 16)

And in some cases, as Cooper and Stoler write, it can be these archives with their systemic biases that were 'themselves cultural artefacts, built on institutional structures that erased certain kinds of knowledge, secreted some, and valorised others' (Cooper and Stoler 17).

This essay responds to the fact that women's lives in particular are subject to archival gaps and takes as a case study the life of Loretta La Pearl, an early twentieth Century circus performer who was the first woman clown in America. Through a discussion of ethics and methods for writing speculative biography, I explore the ethical implications of speculating in relation to the historical record, as well as the methodological challenges, and I argue for the significance of the biographer as a narrative presence within a speculative biographical account. My speculative biography of Loretta will also be a memoir of my journey to find Loretta. Loretta was a circus performer who dressed as a man in order to clown and so this discussion is contextualised by a need to also understand the circus as a particular cultural/social institution that reinforces patriarchal and white supremacist ideas of being. This essay navigates the complexities of finding and writing Loretta's life despite archival gaps.

Women in the archives

In most surviving records of the travelling circus, with animals and performers like the one Loretta performed in during the early Twentieth Century, women performers are sexualised. For example, an eight-hundred-page archived dossier of Australian and New Zealand newspaper clippings contained hundreds of images of women, nearly all in suggestive costumes and poses.[1] This is one of the most dominant ways in which women in the circus are still perceived (Tait 2005). Stories like Loretta's—where a woman performer occupies a traditionally cis male role—are rare or entirely absent in the archives and so, the popular imagination.[2] Loretta passed as a man during her performance (or perhaps more accurately, she passes as a clown—a figure who is often genderless).

Difficulty searching for diverse representations of women is not unique. Schwartz and Cook convincingly show how modern memory is constructed through the archives and by doing so, argue that women have been erased from this mode of imagination. They write of Gerda Lerner who, 'has convincingly traced, from the Middle Ages to the twentieth century, the systemic exclusion of women from society's memory tools and institutions, including archives' (7). Women, despite being a key part of the circus, in performance and through family-based labour, as the circus is often a family enterprise, remain at its borders, out of the spotlight.

It is well established that the archives are shaped by ideological forces. Findlay suggests:

> We need to shake off the vision of the impartial archivist safe in her fortress (and her cardigan) and look to the coder/recordkeeper making truly alternative systems of memory available to the marginalised, the vulnerable, and to the journalist/archivist releasing records with the power to shift the course of global affairs, and making sure they remain available and usable forever. (2016, 158)

Here, Findlay addresses the convergence of archives and journalism (referencing the likes of WikiLeaks and the National Security Archive) to dismantle dominant power structures. For Findlay, it is the duality of the 'journalist/archivist' that allows access to alternative archival memory. The 'journalist/archivist', as constructed by Findlay, is a maker and keeper. This duality of preserving aspects of the past and also creating for the future is a role much like my own: a biographer/archivist.

So, in my own context—researching and writing a biographical account that hopes to position circus women more visibly within institutional and cultural memory—Findlay's argument appeals to me. My methodological and ethical approach to writing Loretta's lost story is to turn the fragments that have survived from other circus women and to redeploy or make these into something new. My biography of the first woman will draw on archival material of women in the circus not only from across the US, but also in Australia. My aim is to create an alternative record of memory.

As Maria Tambakou writes in *Relational narratives: Auto/biography and the portrait*, 'Stories do many things, they produce realities as much as they are produced by them and within their own discursive constraints and limitations, they keep creating conditions of possibilities for other stories to be told, and written' (2010, 170). In writing Loretta, I hope to produce a narrative that will better represent women's erased role in the functioning and evolution of the circus. By choosing to write a speculative biography, I seek to highlight the contribution of women in the circus—showing through in-scene speculative biography the athleticism and dedication of women acrobats, as well as Loretta's subversive inhabitation of the persona of a clown. And in doing this archival and biographical work, as Andrew Flinn writes, I hope to structure 'archival practice as political, loaded with meaning, pressures, and consequences' (2011, 1).

Material that has been lost cannot easily be regained and while loss in relation to what was never 'kept' is hard to measure, it might be read inversely and in contrast to the considerable archival coverage of her husband's career. This contrast shows the skewed attention given to men in the circus, given that Harry and Loretta's achievements were on par (one could even argue hers surpassed his, as her career continued for at least 14 years after Harry died). In light of this absence of archival material, looking back to understand Loretta's life and the circus during its peak requires a different methodological approach. Antoinette Burton in the introduction for a *Journal of Women's History*'s special issue on Finding Women in the Archive discusses the practice of 'recovery' as a balm to the archival absence of women. She writes:

> the histories that have resulted from "researching around" these discrepant subjects remain fragmentary, allusive, and unsatisfactory in the best possible sense ... the stories that can be gleaned from their archival traces are inevitably partial, albeit tantalizingly so. But as this forum also shows, those traces are more than mere documents, more than simply the foundations of historical narrative. In the hands of critical feminist historians, inquisition testimony, personal letters, street strolling, and travel narratives of the kind we have before us are always *already* histories in the making. (2008, 150)

Burton's work highlights that while often fragmentary and partial, these women's histories remain key. My subject Loretta La Pearl, too, has 'archival traces'. What remains of her life cannot alone fill a book. I am caught trying to piece her together through images of the family she married into; posters of her act with her 'boxing dogs'[3]; incomplete census records, and records of women who were like her. Yet, as Burton writes, this in itself is tantalising. It's a compelling pull to turn traces into something more complete. And the tantalising nature of the work is a creative endeavour in itself. But this pull—the allure of the archives as Farge writes (2004)—can create ethical complications where a tantalising completeness risks overwriting the historical figure with a biographer's version instead.

To clarify my own ethical lens and authorship of the text, alongside Loretta's partial biography, my research journey will also become a part of the biographical research project. This methodological approach will convey the intimacy of the relationship between biographer and biographical subject. Caroline Steedman, in *On Not Writing Biography*, discusses how to overcome gaps in the record, specifically discussing relationship between herself and her subject, Frances Hamilton whom she learns much about through her reading list. Steedman reflects on how gaps can be filled and particularly how this can be influenced by how a biographer feels about their subject. Frustrated by the limited archival information available on Hamilton, Steedman writes that,

> a reader and her borrowed books—these are not the same as a life. Frances Hamilton does not know I'm here; and so I escape her level, assessing gaze. Much better not to write biography—especially if your non-subject is a clever woman, given to irony. (2009, 24)

Steedman recognises the complexity of the process of writing on a woman of whom there is little documented information– a 'non-subject' in Steedman's words—and the ethical complications in writing about someone you like.

Loretta is my own 'non-subject' and, as with Steedman, the pull of her 'archival traces' have become part of the biographical story as well as a part of my own ethical considerations in searching for a woman I like. This story of looking and loss of archival material sits alongside and within the biographical project. These gaps are Loretta's history as much as what has been left behind. It is my role as biographer to respect these gaps, enacting a refusal to 'pretend' that her life has not been erased, even as I am trying to speak to and remedy this. To the reader, I will highlight these gaps as well as the way

I have selected and processed archival material. Similarly, Leonie Rowan in *A Different Path: Marginality, Resistance and Drusilla Modjeska's Poppy* writes that in the 'fictional biography' *Poppy*, author Modjeska 'makes the processes of selection and omission that are more commonly kept invisible an explicit topic of discussion' (2001, 48). While writing a 'fictional biography'—which I note is a distinct genre from a speculative biography—Modjeska highlights the writer's role in shaping a biography in a way that many 'traditional' biographies fail to do. Rowan continues:

> the deliberate undermining of narrative authority that occurs throughout the text helps to support a reader who looks for alternative stories about women. It highlights the fact that stories are always produced, and that there is always more then [*sic*] one way to make sense of a given set of 'facts'. (2001, 48)

While Modjeska wrote *Poppy* as a biography of her mother and thus had much more in her personal archives to work with than I do with my subject, she highlights her subjectivity in shaping Poppy's story and this is an ethical claim that life writers and scholars in particular are attentive to and that, as Rowan phrases it—might be even more crucial for 'alternative stories about women' (2001, 48).

Archival traces combined

Because little official record of Loretta's life remains, I supplement the traces of her I can find in the archive through researching other women who lived and worked in the travelling circus in the early twentieth century. Particularly, I have used Burton's concept of 'researching around' which entails utilising supplementary knowledge to better understand the nature of my topic, clowning in the circus. I look for specific circus acts and what they looked like in Loretta's working era of 1920–1960; and the endeavour of moving a travelling circus—part by part—across America before trains were widespread. By piecing together these supplementary archival traces, I hope to have a more complete view of what women's lives in the circus where like at this time.

It is while at a fellowship at the National Library of Australia where I was looking at Australian women in circus that I coincidentally am able reach a fuller understanding of lives like Loretta's. The archive contains Agnes Greenwood and May Wirth's scrapbooks: these self-created records allow me to form an understanding of the everyday nuances of women's lives in the circus at this time and from a woman's point of view. Juliana M. Kuipers argues that 'clipping scrapbooks particularly reveal the efforts of women and girls to interact with and impose order on the world around them' (2004, 85). Ellen Gruber Garvey, too, suggests that scrapbooking is a gendered practice where women and girls are 'gathering the small bits, the leftovers ... a model of gathering that is not passive or compliant, and is decidedly open to feminine participation' (2003, 208; Kuipers 2004, 85). Through scrapbooking, women and girls voice and contextualise the landscape of their own lives. It is a form of everyday auto/biography that Greenwood and Wirth actively participated in.

The first scrapbook I view at the National Library of Australia is by Agnes Greenwood (1885–1977), a circus performer from childhood into adulthood. Greenwood performed roles from animal work to sewing costumes but specialised in acrobatics in her family-run all-woman circus alongside her sisters (The Lilliputian Circus). After marriage (and perhaps due to personal injury—records remain contradictory on this), she established 'Greenwood's Royal Acrobatic Academy' in Melbourne where she taught acrobatics and contortion. I see parallels to Loretta's life in the letters Greenwood writes to secure what was often precarious and scarce work for her performers. Of course, Loretta would have had to advocate for herself; she needed to work after her husband's death. Another lifelong circus performer and scrapbook author, May Wirth was an Australian bareback rider and acrobat at her family run travelling circus, Wirth's Circus (1880–1963). Wirth travelled to America to perform with Barnum and Bailey and the Ringling Circus.[4] Wirth records travelling through America in same era and with similar circuses to Loretta, so these accounts are particularly vital 'researching around'.

Both women scrapbooked across multiple decades of their lives: Greenwood from 1907 to 1976, Wirth from 1900 to 1930. These records document circus posters, personal photos of the performers and circus grounds, newspaper clippings, correspondence and autographed postcards. Greenwood particularly collected newspaper clippings while Wirth scrapbooked photographs of her experiences travelling through Australia, America and Europe with the circus. From the detail of these records, I can speculate on Loretta's life on the road. However, I also acknowledge the different transnational contexts between these three women. Greenwood travelled through Australia only; Wirth travelled through Australia, Europe and America; Loretta travelled through America only (particularly moving through Illinois, Indiana, Ohio, West Virginia, New York and California). While aspects of the travelling circus culture these women experienced would be similar, different aspects of place would have also profoundly affected their experiences.

Scrapbooks are an important archival source for knowledge about historical women's lives. As Katie Day Good writes in *From Scrapbook to Facebook: A History of Personal Media Assemblage and Archives*, these sources are 'messy, fragmentary and highly individualised' (2012, 558). Good is a media scholar exploring how practices of personal record-keeping persist in new technological contexts and she refers to scrapbooks as a 'personal media archive' that 'house personal media assemblages within a bounded setting, with options for both private viewing and public display' (2012, 559). Scrapbooks are a self-documentation tool that are particularly important for women, allowing creators to record their life and to exert control over this as a representation. Yet the issue in relying on scrapbooks as a source is that, as Helfand argues, this self-record means that creators can 'bury the truth or doctor the evidence' of their own lives (Good 2012, 571; Helfand 2008, 9). While the subjectivity of autobiographical primary sources like scrapbooks might sometimes pose an issue for some historians, creative writers tend to be less worried, especially when considering it is impossible for any autobiographical ephemera to not be curated in some way. Memoirist Vivian Gornick writes in 'Truth in Personal Narrative', life writing 'shape[s] a piece of experience out of the raw materials of one's own life so that it moves from a tale of private interest to one that has meaning for the disinterested reader' (2008, 8). Curation is in the shaping of the material, whether memories or a collection of ephemera.

Looking at Greenwood and Wirth's private scrapbooks, I notice that unlike most archived circus material I have seen, which is usually comprised of newspaper clippings and flyers, the images collected here place women at the forefront. Their presence is much more palpable; I am able to see, for example, women being photographed together after a performance. I am able see both the physical visibility of women as well as witnessing Greenwood's correspondence. This allows me to understand her power in advocating for her performers so they are commissioned for shows throughout Australia. These personal archives/assemblages give me—the biographer—a peek into not only these women's interior lives but the politics of the space they inhabited in relation the circus as a public institution.

What ethical and methodological considerations need to be framed in using self-created records be used to supplement Loretta's 'archival traces'? While not all of Agnes and May's experiences relate to Loretta's (for example, both Agnes and May were in the performance space of acrobatics which fared better in terms of gender parity than clowning), there is significant overlap between the shape of their professional lives. The biographer can inhabit liminal space, between these documented experiences and the limited records of Loretta's life as the first woman clown in America. This is significant because it means that biographers can explore the lives of women even when only 'archival traces' remain.

On speculative biography

As a creative nonfiction writer, working with Loretta's 'archival traces' creates ongoing complications for my own creative practice. Yet this is not an unusual predicament; working with limited archival resources is a reality for many biographers and especially those working to uncover women's erased histories. In '"Will the Real Subject Please Stand Up?" Autobiographical Voices in Biography', Karen Lamb reflects on a fellow Australian biographer, Brain Matthews and his biography of Louisa Lawson, the little-known wife of the very famous Australian author Henry Lawson. Lamb discusses how Matthews' creates an 'invented alter-ego biographer' who 'speaks directly to the reader of his hapless quest: he must tell the story of Louisa Lawson ... about whom there is precious little primary source material' (2019, 3). To tell the story of Louisa's life and the difficulties of a limited record, Matthews felt he had to create another persona. Matthews' act of invention allows him to unpack and address biographical material he cannot verify. He is distanced from this material through the persona of 'Owen Stevens' whereas I have chosen to use a different kind of creative biographical method; I wish to engage with the limited record of Loretta's life on an equal footing with the archival documents that remain. My way of distinguishing what is speculation and what is documented in fact is through memoir, rather than a fictionalised persona.

In order to create a nonfiction account from 'archival traces', I am using the form of speculative biography alongside memoir. Donna Lee Brien writes of speculative biography:

> Although the recognition of subjectivity remains a contested issue among historians, speculative biographers assert that, by basing subjective empathy and imaginings in the documented facts (and making clear when this is not thus grounded), biographers can speculate but still ensure their texts are classified as non-fiction life writing (2015, 14–15)

Speculative biography pushes against the problem of how to integrate 'fictional' creative work into biography, an assimilation that Brien calls 'contentious' (2015, 1) or is otherwise viewed as suspicious. But the stories of biography are created by absences; the absence of the biographer often shapes a narrative. Often, the reader is presented with certainty of fact rather than the much more uncertain reality. The writer Siri Hustvedt examines this idea in *Living, Thinking, Looking*: 'the stories of memory and fiction are also made by absences–all the material that is left out' (2012, 181). Virginia Woolf too named the writer's arrangement of a life on the page 'the biographer's imagination', arguing that shaping a life into a narrative was a process of 'being stimulated to use the novelist's art of arrangement, suggestion, dramatic effect to expound the private life' (1960, 155). Much like Woolf's biographer's imagination, Wallace Notestein writes in *The Yale Review* that the biographer 'must use caution as well as imagination at every stage of his work, both in assembling the facts and in giving meaning to them' (1933, 77). Similarly, Lamb, reflecting on her experience of writing a biography of the novelist Thea Astley, argues that

> even though biography as a form presumes to 'edit' a life for 'presentation', that does not mean that a biographer is not at the same time—even subconsciously—editing their own life as part of the writing of a biography. (2019, 1)

For Lamb, 'a biographer's own life story necessarily plays into the creation of biography' (2019, 2). The experience of the biographer informs how they shape and narrate the life of their subject and affects the creative choices made.

The biographical project is thus always to some degree subjective but using speculative biography as opposed to 'traditional' biography amplifies this. As a methodology, speculating on certain detail where no other evidence exists allows me to explore the archival gaps and to 'research around' Loretta's life more openly. Yet this, in turn, inevitably raises ethical issues.

So, where Matthews 'invents' a persona so to make his narrative choices part of the biography and to be transparent about his role in assembling and shaping the life of Louisa Lawson, I will be using a speculative voice. Speculative biography is defined by Brien as 'subjective empathy and imaginings in the documented facts' (2015, 14) and is about imagining past what is known about a subject. As a methodology, speculation can be direct (where it is communicated to the reader through the use of language like 'perhaps') or indirect where, while present, it is not explicitly acknowledged to the reader (Lindsey 2020). Indirect speculation may be what Philip Herring meant when he spoke of a 'biographical licence' (Lindsey 2020). For myself, as a biographer, I will be arranging and assembling as well as using direct speculation[5] to write Loretta's life.

I argue that this methodology is essential to write a biography of women who have little archival information available on them. This argument transforms Brien's methodological approach of 'subjective empathy and imaginings' to an act of feminist intervention that allows a life that would otherwise be 'lost' to become public knowledge. Thus, 'subjective imagining' is not only appropriate within the form of biography, but an essential aspect of fighting the erasure of women's contributions throughout history. It is especially important to treat 'subjective empathy and imaginings' with an intersectional feminist lens—when speculating it is vital to consider not only gender but how it intersects with race, ethnicity, disability, class and sexuality. Reflexively considering how women's lives were impacted by dominant narratives of white supremacy and patriarchy, amongst others, will mean that to a biographer's best ability, the women they write about and the systems they lived within, will be better understood.

Within this consideration of race, ethnicity, disability, class and sexuality, as a biographer using the archives, I am in the complex position of using documents that are subject to systemic cultural bias to build a biographical narrative. These documents are all that are available to me and in trying to understand that they are subject to systemic bias, I use writer Margaret Atwood's work on writing her historical novel *Alias Grace* and her experience in researching Grace Marks, a woman convicted of murdering her employer in nineteenth Century Canada. In her article, 'In Search of Alias Grace: On Writing Canadian Historical Fiction', Atwood discusses her experience of looking for details of women's motivations and daily lives in the archives. Atwood writes that 'the past is made of paper' (1998, 1513) in reference to archival documents, saying that:

> There is—as I increasingly came to discover—no more reason to trust something written down on paper then than there is now. After all, the writers-down were human beings, and are subject to error, intentional or not, and to the very human desire to magnify a scandal, and to their own biases. I was often deeply frustrated, as well, not by what those past recorders had written down but by what they'd left out ... If you're after the truth, the whole and detailed truth, and nothing but the truth, you're going to have a thin time of it if you trust to paper; but, with the past, it's almost all you've got. (1998, 1514)

Atwood, while writing *Alias Grace*, created a methodology of not changing anything she knew to be a 'solid fact' (she uses the example of Grace not witnessing the execution of James McDermott, a stablehand who was convicted of the same crime). When there were suggestions of how events occurred in the archival documents she followed them, but 'in the parts left unexplained ... I was free to invent' (1998, 1515). While Atwood had more archival material to work with, this methodology is not dissimilar to my own, despite Atwood working within the genre of fiction and not biography. She describes her end product as being 'very much a novel rather than a documentary' (1998, 1515). For Atwood, speculating about historical detail within fiction gives her a freedom that is not available to the biographer, yet I believe her methodology for dealing with the limitations of the historical record are still relevant even though her genre is different.

Thinking through the ethics of speculation in nonfiction

Archivist Andrew Flinn discusses shaping archives, particularly independent community-led archives, whose stories have previously been beholden to dominant historical narratives. Flinn writes that when there is little recorded information, it's important to strike a balance in selecting and editing:

> Finding the balance between recovery and celebration in the face of dominant narratives which otherwise ignore and misrepresent on one hand, and an approach which offers a more reflective and complex version of a community's multi-faceted identities on the other is no easy task and one that can result in tensions within an organization or a variety of approaches at different times and in different contexts. (2011, 9)

For Flinn, the ethics of archive assembly are in how to strike the appropriate balance of tone and choice to make an archive that represents a community. For the writer using archives to form a creative work—and in this, a smaller archive of information—this is relevant, especially with speculative biography where it applies to choice and balance in speculation. The speculative biographer faces ethical concerns about what facts to include, what facts to leave out, and what facts to 'speculate'. Particularly in partial histories, the material sits between recovery and celebration. This issue then raises other issues, for example, about the politics of telling a particular story. Loretta lived at a time in US history when women's lives were subject to both social and legal restrictions and these lives (lived in the domestic sphere) were not as often written about or represented. Loretta's story too is important because it is about women's innovation and work in the circus, an experience underrepresented in circus histories and archives.

Atwood addresses the fallibility of collective memory, writing:

> We live in a period in which memory of all kinds, including the sort of larger memory we call history, is being called into question. For history, as for the individual, forgetting can be just as convenient as remembering, and remembering what was once forgotten can be distinctly uncomfortable. As a rule, we tend to remember the awful things done to us and to forget the awful things we did. (1998, 1505)

So how can a biographer write the 'awful things done' without forgetting the 'awful things' our subject might have done? Especially considering that writing biography means a relationship between biographer and subject that is 'formed in imagination' (Lamb 2019, 3). Steedman discusses the propensity to relate to and perhaps project on a biographical subject, writing of Frances Hamilton, 'I like this woman. I do not know if what I am doing is identifying, or projecting onto her; but I like her: her behaviour, her opinions; her confidence in her own judgement' (2009, 16). I, too, like Loretta. I admire her strength in navigating a career that, to this point, had no women performers. I admire her physicality and how she used her own physical strength to perform daily and travel around America in physically taxing conditions. I see myself in her love of canine companionship. Steedman goes on, 'the historian believes she understands; perhaps a spurious kind of intimacy is forged' (2009, 23). I have a relationship with Loretta through writing her biography—in what Tamboukou calls the 'act of narration' which is an 'embodied practice' that 'opens up a political sphere wherein human beings as narratable selves expose their vulnerability and dependence on each other' (2010, 171). All of these relationships exist yet I do not *know* her. The biographer-biographee relationship grapples with this, as Lamb writes of her experience seeing herself in the life of her subject, Thea Astley:

> Perhaps one might lean a bit too much towards being 'accepting of other people's flaws', to use Tomalin's wording. I know that when I came to appreciate that Astley was a passionately devoted mother of a single child, much as I was, to the point where the intensity of her attachment concerned others, I tended to frame any judgement in quoted remarks from other people, slightly shifting the onus of interpretation away from me. (2019, 5)

Writing another's life as a creative practitioner means that this relationship cannot help but be an emotionally murky one. The attachment is intense and ongoing, the 'afterlife' of a biography continues post publication (Lamb 2019, 2). It is perhaps natural, then, to think the best of our subjects as we wish them would be. Yet it is important to be reflexive and interrogate these attachments; in doing so, creating a more emotionally complex creative artefact.

Speculation allows empathic imagining—Brien's notion of 'subjective empathy and imaginings in the documented facts' (2015, 14)—and addresses the need to work with lives that have been overlooked. Speculation also acknowledges the subjective relationship biographers have to their work and allows for an exploration and presentation of this in a way that other kinds of biography might seek to elide. The question then, for the speculative biographer, might be: to what degree is it important to 'speculate' on matters that are not 'sympathetic' to the biographer's imagination?

Intersectionality

Loretta was a white woman in early twentieth century America. The circus is multi-faceted and while being a woman clown would have been difficult, she also benefitted from white supremacy in this era. Writing Loretta raises the issue that while feminists have felt the need to recuperate women's stories, there is an ethical obligation to avoid writing these stories without contextualising certain aspects of these women's experience. Judith Zinsser writes about the 'recovery of forgotten women's lives' through feminist biography, stating the importance of contextualising a woman oscillating between power and powerlessness:

> These women are all portrayed as active agents, not passive victims, however constraining or limiting their circumstances. These are not simple stories of 'power' and 'powerlessness', but rather complex examples of how these supposed poles of experience can co-exist in the same moment of a life. (2009, 45)

Loretta's gender and poverty excluded her from many archival records but being white and being married to a man allowed her certain freedoms that, for example, other kinds of circus performers might have been denied. Perhaps, it was her whiteness and marriage to Harry La Pearl which meant she is in the archive at all (however sparingly). Schwartz and Cook write that:

> Power over the documentary record, and by extension over the collective memory of marginalized members of society—whether women, non-whites, gays and lesbians, children, the under-classes, prisoners, and the non-literate—and indeed over their representation and integration into the metanarratives of history, resides in the decisions that archivists and manuscript curators make in soliciting and appraising collections, the ways in which institutional resources are allotted for procurement and processing of collections, and the priority given to their diffusion through source guides, publication, exhibitions, and web sites. (2002, 17)

There's a tension in Loretta's 'integration into the metanarratives of history' (Schwartz and Cook 2002, 17) that I believe requires an intersectional viewpoint. This perspective goes beyond considering Loretta's place in the archives but permeates through the biography. How much does privilege from whiteness play into Loretta's story, even though she was marginalised due to her gender? Can I speculate, having no information on her political perspective, that she participated in the dominant white supremacy narratives that were popular during that era in the circus?[6] In short, how can I speculate about Loretta's perspective without imposing a modern conception of race, gender, class, disability and sexuality? The speculative biographer must constantly negotiate with what needs to be imagined, and that this is not only about empathy—imagining how a subject feels—but about politics and history: conjuring events that characterise the time/culture/context in order to speculate on how the subject might have responded. Scholar and ex-Ringling Brothers and Barnum and Bailey Circus clown David Carylon writes that the racist practice of blackface began with circus clowns in America in the 1830s and continued on into the next century (2016, 177–178). For myself as a biographer, to what degree can I imagine that Loretta viewed this as acceptable/unacceptable? As it was widespread, ethically I believe I must speculate that Loretta viewed this as acceptable even though I have no proof that she engaged in this practice, no documents (but, I know that her husband did on at least one occasion).

Steedman, researching the life of Francis Hamilton, finds that Hamilton's interest in labour practices is only documented peripherally, through way of her reading list. Hamilton writes: 'got hold of Gilbert Imlay's Topographical Description of the Western Territory of North America in 1794, and cared for it, if her detailed noting of its multiple parts is anything to go by' (2009, 22). Reading anti-slavery literature may indicate Hamilton's opinion on the abolitionism, a stance that is appealing to Steedman herself. However, Steedman resists the temptation to lead the reader to one particular conclusion: 'I do not know whether that was what [Hamilton] actually concluded' (2009, 19). While the circus itself benefitted from and perpetuated racist practice, I cannot know whether Loretta did so. My 'reading-around' reveals that her husband did perform in blackface. It seems likely this was so routine that it would not have troubled Loretta, and that this was indeed a likely attitude for a white performer of the time. In the view of not-knowing, will I write her directly engaging in racist practices? I have no evidence to support it. But I can speculate.

Conclusion

Schwartz and Cook write that 'archives have the power to privilege and to marginalise. They can be a tool of hegemony; they can be a tool of resistance' (2002, 13). They 'are the basis for and validation of the stories we tell ourselves, the story-telling narratives that give cohesion and meaning to individuals, groups, and societies' (Schwartz and Cook 2002, 13). Through speculative biography, archives can be wielded as a tool of resistance; women's stories that were once absent or marginalised can be fleshed out into narratives of lives and movements. Writing women's biographies is an act of recuperation, as academics like Sidonie Smith and Judith Zinsser have shown. From archives, stories grow. Even when the traces left behind need a little massaging to be brought into back into the public realm.

As Tamboukou writes, concluding a paper with a question:

> How is it possible to go on telling and writing the stories we were entrusted with, in ways that are both transparent and meaningful, not in terms of how they represent 'reality' or reconstruct the past—which they can't—but of how they allow lives 'be looked upon in the end, like a design that has a meaning', stories of the feminist imaginary. (2010, 188)

I think, as Tamboukou writes, that we cannot reconstruct the past as it was. But I cannot answer her question, except for the unsatisfying 'we do it the best we can'. For we need women's stories to live on in the feminist imaginary.

Notes

1. The manuscript referenced here is *[Circus, vaudeville, theatrical performers, sports athletes, other curiosities in Australia and New Zealand, 1912–1937: newspaper and magazine clippings, collectables]* [Australia:, 1912]. Web. 29 April 2020 http://nla.gov.au/nla.obj-875549047.
2. See also Barrutia-Wood (2016, 107–116).

3. These dogs were dressed as boxers and were choreographed to appear to be boxing. The dogs were not fighting and were not harmed.
4. Wirth's scrapbook places her at Ringling in 1925 or 1927, Barnum and Bailey in 1912 and 1913. The scrapbook mentioned is: [*Scrapbooks, [ca. 1900]-1930 [microform] by May Wirth*]. [Australia: 1900]. Web. 27 January 2020 <https://catalogue.nla.gov.au/Record/188067?lookfor=may%20wirth&offset=6&max=80> National Library of Australia.
5. At this stage of the project, it is planned that the extent of speculation will be communicated through an author's note. However, I am still working with and interrogating these terms and methodology; I am not settled on them.
6. Earl Chapin May writes of the ongoing connection between circus, the Civil War, slavery and racism in *The Circus: From Rome to Ringling*.

Disclosure statement

No potential conflict of interest was reported by the author(s).

Works Cited

Atwood, Margaret. 1998. "In Search of Alias Grace: On Writing Canadian Historical Fiction." *The American Historical Review* 103 (5): 1503–1516.
Barrutia-Wood, Arantza. 2016. "Archive Piece: Lulu Adams—Female Clown and Circus Performer." *Early Popular Visual Culture* 14 (1): 107–116.
Brien, Donna Lee. 2015. "'The Facts Formed a Line of Buoys in the Sea of my own Imagination': History, Fiction and Speculative Biography." *TEXT Journal* 28: 1–21.
Burton, Antoinette. 2008. "Finding Women in the Archive: Introduction." *Journal of Women's History* 20 (1): 149–150.
Carlyon, David. 2016. *The Education of a Circus Clown: Mentors, Audiences, Mistakes*. New York: Palgrave Macmillan.
Farge, Arlette, Natalie Zemon Davis, and Thomas Scott-Railton. 2004. *Allure of the Archives*. Connecticut: Yale University Press.
Findlay, Cassie. 2016. "Archival Activism." *Archives and Manuscripts* 44 (3): 155–159.
Flinn, Andrew. 2011. "Archival Activism: Independent and Community-Led Archives, Radical Public History and the Heritage Professions." *InterActions: UCLA Journal of Education and Information Studies* 7 (2): 1–17.
Garvey, Ellen Gruber. 2003. "Scissorizing and Scrapbooks: Nineteenth Century Reading, Remaking and Recirculating." In *New Media, 1740-1915*, edited by Lisa Gitelman and Geoffrey B. Pingree, 207–227. Cambridge, MA: MIT Press.
Good, Katie Day. 2012. "From Scrapbook to Facebook: A History of Personal Media Assemblage and Archives." *New Media & Society* 15 (4): 557–573.
Gornick, Vivian. 2008. "Truth in Personal Narrative." In *Truth in Nonfiction: Essays*, edited by David Lazar, 7–10. Iowa: University of Iowa Press.
Helfand, Jessica. 2008. *Scrapbooks: An American History*. Connecticut: Yale University Press.
Hustvedt, Siri. 2012. *Living, Thinking, Looking*. New York: Picador.
Kristeva, Julia. 2001. *Hannah Ardent: Life is a Narrative*. Toronto: University of Toronto Press.

Kuipers, Juliana M. 2004. "Scrapbooks: Intrinsic Value and Material Culture." *Journal of Archival Organization* 2 (3): 83–91.

Lamb, Karen. 2019. "Will the Real Subject Please Stand Up? Autobiographical Voices in Biography." *Life Writing*, 1–6. doi:10.1080/14484528.2019.1672615.

Lindsey, Kiera. 2020. "Intermingling Estuaries: Speculative Biography: Life Writing Experiments that Shift Beyond the Binaries." Paper presented at *Australasian Association of Writing Program* 2020: *Rising Tides*, Griffith University, Queensland, Australia, November 18.

Notestein, Wallace. 1933. "History and the Biographer." *The Yale Review* 22 (Spring): 69–77.

Rowan, Leonie. 2001. "A Different Path: Marginality, Resistance and Drusilla Modjeska's Poppy." *Journal of Interdisciplinary Gender Studies* 6 (2): 47–59.

Schwartz, Joan M, and Terry Cook. 2002. "Archives, Records, and Power: The Making of Modern Memory." *Archival Science* 2 (1–2): 1–19.

Steedman, Caroline. 2009. "On Not Writing Biography." *New Formations* 67: 15–25.

Tait, Peta. 2005. *Circus Bodies: Cultural Identity in Aerial Performance*. Oxfordshire: Routledge.

Tamboukou, Maria. 2010. "Relational Narratives: Auto/Biography and the Portrait." *Women's Studies International Forum* 33 (3): 170–179.

"Women Circus Clowns are Rare." 1939. *Chronicle*, February 23, 54.

Woolf, Virginia. 1960. *Granite and Rainbow: Essays*. London: The Hogarth Press.

Zinsser, Judith. 2009. "Feminist Biography: A Contradiction in Terms?" *The Eighteenth Century* 50 (1): 43–50.

'A Man of Violent and Ungovernable Temper': Can Fiction Fill Silences in the Archives?

Katherine E Collins

ABSTRACT

Biofiction can be defined as fiction about a named, real person and is characterised by creativity, invention, and imaginative exploration. In this essay I deploy a mixture of nonlinear narrative and theoretical writing to explore the argument that creative ways of responding to archival silences illuminate, and also complicate, our attempts to recover women's lives from obscurity. As the text evolves, the narrative sections become more invented, more experimental, something more like fiction.

Maggie had written the story of the beginning over and over. The day when her granddaughter, Emily, had flatly refused to bring a coat, so Eve's big cream scarf was wrapped around the nine-year-old girl like one of those crossover beach dresses advertised in the glossy magazines that come with Saturday newspapers. It reminded her of the day she had tried to help Eve learn for herself why sensible people brought coats with them on cold days – unpleasantly bulky around their arms though they may be – by allowing her to walk to school without one, one freezing February morning. She doubted Eve would even remember it, but it made Maggie smile to think of her finally seeing things from her mother's point of view, thirty years later.

Their usual café was full, so they walked back along the high street hoping somewhere else would have room. Nearly at the end of the row of shops they tried a tiny side street, the last possibility. And there they found a row of little windows painted in that grey-apple-green that ex-Londoners like to use for the woodwork on their restored cottages. *The Milk-shake Café*, the sign said. Soon a hot chocolate, a pot of tea snuggled in a knitted cosy, and a frothy mocha jostled together on the chunky table. In the steamy warmth Maggie felt almost trapped in time, as if everything outside had speeded up while they were marooned on a 1950s island. Perhaps that was what made her think of her grandmother, Ethel, the teapot on a tray reminding her of cups and saucers and rich tea biscuits in bed, brought on a silver tray by a silver-haired, straight-backed old lady in a navy polka dot dress. Eve and Emily sat enthralled as Maggie told her granny's story: a young woman who lived in a big house with servants in the attic, and the man she wanted to marry against the wishes of her father.

'What did Granny's family have against Clifford?' asked Eve.

'I don't know,' Maggie said. 'It must have been some bust up, when you think about it. They cut her out completely.'
***

In 2006 David Lodge expressed surprise at how popular biographical novels have become. Also described in academic literature as 'biofictions' (Lackey 2016a, 3), these can be defined as fiction about a named, real person, and are characterised by creativity, invention, and imaginative exploration. The authors of such texts venture beyond the core postmodern argument that all textual representation is to some extent a creation by deliberately inventing 'stories that never occurred in order to answer perplexing questions, fill in cultural lacunae, signify human interiors, or picture cultural ideologies' (Lackey 2016b, 14). Well-known examples of contemporary literary biofictions include *In the Time of the Butterflies* by Julia Alvarez (1994); Michael Cunningham's *The Hours* (1998); and Joyce Carol Oates's *Blonde* (1999). Biofiction is not confined to postmodernist innovation though: Max Saunders traces the roots of these ideas back through Modernist, *fin de siècle*, and late-Romantic works. He prefers the term 'autobiografiction' (Saunders 2010, 7), which, he argues, complicates what at first might seem to be a straightforward relationship between Postmodernism and literary-biographical experimentation. Saunders's thesis holds that conflicting responses to life-writing, as well as helping to define the field, canon, and modes of interpretation of modern English literary history, have provoked new life-writing practices. These practices turn life-writing – biography and autobiography – into 'something different, something more like fiction' (Saunders 2010, 9).

Why might we want to transform life-writing, through literary experimentation, into something more like fiction? One reason might be to smuggle vitality into the absences that seem to echo through the archives when it comes to women's lives. In a period when the majority of biography and formal autobiography concerned itself primarily with the lives of men, as Saunders observes, 'fiction paradoxically becomes an arena for granting female experience an equivalent reality in the public sphere' (Saunders 2010, 10). No less of an issue today, it has been argued that elements of this formal, 'truth telling programme' (O'Brien 1991, 125) of realist biography continue to hold strong sway in the standards to which contemporary biographical and autobiographical texts are held, while the battle for experimentation must be 'fought anew in every generation' (Cline and Angier 2010, 58). The rewards, though, appear to be worth the struggle for feminist scholars and writers: to challenge the gendered assumptions associated with 'the linear development of a sovereign subject' (Novak 2017, 6). In this way, as Novak argues, experimenting with genre can be read as a 'form of symbolic action' (Frow 2006, 1–2). In this short essay I use a mixture of nonlinear narrative and theoretical writing to explore the argument that creative ways of responding to archival silences illuminate, and also complicate, our attempts to recover women's lives from obscurity. As the text evolves, the narrative sections become more invented, more experimental, something more like fiction.
***

'I think I've solved the mystery of Ethel's father!' Eve launched in as soon as she heard Maggie's voice on the phone.

'Oh yes?'

'Yes. Have you looked at the Southall divorce documents? I think they explain what he had against Clifford.'

Maggie had skimmed through when she added them to Clifford's parents' Ancestry profiles. The phrase that had stuck in her mind was 'a man of violent and ungovernable temper and intemperate habits'.

She sat down at her desk and switched on her computer, sipping her tea as she waited for the website to load. She didn't get any sense of Clifford's mother, Tishie, from these glimpses of her life through the straight-edged windows of census documents and parish records. Born Emma Jane Kentish – which must be the source of her nickname – in 1858, Tishie's childhood home was a substantial red brick house in Church Road, Moseley, a Victorian version of a commuter village about two miles south of the busy, smoky whirl of Birmingham. At some point before the 1871 census the Southall family moved in next door: Horatio, his wife Caroline, their three children, and two servants. The eldest son, Horatio William, was a solicitor like his father. Four years after that census, on 31st March 1875, Tishie and Horatio William were married at St Mary's Church, Moseley. She was 17, and he was 27. Their son, yet another Horatio, was born when Tishie was 19. The births of their daughter, Gladys, and their second son, Clifford – Ethel's Clifford – followed five and eight years later.

The documents reminded Maggie of the sort of zoetrope Tishie might have played with during her middle class Victorian childhood. She could use them to sketch out a series of frames in stale legal language – adultery and debts, a husband's violence and the humiliations he visited upon his wife – and then set them spinning until a jerky animation played to a whirring soundtrack.

Their house was built in the Arts and Crafts style, from what Maggie could tell online. Red brick topped by a tiled roof that ended its slope with an outwards flick, like a bell. Three small cottage style windows punctuated the upper frontage above an ornately latticed front door framed with thick white stonework, like the pillars and swirling icing on a wedding cake. Maggie had no way of knowing what their house was like inside, but she found herself swept up in the idea that they would have remained true to the aesthetic principles that informed the exterior: chalky, muted colours, natural materials, and simple floral motifs rather than the heavy, dark clutter of the more traditional Victorian home. As she added the layers of embroidery that brought colour to the white squares of the documents, Maggie imagined Tishie and Horatio William in their parlour, the walls behind the fireplace panelled with glowing rectangles of mid-brown oak, flanked with shelves from the same wood, groaning with leather bound volumes. On the floor a rug, woven in a pattern of flowers twining around a diamond of faded red, the homely airiness of the décor incongruous with the heavy, dark, and cluttered atmosphere as Horatio William slid his silver letter opener into a hand-addressed envelope. Inside was a letter from Mrs Benion asking for the repayment of a sum of £2, which she had advanced some weeks before. The letter prompted a fierce argument, during which Tishie called her husband a scamp, a rogue, a thief, and a liar, and then hurled a boot at him, which struck him on the head.

***

In June 2017 I presented a paper at the Centre for Life History and Life-writing Research conference, *Critical and Creative Approaches*, in which I explored the process of creating an autofictional character (Collins 2017). I read extracts from a novel-in-progress about Ethel, my great-grandmother, and the autofictional character herself, Eve, and I posed some straightforward questions about ethics and representation. During the discussion a doctoral student raised her hand. Are you saying, she asked, that I can simply *create* the internal narrative of the historical figure I'm researching? Forty sets of eyes turned to me, expectantly.

If life-writing should be judged according to conventional, realist criteria, then my answer to that student has to be emphatically no, but if, as I have outlined in a previous section, we accept the legitimacy and value of thinking differently about life-writing, then how might we assess the quality, the ethics, the aesthetic and historical value of these experimental texts? How to decide if a particular biofictional representation is an unethical 'misappropriated life' – a particularly unfortunate outcome if the life itself is already just a few curling archival scraps – or whether it is a valuable 'truthful fiction' (Lackey, 2016b, p. 229)?

It's tempting to turn to the comfortable domain of extensive and detailed research and seek reassurance there. Well, naturally the research must be beyond reproach, but there can be pitfalls: Barbara Mujica, who has herself written biographical novels about Diego Velazquez, Saint Teresa of Ávila, and Frida Kahlo, cautions that facts 'can overpower your characters and drain them of their vitality' (2016, 12). Which rather defeats the point of this kind of experimentation. So, whether a writer has produced a truthful fiction – rather than exploited a stolen identity – then, seems to come down to, in the simplest of terms, the skill, sensitivity, keen historical awareness and interpretive abilities of the writer to convey some sense of 'realness' without undermining what has been called the 'pact' that the writer will tell the truth (Lejeune 1989; see also Kacandes 2012, 386). This argument is similar to that of Jeanette Winterson, who wrote, in the context of how much fiction might be based on the author's own experience: 'The fiction, the poem, is not a version of the facts, it is an entirely different way of seeing' (2013, 28). The goal, then, is to 'persuade through the communicative forces of fantasy … to spin magic that engrosses and convinces the reader' (Vargas Llosa, trans Mujica p. 12).

At the conference in Sussex I answered the student with caution. I don't think we should 'make up' the thoughts and feelings of our subjects and call it history. I think that whenever we produce work, whether scholarly or creative, we offer it up to judgement by peers and readers, and we have to be clear about what sort of claims we make for it. If I'd had Lackey's book on the table in front of me, I might have quoted directly from that text, advising us all to consider whether the author has 'done the necessary work' and if they have demonstrated the ability to 'fulfil the mandates of their implicit truth contract?' (Lackey, 2016, p. 254).

***

The walls around the pale fireplace bloomed with William Morris' Daisy print; morning light from the small window fell on a box of books on the table beside a small, periwinkle seat. The only thing that jarred was the bed where Tishie sat in her nightgown, reading. A solid four-poster, made up with soft pillows and counterpane in delicate shades of summer skies to match the walls, ornate pillars carved from a wood so dark it appeared almost black, a relic of an earlier time.

Horatio William stormed into the room and caught sight of her sitting, content. He picked up the chamber pot in both hands, and tipped it over her head. For a moment she froze, cold ammonia-scented liquid trickling down her face, dripping from her hair. Then she threw her damp bedcovers aside and flew across the room, teeth bared.

'Stay away from me woman,' he said, dodging her with a cruel smirk, 'until you have taken a bath.'

'A bath!' Tishie raised her fists to strike. Horatio William grabbed her wrists, one in each hand, and held her away, squeezing hard enough to bruise, twisting one arm until Tishie cried out in a mixture of pain and frustration.

'I wish you were dead!' her voice cracked. 'If you were dying in the gutter I would not go across the road to help you!'

Horatio William tightened his hold on Tishie's wrists, straightening his arms to force some space between them before loosening his grip, only for her to try to strike him again. He hit out first, catching her a blow on the upper arm and knocking her to the floor where she remained, kneeling, still dripping with stale urine, fists clenched.

'Dad,' came a shocked voice. Horatio William turned to find his adult son standing outside the open door, the young man's expression making his contempt perfectly clear. 'Very few men would strike a woman like that!'

'Very few men must put up with such a woman. And one who neglects her most basic natural duty to her husband. It is a wonder that any man in such a marriage doesn't seek to fulfil his needs elsewhere.'

'Why don't you then?' screamed Tishie. 'Just go, go away from me and my children, go with any woman you please. Just leave us in peace.'

***

According to the divorce documents, Horatio William took Tishie's words, reproduced above, as conducive to his adultery with a woman named Alice Bembridge, of 4 Grosvenor Road in the parish of Houndsworth. On that basis, he asked the court that Tishie's petition for divorce be dismissed.

The 1901 census shows Alice Bembridge of 4 Grosvenor Road in the parish of Houndsworth was 28 years old, and lived with her two sisters: Martha, a dressmaker, and Rebecca, a Lacquer-ware worker. Alice was recorded as the head of that household; her occupation 'lets apartments'. Her father, Nicholas Bembridge, at that time was 53, lived in Balsall Heath, and was employed as a photographer. Horatio William was a year younger than Alice's father, and was living separately from Tishie and his children, in a boarding house in the parish of St Jude, along with the landlord, Richard Bradshaw, and 17 other boarders. I was curious to imagine why a 28-year-old woman of apparently independent means would be interested in a relationship with a man more than twenty years her senior, a bankrupt with a string of failed business ventures (Birmingham Daily Post 1887), embroiled in an embarrassing marital situation.

The 'character' of Alice Bembridge could be written as a calculating Madam (if the profession of 'letting apartments' were to be interpreted euphemistically). But what would such a person gain from a relationship with Horatio William in his present circumstances? This version of Alice might be playing the long game, encouraged by Horatio William to believe that he'd win his case in the High Court and gain his requested relief from Tishie who, according to the Rate Books of that year, by 1901, was the owner of nine houses in Pershore Road. This Alice might also have an eye to the circumstances of Horatio William's father-in-law (William Kentish was a wealthy man: when he died in 1913 he left £28,094 3s 6d – about £3 million today, according to the Bank of England's online inflation calculator). But that version of a long game seems like a long shot, and couching a story in these terms a breach of the implied truth contract. What seems more possible is that at 52, Horatio William, who was, from documented accounts, a handsome and charismatic man, was attractive, and Alice simply fell for him.

***

Dear God. When she looked at him properly, in daylight, he wasn't even that handsome. The little wet snuffles increased in volume until a snore caught in his throat and he coughed, foetid stale whiskey breath washing over her. He was not handsome at all in fact. Dear God. And his wife had given them her blessing. Or at least, that's what he shouted as he lurched up the narrow staircase last night, deaf to her pleas to lower his voice, to have a care for her sisters, their neighbours. Dear God.

This stooped paunchy brute who hawked in his throat and scratched his balls was nothing like the powerful, untouchable businessman with his starched white collars and silk cravats, whose hair glowed in flickering lights as he threw back his head with laughter and charmed his investors with promises of high returns. He was the most sophisticated man she'd ever met. Named for the Admiral, he'd say, and call her Lady Hamilton as he knelt to run his hands up the silk stockings he'd bought.

This shuffling stranger with unkempt moustaches and white hairs sprouting on his cheeks had snatched away the man who'd consumed her, whose cologne she'd splashed on her sheets so she could inhale his memory in the morning. She resented the deception bitterly, but not as much as she begrudged his continued presence.

Horatio William didn't ask to stay with Alice and her sisters, he simply didn't leave. She needn't have worried about her neighbours or tenants because no one saw him. He only ever had one visitor, his solicitor, Mr Gough, a compact closed-in pinstriped man who would bring sheaves of papers covered in copperplate script. Papers Horatio William would seize and scrutinise until the early hours of the morning, grunting and muttering odd phrases as he scored the paper with red ink. 'Cruelty! Cruelty be dammed' and 'kicked, kicked? Ridiculous.'

He lost his case in the High Court. He lost his assets and custody of his two younger children. Worse than that it was all over the national newspapers, even quoting his eldest son's testimony against him. But worse still, much worse, was the papers naming Alice herself. 'How could you, how could you let this happen?' she sobbed, her face buried in print-smudged hands.

The despised creature lifted its greying dishevelled head and bellowed, 'It's you that's brought this misfortune to *my* door. Adultery with *Alice Bembridge*, isn't that your name, hmm? The reason they sided with that ... *woman*?' He swiped at her head with the newspaper, the thick fold catching the corner of her eye. A trickle of red oozed down, a single furious tear. It would be the only one she shed for him.

Acknowledgements

Thanks are due to Eve Wedderburn for insightful comments on drafts of this article.

Disclosure statement

No potential conflict of interest was reported by the author.

ORCID

Katherine E Collins ⓘ http://orcid.org/0000-0001-5333-7377

References

"1901 England Census" [database on-line]. Provo, UT, USA: Ancestry.com Operations Inc, 2005. Class: *RG13*; Piece: 2712; Folio: *82*; Pages: *5, 41, 1*.

Birmingham Daily Post. 1887. Monday May 9, 1887 (p. 6); Wednesday August 3 1887 (p. 6); Tuesday October 4 1887 (p. 6).

"Civil Divorce Records". 2012. *The National Archives of the UK; Kew, Surrey, England; Class: J 77; Piece: 719. Ancestry.com. England & Wales, 1858-1916 [Database on-Line].* Provo, UT, USA: Ancestry.com Operations, Inc. (p. 83).

Cline, Sally, and Carole Angier. 2010. *The Arvon Book of Life Writing: Writing Biography, Autobiography and Memoir.* London: Methuen Drama.

Collins, Katherine. 2017. "The fiction in truth: creating an autobiographical character" Paper." Paper presented at the 9th annual Brighton-Sussex postgraduate conference at the University of Sussex, 16 June.

Frow, John. 2006. *Genre, The New Critical Idiom.* London: Routledge.

Kacandes, Irene. 2012. "Experimental Life-Writing." In *The Routledge Companion to Experimental Literature,* edited by Joe Bray, Alison Gibbons, and Brian McHale, 386. London: Routledge.

Lackey, Michael. 2016a. "Locating and Defining the Bio in Biofiction." *A/b: Auto/Biography Studies* 31: 3–10.

Lackey, Michael. 2016b. *The American Biographical Novel.* London: Bloomsbury.

Lejeune, Philippe. 1989. *On Autobiography,* 3–30. Minneapolis: University of Minnesota Press.

Lodge, David. 2006. "The author's curse", *Guardian,* 20 May 2006 https://www.theguardian.com/books/2006/may/20/featuresreviews.guardianreview2 [accessed 1 August 2018].

Mujica, Barbara. 2016. "Going for the Subjective: One way to Write Biographical Fiction." *A/b: Auto/Biography Studies* 31: 11–20.

Novak, Julia. 2017. "Experiments in Life-Writing: Introduction." In *Experiments in Life-Writing. Palgrave Studies in Life Writing,* edited by L. Boldrini, and J. Novak, 1–36. London: Palgrave Macmillan.

O'Brien, Sharon. 1991. "Feminist Theory and Literary Biography." In *Contesting the Subject: Essays in the Postmodern Theory and Practice of Biography and Biographical Criticism,* edited by William H. Epstein, 123–133. West Lafayette: Purdue University Press.

"Rate Books". 2014. *Textual Records. Library of Birmingham, Birmingham, England. Ancestry.com. Birmingham, England, Rate Books, 1831-1913 [Database on-Line].* Provo, UT, USA: Ancestry.com Operations, Inc.

Saunders, Max. 2010. *Self Impression: Life-Writing, Autobiografiction, and the Forms of Modern Literature.* Oxford: Oxford University Press.

Vargas Llosa, Mario. 1999. *La Verdad de las Mentiras [The Truth of Lies].* Barcelona: Seix Barral. quoted in Barbara Mujica (p. 12).

Winterson, Jeanette. 2013. *Art Objects: Essays on Ecstasy and Effrontery.* London: Random House.

Killing the Silent Witness: The Benefits of an Authorial Stance as Interpreter in Future-focused Natural Biography

Sarah Pye [ID]

ABSTRACT

The traditional role of biographer as 'silent witness' has been replaced by a spectrum of subjective authorial points of view which include that of omniscient narrator and authorial fictional character. This essay argues that the lesser discussed perspective of 'interpreter' is more effective in scientific and conservation biographies which aim to elicit environmental engagement from the reader. It uses the interdisciplinary scholarship of environmental interpretation, which 'involves translating the technical language of a natural science or related field into terms and ideas that people who aren't scientists can readily understand' [Ham. 1992. *Environmental Interpretation: A Practical Guide for People with big Ideas and Small Budgets*. Golden, CO: North American Press, 3] and examples from my own research into the life of Malaysian ecologist Dr Wong Siew Te to explore this perspective.

Introduction

Mark Schorer, biographer of American novelist Sinclair Lewis (Schorer 1963) said the biography has two subjects—'the figure whose life is being recreated and the mind that is recreating it' (Schorer 1962). Traditionally, that second subject was expected to remain hidden, ostensibly to prevent subject bias and ensure objectivity, but, in the early twentieth century, biographers, such as Virginia Wolf and Lytton Strachey, experimented with the genre's form, prompting a tsunami of varying authorial perspectives which included those of omniscient narrator and the inclusion of the author as fictional character. In 2016, as I embarked on writing the biography of Malaysian biologist and tropical ecologist Dr Wong Siew Te, I considered how my presence in the narrative affected how my work was written and read (Ricketson 2014; Gutkind and Buck 2008), and found myself grappling with these and other perspectives just as Virginia Woolf had before me (Backscheider 1999). My decision to take the role of 'interpretive narrator' (Nadel cited in Allen 1986) was informed by the interdisciplinary scholarship of Environmental Interpretation. This paper explores the benefits of this perspective.

Biographical subject

I chose Dr Wong Siew Te as my biographical subject for three reasons. First, his ground-breaking and important research was little known and had not been the subject of a long-form non-fiction narrative before. When Wong began studying the Malayan sun bear in the 1990s, he was one of only three researchers in the world focusing on this species and the only researcher native to the country in which sun bears are endemic. His quest to save this vulnerable species spans three continents and more than three decades.

Second, the focus of his research and life's work, the Malayan sun bear (*Helarctos malayanus*) is both relatively unknown, and integral to the health of the tropical rainforest of SE Asia. Wong spent six years trapping and researching sun bears in the rainforest. During this time, he identified captive rescued bears living in appalling conditions and raised funds to create the Bornean Sun Bear Conservation Centre on the edge of the Kabili Sepilok Forest Reserve in Sabah, Malaysia. It opened to the public in 2014 and now houses approximately 40 rescued bears. In addition, Wong's team has reintroduced eight adult bears back into the wild. BSBCC offered me an unparalleled opportunity to use individual bear histories to illustrate issues such as habitat loss, poaching and the illegal wildlife pet trade.

Third, Wong is a Malaysian working on conservation in his own country. He was named both '*Wira Nagaraku*' (Malaysian Hero) by his own government, and one of 25 CNN World Wildlife Heroes in 2017 (Koshy 2017). Ethnic diversity is lacking in the conservation movement, which has been called a form of white middle class nature-protection elitism (Pepper 1993). A better understanding of how communities interact with wildlife is needed in the field (Bakels et al. 2016) and life stories can help facilitate. Wong's connection to country allowed me to develop culturally nuanced biography with the capacity to become an important environmental engagement tool providing inspiration for the edification of would-be scientists or armchair conservationists by exposing them to 'people doing great things with courage, stamina and creativity' (Orr 1999, 1244). In biography, however, the subjective voice of the author can impact the level of engagement. I investigated a range of authorial perspectives, which included those of omniscient narrator and fictional character, before settling on positioning myself as interpreter. This paper compares those three stances and proposes that a subjective interpretive stance is the most appropriate in a biography which aims to elicit environmental behavioural change.

Silent witness

Traditionally, biographic writing assumes the writer is a silent witness and this objective treatment is still preferred by many. For instance, Backscheider (1999) criticizes biographies where the author present in the work, believing this practice confuses the narrative structure. Rhiel and Suchoff (1996, 3) maintain 'If you believe the myth of objective fact and objective biography, the self is not supposed to be in biography at all'. During the early part of the twentieth century the conventional position of the biographer evolved and biographies began to incorporate narrative innovation (Nadel 1984). One of the early innovators of the new style, Lytton Strachey (1880–1932), believed a biographer needs to have a point of view, pushing the objective boundaries. Strachey said that uninterpreted truth is 'as useless as buried gold'(Edel 1984, 182) and Edel acknowledged that the author is never really silent, opening the opportunity for representational perspective and widening the spectrum of subjective authorial points of view. My practice-led research included investigation of the spectrum including those of omniscient narrator and author as fictious character.

Omniscient narrator

The omniscient biographer is a metaphoric 'fly on the wall' who constantly characterises, comments and analyses (Edel 1984, 183). This perspective is the closest to the traditional silent witness, but it is difficult to maintain. In his work *Evil Angels*, (1985) a retrospective look at Australia's most publicised miscarriage of justice in which Lindy Chamberlain was jailed for the murder of her baby Azaria (Ricketson 2014), Bryson assumes this perspective. Although he writes numerous scenes he witnessed as a court reporter, Bryson chooses not to acknowledge his presence, going so far as to recount an altercation between three journalists and two radio reporters without acknowledging himself as one of the journalists (Bryson 1985, 529–530). By not declaring—or worse hiding—his subjectivity, Bryson undermines the trust between writer and reader. All-knowing omniscience erroneously suggests a level of knowledge about the subject which can never be completely substantiated, prompting Ricketson to question 'is the omniscient authorial voice appropriate in narrative non-fiction when, by definition, practitioners cannot know everything about the people and events they are writing up?' (2014, 6) and Bobinski's (1982) to comment that 'novelists have omniscience, biographers never do'. I resisted the use of the omniscient voice because I was aware that I was telling only one version of the truth (Pearson cited in Brien 2014; Edel 1984; Gerard 1996) and I felt it important to acknowledge and address the possibility of cultural and colonial bias within the narrative. With my target audience being primarily Western, I also felt the effectiveness of the narrative depended, to a large extent, on my narrative presence (Gutkind and Buck 2008). This excerpt, told through the eyes of an 'outsider' (Root 2008, 160) on a grocery shopping trip, would not have been possible using an omniscient voice:

> … as Wong discusses cuts of beef in Mandarin, I try to identify fragrances and decipher products. The shelves tell a story of a colonial past, a multicultural present, and a reluctance to dismiss tradition. To my surprise, along with a splattering of Malay, Arabic and Mandarin, every label includes English titles. Heinz salad dressing and mint sauce placate British expatriates next to two-kilo tins of Mother's Choice margarine. A row of MasterFoods spice jars stands to attention next to haphazardly hanging plastic bags of Chinese spices with hand-written stickers, their corners curling. (Pye 2020, 183)

Fictitious character

In many instances, biographers have dealt with the subjectivity of their craft by fictionalising themselves as a character within the story to acknowledge alternative perspectives (Ricketson 2014) and observe from within (Root 2008, 160). Pulitzer Prize-winning biographer Edmund Morris wrote himself into his authorised biography of Ronald Reagan, *Dutch* (1999), as a fictional character in order to 'flesh out Reagan's hidden and puzzling personality' (Gutkind 2012, 39) but he was highly criticised for blurring the boundaries between fact and fiction (Brien 2014). Other attempts at fictionalisation, such as *In Search of J.D. Salinger* (Hamilton 1988), and *The Australian Love Letters of Raymond*

Chandler (Close 1995), were considered more successful because the character was used to render apparent the nature of the research and narrative construction (Brien 2014). However, the inclusion of a fictional narrator blurs the lines between genres (Straight 2012) and readers are often unsure if they are reading fact or fiction unless they are told (Abbott 2008). Some have purported to write memoirs which were later found to be complete fiction (Gutkind 2012, 35). *A Million Little Pieces* (Frey 2003) for instance, sold more than 1.77 million copies in the US in 2005, marketed as a non-fiction memoir (Dahmen 2010). It chronicled the author's battle with alcohol and drug addiction making substantive but fabricated claims which, because of its nonfiction label, resulted in a US federal class-action lawsuit costing Random House over \$US2 million (Dahmen 2010). In *Misha: A Memoire of the Holocaust Years* (Defonseca 1997), the author claimed she was adopted by a pack of wolves as she searched for her deported parents. When Monique de Wael (Defonseca's real name) was cornered, she defended the book as *her* reality. In order to consider my work a nonfiction narrative, I felt it important to remain as true to the spirit and facts as possible (Gutkind 2012; Edel 1984) and I decided not to fictionalise myself because I believe this treatment blurs the lines between genres (Straight 2012). Including myself as a *nonfictional* character, however, gave me licence to draw conclusions from Wong's witnessed emotions (Gerard 1996) which is impossible in nonfiction when using third person limited point of view (Gerard 1996). For instance:

> Exactly a decade after Chai's death, Wong and I are working next to each other on his bench desk. He has been remote and pensive all day. Before I close my laptop for the night, he recounts the conversation. It's one he hopes he will never have to make again. Wong puts down his steaming mug, diverting his eyes. Outwardly, he stares into the depths of his fish tank; inwardly, into the depths of his soul. Time may have dulled the pain's immediacy, but Wong is still visibly shaken. (Pye 2020, 155)

Interpreter

Crafting a 'jumbled assortment of recollections and anecdotes' into a story about someone else's experiences always requires an 'interpretive filter' (Carey 2008), but Nadel believes interpretation is more than just choosing what to discard, and what to keep. He defines an 'interpretive narrator' (cited in Allen 1986) as someone who guides the reader by establishing meaning—facilitating connection between the reader and the content from within its pages (Nadel 1984). When the content is alien to the reader, an interpretive narrator can smooth challenging material and aid understanding. Although the interpretive stance is the most difficult perspective to sustain, Nadel (1984, 171) says it is the 'most absorbing to read'. Since he coined the term in 1984, it has not gained traction in creative writing literature, but the stance is certainly evident in practice.

The Immortal Life of Henrietta Lacks is a powerful example of the author positioning herself within the narrative in an interpretive stance. It is a compelling historiographic biography in which author Rebecca Skloot is a pivotal character as she uncovers the story of Henrietta Lacks, an African American woman diagnosed with aggressive cervical cancer. In 1951 and without her consent, doctors removed a sample of Ms Lacks' tissue and gave it to a laboratory attempting to grow human cells. The resulting HeLa immortal cell line has been responsible for many scientific discoveries in the last seventy-five years (Skloot 2009) and it has also tested the ethics of biospecimens (Beskow 2016). Skloot incorporates details of her investigation into both the scientific community and the Lacks family, particularly her developing relationship with the dead woman's conflicted daughter, Deborah. The complexities of the relationships between the author and Deborah add to the richness of the biography in a 'narrative pictorial' style (Edel 1984). Skloot weaves the heart-breaking family history with ethical and legal issues surrounding the use of the HeLa cell line (Bloom 2010), creatively interpreting complex, and often dry, scientific events or facts for a general audience:

> Years later, Robert Stevenson, who became president of the American Type Culture Collection, described Gartler's talk to me this way: 'He showed up at that meeting with no background or anything else in cell culture and proceeded to drop a turd in the punch bowl'. (Skloot 2009, 154)

I explored how I could position myself as interpreter of culture and science, taking my reader on a journey of discovery as Skloot does. Just as her narrative has three strands: the scientific story, the story of Deborah, and her own investigative journey, mine had the science of sun bears, the story of Wong, and my own journey of discovery. Like Skloot, I was a cultural outsider—a 'four-eyed traveller' trying to see the world through the eyes of the subject, yet also through my own (Edel 1984, 236). Just as Skloot's used the story of one woman's cells to delve into a wide history of cell discovery and application, I used one man's extraordinary life to incorporate a wider conservation narrative. However, unlike *The Immortal Life of Henrietta Lacks*, which was a historical retrospective narrative, my story aimed to evoke future environmental behavioural change. Once I decided to position myself as an interpreter, I found the subgenre of natural biography, coupled with the discipline of environmental interpretation assisted in nuancing my subjective perspective.

Natural biography

Saving Sun Bears can be considered an eco-biography—an ecology-based life writing narrative that considers the relationships of living organisms with their physical environment (Funda 2014) in which it is impossible to see where 'nature ends and the Self begins' (Farr and Snyder 1996, 203). It is an important definition as humans try to address a real disconnect with natural systems. However, the term eco-biography is insufficiently differentiated from what was previously called natural biography, described as 'place-based, ecological literature of the self' (Straight 2012, 12). Such stories recognise that the subject exists only in relation to the environment. They associate 'good' science with its application. What differentiates natural biography from general scientific biography is a future projection which attempts to elicit engagement in an ethic of care. This is the sub-genre's unique strength since, in the Anthropocene era, environmental impacts and the associated damaging societal outcomes, will continue unfettered if nothing is done and human ignorance and inertia prevails (Betzold 2015; Spires, Shackleton, and Cundill 2014; Piggott-McKellar et al. 2019). As Lawrence Buell (2005, vi) pointed out, 'For technological breakthroughs, legislative reforms, and paper covenants about environmental welfare to take effect … requires a climate of transformed environmental values, perception, and will' and without significant change by a majority, human behaviour has the capacity to lead to our eventual demise (Tonn and Stiefel 2014). Unfortunately,

Hayes (2006) and others since (Redford et al. 2018; Agol, Latawiec, and Strassburg 2014) found recent conservation projects have had little or mixed impact on reversing or reducing biodiversity loss, due to a lack of community, political and industrial commitment. Because many studies have shown a correlation between pro-environmental behaviour and an individual's level of environmental knowledge (Rickinson 2001), more creative communication of conservation science to the general public is a pre-requisite for the survival of the human race and the natural environment (Root-Bernstein and Scott 1999; Hobbs 1998a, 1998b). Faced with a potential apocalyptic future, Straight (2012, 13) said natural biographers 'write in order to envision and to construct more sustainable lives'. Biographies of conservation scientists, such as Wong, have the capacity to elicit positive change in social and political behaviour (Straight 2012) while improving environmental literacy (Verdier and Collins 2017) and evoking global stewardship.

Although natural biography is a recent term, its roots can be traced to the transcendentalism movement of the 1820s and 1830s when American Henry David Thoreau moved from Waldo Emerson's homestead and 'squatted' in a cabin on the banks of Walden Pond (still on Emerson's land) (Killingsworth 2013). The diaries he wrote during this transient period formed the basis of *Walden* (Thoreau and Fender n.d.). Within its pages, Thoreau resisted traditional disciplinary and generic boundaries (Kuhn 2009), while simultaneously conducting scientific study. As the railway impinged on life in the village of Concord in 1849, heralding the new epoch, Thoreau protested against the changes taking place around him, suggesting a return to a simpler life. Rather than look backwards, as most biographies and memoirs of his time did, Thoreau spearheaded life-writing which interpreted the present and projected it into the future. It is this future-focus for which *Walden* is regarded as a seminal natural biography (Edlich 2010). It was a focus which also defined *A Sand County Almanac,* a series of autobiographical place-based essays first published in 1949 (Leopold 1992), advocating ethical connection to the environment and informing the emerging U.S. conservation movement.

Richard Nelson's natural life narrative essay compilation, *The Island Within* (Nelson 1989), is based on the author's journals, and was heavily influenced by the work of Thoreau and Leopold. It recounted a series of expeditions to an unnamed island in Alaska, where Nelson learned ancient wisdom from the Native American residents and incorporated it into his book. *The Island Within* was published during another environmental upheaval—the American Republican party's opposition to environmental policies of the 1960s and 1970s (Edlich 2010). Nelson's future-focus questioned and critically examined human impact, clearly encapsulating challenges of the Anthropocene. I found myself agreeing when he wrote 'I have come seeking a better sense of how I fit into this place, not only as a visitor and watcher, but as a participant' (Nelson 1989, 172). I aimed to connect a predominantly Western audience questioning its own place in the world with a different way of being. Incorporating my own evolving conservation journey within the narrative, positioned me as interpreter of the world which I temporarily inhabited:

> A wave of complicit survivor guilt washes over me. Was the release a mistake because the ending might not be a happy one? What part did I play in that? Am I complicit for consuming too many resources which impact climate change —the real culprit? Am I at fault simply by being human? In a split second, my admiration of Wong's unrelenting commitment deepens. So too my understanding of apathy and inaction around climate change. I fight

the fear of doing the wrong thing, while knowing inaction is decision by default. (Pye 2020, 281)

In a similar way, Barry Lopez's reflection in *Arctic Dreams* (2001) leaves the reader in no doubt of the authors presence in the narrative and of his environmental concerns: 'We have irrevocably separated ourselves from the world that animals occupy … We manipulate them to serve the complicated ends of our destiny' (Lopez 2001, 200). Safina (2002), too, ends his research narrative of an albatross called Amelia with the question: 'Could we not recognise ourselves as part of the same chain of life, originated from the same hotspot?'

Environmental interpretation

The emotive language, future-focus, and the attempt to evoke action which are important elements in natural biography, are mirrored in the scholarly discipline of environmental interpretation which 'involves translating the technical language of a natural science or related field into terms and ideas that people who aren't scientists can readily understand' (Ham 1992, 3). Freeman Tilden (1883–1980), referred to as the father of the discipline (Beck 2002), uses an example from the writings of Charles Darwin to illustrate good environmental interpretation. While in South America in the 1830s, on the second voyage of HMS Beagle, Darwin describes the landscape as consisting of 'various kinds of submarine lava, alternating with volcanic sandstones and other sedimentary deposits' (cited in Tilden 1977, 20) which is a factual and objective delivery of information. Darwin then elaborates, interpreting the information by bringing geology to life and making his observations relevant to the reader:

> It required very little geological practice to interpret the marvellous story which this scene at once unfolded … I saw the spot where a cluster of fine trees once waved their branches on the shores of the Atlantic, when that ocean came to the foot of the Andes … the trees now changed into silex, were exposed, projecting from the volcanic soil, now changed into rock, whence formerly, in green and budding state, they had raised their lofty heads. (Darwin cited in Tilden 1977–21).

Good environmental interpretation should lead the reader to personal discovery or revelation with elements of suspense and surprise, provoking interest and curiosity while connecting the audience with the subject matter (Beck 2002; Tilden 1977). I experimented with the element of revelation in the opening paragraph of my story. Rather than delivering just the basic and 'dry' information about the rehabilitation of sun bears, I used the readers' perceived anthropocentric assumptions as to how they might bid farewell to a friend, to craft a scene between Wong and a character called Natalie. When I had captured the reader's interest, I used the element of surprise to reveal that Natalie was a sun bear, leading to revelation as I took the reader on the journey with me by exposing the truth (Tilden 1977):

> May 16th 2015 was Wong's birthday and his dreams were about to come true. Yet emotions seldom travel alone, so he also suppressed a sadness as he prepared to say farewell to a close friend. Wong hoped he would never see her again and took a few minutes to say his goodbyes before moving to a safe distance. The translocation cage had been tipped ninety degrees on its side and he knew once he pulled the rope in his sweaty hand, there was no turning back. He glanced at his watch. 10.40 am. Then tugged. (Pye 2020,15)

Just as biography has always been the 'dynamic interaction of lives—those of biographer, subject, and the reader' (Backscheider 1999, 162) the audience is central in effective environmental interpretation. Tilden (1883–1980) saw it as an approach to communication which uses relationships and meanings, rather than isolated 'cold' facts (Ham 1992, 3; Tilden 1977). The interpreter's role is to reveal connections which are relevant to the audience based on their values, motivations and satisfactions (Beck 2002; Lee 1986). An interpretive narrative, therefore, adopts a constructionist viewpoint which understands readers are not blank slates. They are, instead, active participants (Australian Education Council cited in Ballantyne 1998, 83) influenced by their prior knowledge and experiences (Ballantyne and Bain 1995; Roschelle 1992; Ballantyne 1998). By including myself as interpreter and offering differing viewpoints and insights (Beck 2002) into sun bear science and Malaysian culture, I was essentially guiding the reader through material which they may find challenging. My subjective experience, therefore, had the capacity to help reconcile conflict by 'making new things familiar, and familiar things new' (Johnson, S cited in Beck 2002, 117). For instance, my reader would not have taken a sun bear to a medical centre, but they may have taken their child, so I smoothed understanding by making the connection:

> Taking a child for an x-ray can be an inconvenience but taking a sun bear for an x-ray is an adventure with a whole different level of complexity ... [Wong] smiles as he recounts the startled look on the other patients' faces as a sun bear was carried through the front door on a canvas stretcher. (Pye 2020, 227)

I incorporated global conservation milestones in my story to add significance to Wong's experiences and draw connections to an international reader. My subjective interpretive stance enabled me to illustrate such milestones with scenes. For example, I illustrated the scientific importance of the Rajah Brooke's birdwing butterfly (trogonoptera brookiana), which helped Alfred Russel Wallace formulate his own theory of evolution, by combining Wong's experience in Borneo with my own in London:

> An iridescent green Rajah Brooke's birdwing flitted past. Wong turned full circle to follow, his arms outstretched, lungs expanding with fresh air.

> I am trying to track down the same butterfly, but this time I'm a long way from the pulsating jungle. I'm in London for a writing conference and I've taken a few hours off to visit the British National History Museum. Beneath cathedral ceilings, I face a palatial staircase. On the first landing, a white marble effigy of Charles Darwin surveys the exhibits with surety. Without the man I am searching for, however, Darwin's greatest work might have never seen the light of day. (Pye 2020, 111)

Environmental interpretation plays a role in framing engaging narratives and has the potential to evoke action (Tedlock 2011). This was directly related to my own goal of helping the reader 'perceive more acutely the world around them, the cultures that preceded and coexist with their own, and how they can affect the future ways in which humans will live in this world'(Knudson, Cable, and Beck 2003, 115). I wished to leave the reader with both the understanding that one person *can* make a difference in environmental conservation and engender the impetus to become a change-maker. As the US Park Service Administration Manual says 'through interpretation, understanding; through understanding, appreciation; through appreciation, protection'(cited in Tilden 1977, 38).

Cultural interpretation

Interpreting the experiences of someone from a different culture came with a unique set of challenges and opportunities but they were not solely informed by the Western/Asian or the Christian/Taoist binary I first suspected. Wong was born a Taoist; appropriated a Buddhist world view; lived in Taiwan for several years, and the US for a decade; lives in a predominantly Muslim country; and embraces elements of Indigenous animist beliefs. I could also be classified as a global citizen having been born in Europe, spent my early years in England, my formative years in the Caribbean; a decade in the US; and immigrating to Australia. However, I was cognizant that some of my own values were anchored in colonial thinking. I attempted to address this by acknowledging the potential for colonial or Western bias in my subjective perspective (Lawrence 2015; Snodgrass 1992; Tedlock 2011):

> The documentary's London premiere is a few short hours away. As he counts down the hours, Wong spends the day contemplating the ostentatious architecture of an imperial past, built partly on the bent back of his own nation. (Pye 2020, 161)

A colonial perspective is also evident in the conservation movement which is underpinned by an insipid undercurrent of Western superiority which has privileged Western doctrines over indigenous knowledge (Vivanco 2002; Stronza 2001; Pyhala, Osuna Orozco, and Counsell 2016). Much of the current debate over species protection, for instance, is based on colonial patterns (DeMello 2012) which perpetuate a popular conservationist narrative of sending 'white Westerners abroad to save the wildlife from the natives' (Vivanco 2002, 1199). This perceived lack of non-Western voices in the conservation discourse is potentially dangerous because it turns poor nations into 'targets for social and political intervention by privileged countries' (Huggan 2013, 42; Escobar 1995). If written well, biography has the capacity to open up a 'cultural marketplace' (Rhiel and Suchoff 1996, 3) and expand the conservation discourse. Passages like this one addressed that imbalance:

> Wong was grateful for the weight of Attenborough's voice, yet he hoped by the next globally significant challenge in Sabah, the protests of the local conservation community would be loud enough. Intuitively, he knew Sabah needed a local figurehead, rather than a colonial one. (Pye 2020, 341)

While this passage, which compares the Taoist Metta Sutta, (an important ethical guide for Wong), with a work I call 'my own kindness code' used my interpretive voice to draw attention to similarities which cross cultural boundaries:

> I read on: "So, with a boundless heart, one should cherish all living beings; radiating kindness over the entire world ... freed from hatred and ill-will." The Desiderata interrupts my thoughts again, "You are a child of the universe, no less than the trees and the stars. You have a right to be here ... The universe is unfolding as it should." (Pye 2020, 289)

I felt, like Nadel, that my 'outsider's gaze' proved beneficial to highlight 'simultaneous connections or contrasts' (Nadel 1984, 202) between Wong's cultural upbringing and my own. As Lawrence explains, 'It is only in the eyes of an *other* culture that the alien culture reveals itself more completely and more deeply' (2015). By exploring Wong's culture, world view and environmental ideology then comparing it to my own but including an interpretive subjective voice, I attempted to broaden the conservation discourse and help the reader understand how different perspectives impacted wildlife protection (Kessler-Harris 2009; Pimlott 1998; Thornber 2014).

Conclusion

My practice-led research into differing representations of authorial subjective perspective led to the conclusion that, in the case of future-focused natural biographies, the interpretive stance is the most appropriate. What differentiates this sub-genre is its future-focus and predictive nature. While a certain level of 'mental unease' or questioning the status quo is necessary in the process of changing behaviour (Ballantyne 1998, 89), cognitive conflict can occur when a reader is presented with new knowledge which is 'incompatible with their present understanding' (Ballantyne 1998, 88) and this can lead to apathy, anxiety and inaction. However, a skilled interpretive narrator has the capacity to smooth the impact of challenging material by guiding the reader on their explorative journey. This subjective stance is, therefore, more effective in future-focused natural biography which aims to evoke behavioural change.

Disclosure statement

No potential conflict of interest was reported by the author.

Funding

This work was supported by an Australian Research Training Program scholarship.

ORCID

Sarah Pye ⑩ http://orcid.org/0000-0002-6799-2839

References

Abbott, H. Porter. 2008. *Cambridge Introduction to Narrative*. 2nd ed. Santa Barbara: University of California.
Agol, Dorice, Agnieszka E. Latawiec, and B. N. Strassburg. 2014. "Evaluating Impacts of Development and Conservation Projects Using Sustainability Indicators: Opportunities and Challenges." *Environmental Impact Assessment Review* 48: 1–9.
Allen, Peter. 1986. *Biography: Fiction, Fact and Form by Ira Bruce Nadel (review)*.
Backscheider, Paula. 1999. *Reflections on Biography*. Oxford: Oxford University Press.

Bakels, J, S Bhagwat, E Drani, M Infield, and C Kidd. 2016. Culture and Conservation: Investigating the Linkages Between Biodiversity Protection and Cultural Values and Practices. In *Culture and Conservation*. Cambridge, UK: Arcus Foundation.

Ballantyne, Roy. 1998. "Interpreting 'Visions': Addressing Environmental Education Goals Through Interpretation." In *Contemporary Issues in Heritage and Environmental Interpretation: Problems and Prospects*, edited by David Uzzell and Roy Ballantyne, 77–97. London: Stationery Office.

Ballantyne, R., and J. Bain. 1995. "Evaluating the Impact of Teaching/Earning Experiences During an Environmental Teacher Education Course." *International Research in Geographical and Environmental Education* 4 (1): 29–46.

Beck, Larry. 2002. *Interpretation for the 21st Century: Fifteen Guiding Principles for Interpreting Nature and Culture*. Edited by Ted T. Cable, 2nd ed. Champaign, IL: Sagamore.

Beskow, Laura M. 2016. "Lessons From HeLa Cells: The Ethics and Policy of Biospecimens." *Annual Review of Genomics and Human Genetics* 17 (1): 395–417. doi:10.1146/annurev-genom-083115-022536.

Betzold, Carola. 2015. "Adapting to Climate Change in Small Island Developing States." *An Interdisciplinary, International Journal Devoted to the Description, Causes and Implications of Climatic Change* 133 (3): 481–489. doi:10.1007/s10584-015-1408-0.

Bloom, Stacie. 2010. "The Immortal Life of Henrietta Lacks." *Journal of Clinical Investigation* 120 (7): 2252. doi:10.1172/JCI43410.

Bobinski, George. 1982. "'New Directions in Biography Review.' Review of New Directions in Biography: Essays by Phyllis Auty, Leon Edel, Michael Holroyd, Noel C. Manganyi, Gabriel Merle, Margot Peters, and Shoichi Saeki, Anthony M. Friedson." *The Library Quarterly: Information, Community, Policy* 52 (4): 403–404.

Brien, Donna Lee. 2014. "'Welcome Creative Subversions: Experiment and Innovation in Recent Biographical Writing." *TEXT* 18 (1).

Bryson, John. 1985. *Evil Angels*. Melbourne: Penguin Books.

Buell, Lawrence. 2005. *The Future of Environmental Criticism: Environmental Crisis and Literary Imagination*. Malden, MA: Blackwell Publishers.

Carey, Janene. 2008. "Whose Story is it, Anyway? Ethics and Interpretive Authority in Biographical Creative Nonfiction." *TEXT* 12 (2).

Close, Alan. 1995. *The Australian Love Letters of Raymond Chandler*. Carlton: McPhee Gribble.

Dahmen, Nicole Smith. 2010. "Construction of the Truth and Destruction of a Million Little Pieces: Framing in the Editorial Response to the James Frey Case." *Journalism Studies* 11 (1): 115–130. doi:10.1080/14616700903172080.

Defonseca, Misha. 1997. *Misha: A Mémoire of the Holocaust Years*. Boston, MA: Mt. Ivy Press.

DeMello, Margo. 2012. *Speaking for Animals: Animal Autobiographical Writing*. NY: Routledge.

Edel, Leon. 1984. *Writing Lives – Principia Biographica*. New York, NY: WW Norton and Company.

Edlich, Micha. 2010. "Richard K. Nelson's The Island Within: Environmental Life Writing as Ecological Identity Work." *A/b: Auto/Biography Studies* 25 (2): 203–218. doi:10.1353/abs.2010.0035.

Escobar, Arturo. 1995. *Encountering Development the Making and Unmaking of the Third World, Princeton Studies in Culture/Power/History*. Princeton, NJ: Princeton University Press.

Farr, Cecilia, and Philip Snyder. 1996. "From Walden Pond to the Great Salt Lake: Ecobiography and Engenered Species Acts in Walden and Refuge." In *Tending the Garden: Essays on Mormon Literature*, edited by E. England, and Fielding Anderson, 197–212. Salt Lake City: Signature Books.

Frey, James. 2003. *A Million Little Pieces*. London: John Murray.

Funda, Evelyn I. 2014. A Bushel's Worth: An Ecobiography by Kayann Short (review).

Gerard, Philip. 1996. *Creative Nonfiction: Researching and crafting stories of real life*. Long Grove, IL: Waveland Press.

Gutkind, Lee. 2012. *You Can't Make This Stuff up: the Complete Guide to Writing Creative Nonfiction-From Memoir to Literary Journalism and Everything in Between*. 1st ed. Boston, MA: Da Capo Press/Lifelong Books.

Gutkind, Lee, and Hattie Fletcher Buck. 2008. *Keep it Real: Everything you Need to Know About Researching and Writing Creative Nonfiction*. New York, NY: W. W. Norton.

Ham, Sam H. 1992. *Environmental Interpretation: a Practical Guide for People with big Ideas and Small Budgets*. Golden, CO: North American Press.

Hamilton, Ian. 1988. *In Search of J.D. Salinger*. NY: Vintage Publishing.

Hayes, Tanya. 2006. "Parks, People, and Forest Protection: An Institutional Assessment of the Effectiveness of Protected Areas." *World Development* 34 (12): 2064–2075. doi:10.1016/j.worlddev.2006.03.002.

Hobbs, Richard. 1998a. "Ecologists in Public." In *Ecology for Everyone*, edited by Ray Willis, and Richard Hobbs, 20–25. Chipping Norton: Surry Beatty and Sons Pty Ltd.

Hobbs, Richard. 1998b. "Ecologists in Public." In *Ecology for Everyone: Communicating Ecology to Scientists, the Public and the Politicians*, edited by Ray Wills and Richard Hobbs, 20–25. Chipping Norton: Surry Beatty and Sons.

Huggan, Graham. 2013. *Nature's Saviours*. Abington: Routledge.

Kessler-Harris, A. 2009. "Why Biography?" *The American Historical Review* 114 (3): 625–630.

Killingsworth, M. Jimmie. 2013. "Occupy Walden." *South Central Review* 30 (1): 83–96. doi:10.1353/scr.2013.0007.

Knudson, Douglas M., Ted T. Cable, and Larry Beck. 2003. *Interpretation of Cultural and Natural Resources*. 2nd ed. Urbana, IL: Sagamore-Venture Publishing.

Koshy, Elena. 2017. "An Unconventional Hero." In *New Straits Times*. Malaysia.

Kuhn, Bernhard. 2009. *Autobiography and Natural Science in the Age of Romanticism: Rousseau, Goethe, Thoreau*. Burlington, VT: Ashgate.

Lawrence, Annee. 2015. "Excruciating Moments: On Writing Cross- Cultural Agency in the Novel." *New Writing*, 1–10. doi:10.1080/14790726.2015.1083590.

Lee, T. R. 1986. "Effective Communication of Information About Chemical Hazards." *The Science of the Total Environment* 51: 149–183.

Leopold, Aldo. 1992. *A Sand County Almanac; and Sketches Here and There*. Edited by Aldo Leopold, Charles W. Schwartz and Robert Finch. Special commemorative edition. New York, NY: Oxford University Press.

Lopez, Barry Holstun. 2001. *Arctic Dreams: Imagination and Desire in a Northern Landscape*. 1st ed. New York, NY: Vintage Books.

Morris, Edmund. 1999. *Dutch*. New York: Modern Library.

Nadel, Ira Bruce. 1984. *Biography: Fiction, Fact and Form*. Somerset: Macmillan Press.

Nelson, Richard K. 1989. *The Island Within*. New York, NY: Vintage Press.

Orr, David W. 1999. "Education, Careers, and Callings: the Practice of Conservation Biology." *Conservation Biology* 13 (6): 1242–1245. doi:10.1046/j.1523-1739.1999.00005.x.

Pepper, David. 1993. *Eco-socialism: From Deep Ecology to Social Justice*. London: Routledge.

Piggott-McKellar, Annah E., Karen E. McNamara, Patrick D. Nunn, and James E. M. Watson. 2019. "What are the Barriers to Successful Community-Based Climate Change Adaptation? A Review of Grey Literature." *Local Environment* 24 (4): 374–390. doi:10.1080/13549839.2019.1580688.

Pimlott, Ben. 1998. "It's all in the life." *New Statesman*, 6/11/1998.

Pye, Sarah. 2020. *Saving Sun Bears*. Hong Kong: Signal 8 Press.

Pyhala, A., A. Osuna Orozco, and S. Counsell. 2016. *Protected Areas on the Congo Basin: Failing Both People and Biodiversity?* London: Rainforest Foundation – UK.

Redford, Kent H., Kristin B. Hulvey, Matthew A. Williamson, and Mark W. Schwartz. 2018. "Assessment of the Conservation Measures Partnership's Effort to Improve Conservation Outcomes Through Adaptive Management." *Conservation Biology* 32 (4): 926–937. doi:10.1111/cobi.13077.

Rhiel, Mary, and David Bruce Suchoff. 1996. *The Seductions of Biography*. New York, NY: Routledge.

Ricketson, Matthew. 2014. *Telling True Stories: Navigating the Challenges of Writing Narrative non-Fiction*. Crows Nest: Allen & Unwin.

Rickinson, M. 2001. "Learners and Learning in Environmental Education: A Critical Review of the Evidence." *Environmental Education Research* 7 (3): 207–320. doi:10.1080/13504620120065230.

Root-Bernstein, Michelle, and Robert Scott. 1999. *Sparks of Genius: The Thirteen Thinking Tools of the World's Most Creative People*. Edited by Michèle Root-Bernstein. Boston, MA: Houghton Mifflin Co.

Root, Robert. 2008. *The Nonfictionist's Guide: on Reading and Writing Creative Nonfiction*. Lanham, MD: Rowman & Littlefield.

Roschelle, J. 1992. "Learning by Collaborating: Convergent Conceptual Change." *Journal of the Learning Sciences* 2: 235–276.

Safina, Carl. 2002. *Eye of the Albatross*. New York: Henry Holt and Company.

Schorer, Mark. 1962. *The Burdens of Biography*. Ann Arbor, MN: University of Michigan.

Schorer, Mark. 1963. *Sinclair Lewis: An American Life*. NY: McGraw-Hill Book Company.

Skloot, Rebecca. 2009. *The Immortal Life of Henrietta Lacks*. New York, NY: Crown Publishers.

Snodgrass, Adrian. 1992. "Asian Studies and the Fusion of Horizons." *Asian Studies Review* 15 (3): 80–95.

Spires, Meggan, Sheona Shackleton, and Georgina Cundill. 2014. "Barriers to Implementing Planned Community-Based Adaptation in Developing Countries: a Systematic Literature Review." *Climate and Development* 6 (3): 277–287. doi:10.1080/17565529.2014.886995.

Straight, N. 2012. *Autobiography, Ecology, and the Well-Placed Self: The Growth of Natural Biography in Contemporary American Life Writing*. New York, NY: Lang, Peter, Publishing Inc.

Stronza, Amanda. 2001. "Anthropology of Tourism: Forging new Ground for Ecotourism and Other Alternatives." *Annual Review of Anthropology* 30: 261–283.

Tedlock, Barbara. 2011. "Braiding Narrative Ethnography with Memoir and Creative Nonfiction." In *The SAGE Handbook of Qualitative Research*, edited by Norman K. Denzin and S. Yvonna, 331–340. Lincoln. Thousand Oaks, CA: SAGE Publications.

Thoreau, H. D., and S. Fender. n.d. *Walden*. Oxford: Oxford University Press.

Thornber, Karen L. 2014. "Literature, Asia, and the Anthropocene: Possibilities for Asian Studies and the Environmental Humanities." *The Journal of Asian Studies* 73 (4): 989–1000. doi:10.1017/S0021911814001569.

Tilden, Freeman. 1977. *Interpreting our Heritage*. 3rd ed. Chapel Hill, NC: University of North Carolina Press.

Tonn, Bruce, and Dorian Stiefel. 2014. "Human Extinction Risk and Uncertainty: Assessing Conditions for Action." *Futures* 63: 134–144. doi:10.1016/j.futures.2014.07.001.

Verdier, James M., and Scott L. Collins. 2017. "Science Communication." *BioScience* 67 (6): 487. doi:10.1093/biosci/bix063.

Vivanco, Luis A. 2002. "Seeing Green: Knowing and Saving the Environment on Film." *American Anthropologist* 104 (4): 1195–1204. doi:10.1525/aa.2002.104.4.1195.

How to be a Fan in the Age of Problematic Faves

Matt Bucher and Grace Chipperfield

ABSTRACT

In 2018, author Mary Karr tweeted about her abusive relationship with David Foster Wallace. This was at the height of #MeToo and cancel culture, where the phrase 'problematic fave' was commonplace. Wallace, dead for ten years but still alive in the public imagination, was suddenly brought into the conversation. Wallace's fans, too, were implicated in his bad behaviour, particularly by their reputation for being 'lit-bros'. At the time, Grace Chipperfield was writing a doctoral thesis on Wallace, which eventually turned into a collection of essays that reckoned with both Wallace's complicated legacy and her relationship to him as a fan, a scholar, and a woman. The final essay in the collection was a deep dive into Wallace fandom, and to write this Grace corresponded with members of the Wallace community, including one of its most dedicated and active participants: Matt Bucher. Here, then, is a sample of that correspondence. This essay is a series of letters between Grace and Matt throughout which they consider their moral obligations as fans in the age of the problematic fave.

Dear Grace,

When you first broached the idea of writing about 'the Wallace community' rather than Wallace's work—and I should add your *own* experience identifying as a Wallace fan—it reminded me of an experience I had attending my first ever David Foster Wallace Conference. This was a one-day symposium at the City University of New York in late 2009. I was a bit sheepish because I was there to give a paper on the history of the DFW listserv and pretty much everyone else was there talking theory, philosophy, and literary criticism. I felt slightly out of place, an impostor. And when, during the casual breakfast small talk, I tried to explain the premise of my paper to another conference-goer, her reply was something like 'Oh cool, fan studies, that's a very hot topic in academia'. And my first thoughts were 'Really? Academia even recognizes fan studies, much less thinks it's cool?' I was sceptical of this claim. Still am, really. Frankly it didn't seem like a serious enough topic to study in depth—sort of like studying the map rather than the territory. And at root, it's simply uncool, unprofessional, and anti-intellectual to identify as fan. Add to that the 'problematic' status of someone like

David Foster Wallace and you have transformed yourself from a mere fan into a loathsome pariah.

I won't bother to rehash all the lit-bro stereotypes here. The cliché is too well known; I have fit all the characteristics: white, male, cishet, beard, young (not any more though! How long until we have a septuagenarian lit-bro cliche?), appears pretentious. And, if I am able to change any of these attributes, the easiest, besides shaving the beard, would be to lose the DFW fan status. After all these years, why haven't I? It's not due to any particular devotion to the man himself or to every scrap of his writing, but, as I hope to explain to you, the community that has grown up around his work.

And, to my relief, in my 20+ years of DFW fandom, I've always felt the cliché of the DFW lit-bro was just that: a half-truth, a stereotype. Since the beginning of my participation in what we are calling this fandom I've noticed a significant population, maybe as high as 40 percent, that does not fit the cliché: women, some people of colour, LGBT, senior citizens, non-English speakers. Is that your experience, too? I'm sure it's more than half young, white, males, but is it enough to justify the stereotype? Just saying that sounds awful: 'justify a stereotype'. And why do we expect this of every readership or fandom? What are the racial demographics of a George Saunders fandom, a Franzen fandom, a Zadie Smith fandom, a Jeffery Eugenides fandom, a Jennifer Egan fandom, a Ben Lerner fandom, a Pynchon fandom? Surely there is a massive amount of overlap among all these groups. The DFW lit-bro is a mirror image of the Ben Lerner superfan, I'd imagine. But is it the particular brand of passionate intensity of the Wallace fans that inspires such a visceral reaction against them? My guess is that is so. While there are plenty of people who love other contemporary writers, we hear very few stories about how *The Corrections*, or *Middlesex*, or *CivilWarLand in Bad Decline* or *Leaving the Atocha Station* 'saved' someone's life,[1] or made them feel less alone, or brought them into recovery, or brought them into a community of like-minded folks. What's your take on that?

Matt

Dear Matt:

It's funny (in an ironic sort of way) that you felt like an impostor at the 2009 DFW conference. I feel like one of the things most PhD students share, and probably even seasoned academics, depending on their confidence levels, is that most of us feel like frauds. Like someone's gonna point at us and say 'You there. You are not good enough to be here. Put that down!'

Throughout my PhD, I've felt like two kinds of impostor: the first is the one just mentioned; the second, and the more significant one, as far as my thesis went, was that I felt like I was writing something disingenuous. This is why I ended up changing my thesis project with only 18 months left of my degree. I always tied my sense of uncertainty about my original PhD project to the first kind of impostor syndrome, but in hindsight I can see the problem was really that I felt like I was holding something back in my writing, and that I felt I was meant to hold this part back to be taken seriously as a scholar (this part being, in short, admitting that I was very personally attached to Wallace, and also admitting that I was this attached because reading his work helped me recover from my eating disorder). So anyway, it's funny (in that ironic sort of way) that you mention being at that conference and feeling the way you did. It's also funny, or maybe just coincidental, or serendipitous, that the academic you mentioned brought up fan studies in the context of your paper. Fan studies has been the thing that cracked open the thesis I actually and eventually wrote about Wallace, and this area of scholarship gave me a way to write about why I'm so attached to him, his work, and the community. And it's why you and I are writing these letters.

Actually fan studies came to me after Rita Felski and her (and many other scholars') work on postcritique. And postcritique only really came to me after our mutual friend Matt Luter gave his paper at the 2017 Wallace conference, also where you and I first met, when he talked about academia and how it demands a split between our public and private selves, not only in relation to the criticism we produce but on the level of our lived reality, if graduate students want to survive in this environment.[2] Matt L. drew on Felski's work to highlight how 'the dominant reading mode of the academic critic' can't 'address fundamental questions about what literature accomplishes in the world and how it operates fruitfully in the everyday emotional and intellectual lives of actual readers' (Luter 2017, 2). In *The Limits of Critique* (2015), Felski writes about how in academia, and specifically in literary studies, our dominant mode of critique is one predicated on detachment. The more detached the critic, the more able, in theory, she is to see and understand what a text is 'doing', and so the work of a critic has become associated with a specific intellectual persona, one 'that is highly prized in literary studies and beyond: suspicious, knowing, self-conscious, hardheaded, tirelessly vigilant' (Felski 2015, 6). Felski wants us to displace critique (at least, the dominant version described above) and explore other options—like writing about literary texts from a different affective position, like love rather than suspicion, and from places of attachment, rather than detachment—that can be broadly collected under the name 'postcritique'. But it's risky to make this shift, because when you admit you love something, you open yourself up to charges of naïveté, and there's an assumption that you won't, or can't, be critical of that thing (love is blind and all that).

You wrote that it's simply uncool, unprofessional, and anti-intellectual to identify as fan, and the word fan may well be implicit in what Felski's saying here. Fan studies was something that I looked into because I wanted to write about the Wallace community as part of working through my attachment to Wallace, and it was really cool to find this area of research that, as early as the 1990s, was already attempting and succeeding to do what literary studies has only seemed to become cognizant of wanting to do since around the 2010s.[3]

This stuff seemed even more relevant when Mary Karr tweeted in 2018,[4] and Wallace was implicated in #MeToo, and became a problematic fave. The lit-bro stereotype existed before then, of course, but that seemed to be another turning point in Wallace's legacy and his fandom (although I'm not sure if you'd agree? Maybe for newer fans, like myself, it was a bigger deal than for those who'd been following his career while he was alive?). Being a Wallace fan in 2018 seemed to connote more than a lack of cool, seeming at times almost synonymous with being misogynist—as you say, a 'loathsome pariah'.[5] I was having trouble working out how to reconcile my love of Wallace and the community with cultural movements like #MeToo and cancel culture, and that's why I ended up writing the thesis that I did.

Re: your questions about the Wallace community/fandom. Yes, it's been my experience that we are a more diverse group than the Wallace lit-bro stereotype would otherwise suggest. I also agree that at least 50% probably are white men, though it would still be reductive to lump them all into the Wallace fan stereotype (which, I mean, by virtue of even calling it a stereotype gestures towards a level of generalisation and shallowness). But/and I don't think you or I or anyone in the community would delude themselves that the stereotype springs from nothing. I do think Wallace fandom is an exception in the way that there doesn't seem to be a similar demand for diversity of more readerships; the demographics of a Ben Lerner fandom, etc., while probably idiosyncratic in their own way, haven't had numerous opinion pieces or scholarly articles written on them (at least, not to my knowledge? Do you think that's a fair call?). Nor are these fandoms necessarily conflated with the identity of the author they like. You only have to Google DFW and his fans to see that we're on people's radars in ways that a reader of George Saunders simply isn't, that Wallace's behaviour can be read into his fans and his fans behaviour can be mapped onto our cultural imagination of who Wallace was—this idea that you love something because you are like that thing.

The particular bar set for Wallace and his fans is, I think, down to a number of factors, some of which are to do with both Wallace's reputation and, as you say, the level of devotion he and his work inspire in his readers (the kind of devotion that could lead to you and I having this exchange here). That Wallace and his fans can even be said to be cultish puts him in a different category and different company to other popular writers, which is tied to this idea of 'Saint Dave'[6] and the hagiography that happened after his suicide. The figuring of Wallace as some kind of moral guide no doubt amplified the reaction that came after Karr's tweets. But yeah, reader devotion can be read as evangelism, can be read into the whole 'men recommend DFW' phenomenon,[7] can, overall, and post-2018, be read in a very unflattering light. Which I guess was the motivation behind writing about Wallace fandom. If what you like says something about you, what does it mean to be a Wallace fan? What does it mean to you?

Grace

Dear Grace,

In Nick Hornby's *High Fidelity*, the music-obsessed protagonist says 'I agreed that what really matters is *what* you like, not what you *are like* …. Books, records, films—these things matter. Call me shallow but it's the truth' (Hornby 17).

Your question about what it means to be a Wallace fan has me thinking about the practical side of reading a thousand-page novel. Like many of the sad young literary men, I read the book in university, when I was afforded large swaths of time to do nothing but read, study, and contemplate reality. And carrying the book around for weeks on end, I admit that I see how some people used that as a weird status symbol. 'Look how smart I am' naturally repulses us. But from earnest-but-naive student the stereotype has evolved into the complicit, the subtle misogynist, the lit-bro who excuses an abusive art monster like DFW. Rough, right? Makes sense to me that you'd want to grapple with that idea of a fan, especially when you find the word applied to yourself.

I feel like the word 'fan' is inadequate to describe my experience in David-Foster-Wallace-Land (as you call it in your thesis). Like, I can watch a new show on Netflix tonight, binge a few episodes, follow the actors on Instagram, read the recaps on Reddit, and boom, in a few hours I am a 'fan' of that show. But the DFW thing is decades-long for me, part of my identity now. I'm not just a fan, I'm somehow working in service to the fandom (which I would only call 'the community'). For me, and other fans like me I know and have talked to about this, we don't really even re-read DFW's work that often. We've long since digested all that—and he isn't around to produce new material. The community of scholarship, 'Wallace Studies', that has grown around the work interests me more than the original work. I'm not sure that many non-literary fandoms function this way, maybe within a subset of *Star Wars* fans?

Beyond just personal taste, we learn at a young age that liking things, especially art created by fallible beings, can have political consequences. A whole generation is undergoing that process of discovery—and the requisite crisis of faith—because they grew up reading and watching Harry Potter. While Rowling is not accused of personally abusing anyone, using her global, billion-dollar, platform to spew anti-trans bigotry is arguably doing far more damage than any one abusive boyfriend could ever do (Hardwick 2020).

There's also the issue of what's cool or not at this particular moment in history. For a writer, or a work of art to fall out of fashion is perhaps a worse fate than being cancelled. To be remembered for being a bigot or an abuser at least gets you into the history books. Libraries and used bookshops are filled with the works of the irrelevant, names that commanded audiences and salaries, now condemned to the recycling bin out of indifference rather than malice. What happens to those fans? They have little choice but to 'move on' or 'outgrow' their obsession.[8]

When I first read *Infinite Jest*, I had no idea that any other 'David Foster Wallace fans' even existed. I had discovered the book almost by accident and had never heard anyone in my life mention Wallace or *Infinite Jest*. Over the past 24 years, I have watched a fandom mature. What is the natural lifespan of a fandom? I assume some of it depends on the production of new content. How many *Star Wars* movies will be produced in our lifetimes? Without new content, does a fandom become simply a nostalgia machine? What do you think?

Matt

Dear Matt:

You recently sent me a link to an interview with Hanif Abdurraqib[9] where he reflected on how to be critical of the thing you love. Abdurraqib said fans deserve as much attention as the artist they've attached themselves to. Trying to understand and articulate fans' persistent love for something seems important, or at least informative, in an age where we're finding it hard to separate artist from art (and in this case, also finding it hard to separate fans from the artist and their art), and in which we're not comfortable or assured about how we reckon with artists' flaws. In that same interview, Abdurraqib talks about the 'exhausting question of separating the art from the artist'. He describes the argument for this separation as really being a request for absolution by fans, so they can feel okay about continuing to love what they've discovered is problematic—this was the thing that I was worried/self-conscious about when it came to the essays I wrote for my thesis. It's very easy to find scholarly reasons to keep studying Wallace, but I was less convinced that those reasons, which sometimes just felt like excuses, held up for me as a fan.

You asked if a fandom might become just a nostalgia machine, and I think this can be true with or without new content. Even in fandoms that continue to have new content produced for them (e.g. as you point out, *Star Wars*), if fans' relationships to that content don't evolve, or don't involve a level of critical awareness, then, yes, I think fandom becomes a nostalgia machine. Abdurraqib says our nostalgia for the object of our affection 'can train a person to imagine that their brightest and most beautiful moments only have a single soundtrack'. Despite my sentimentality about Wallace and his fans, I have a low tolerance for nostalgia. Nostalgia is misleading, and we know, especially as of 2016, that it can be dangerous. And so I don't yearn to return to a time when Wallace was 'Saint Dave' and could do no wrong. Holding Wallace fandom in some static heyday benefits nobody.

You bring up the political consequences of liking art created by fallible people, and I think that cancel culture has really turned the volume up on this whole question of our political and ethical/moral responsibilities as consumers and fans. Before 2018 I probably never even considered that the stuff I liked had political consequences. I know how naïve that sounds (and is)—I was old enough by that point to know better! But I was naïve about it anyway. I didn't think that there was any connection between an author I liked and bigger political questions. I used to be a fan of the TV show *Supernatural*, and then when I was researching stuff for my thesis I fell down a hyperlink rabbit-hole about Jensen Ackles, one of the lead actors in the series, making comments that fans interpreted as homophobic, and what that meant for that fandom, especially for those fans who wrote slash fiction about his character (this had nothing to do with my waning interest in the show – that happened earlier, around season six, when I was no longer hooked). With Wallace, I really struggled with the idea that I had any sort of political or moral responsibility as a fan of his work. Abdurraqib says the political responsibility of a fan is to challenge their nostalgia, and their attachments to the object of their affection. He says it's the responsibility of fans to 'love themselves more than they love their icons. To love themselves even more than they love their memories, and to love the evolution of all those things in harmony: the evolution of themselves, the evolution of their memory, and the evolution of the artist—for better or worse' (Abdurraqib 2019).

This idea of fans loving themselves more than their icons may be why the Wallace community has in many ways overshadowed Wallace for me. The community has perhaps superseded any other attachment I have to Wallace, and the people who make up that community are the reason I felt like digging my heels in when it became controversial to be a fan of Wallace. I've only been aware of this community for like four years, though; what's it been like to watch Wallace fandom mature over 24 years? The thing that's kept me optimistic about the fandom is that I do think we have evolved, even in the short span of time that I've been an active part of it. This was something I tried to show in the final essay of my thesis, 'What it's like in David-Foster-Wallace-Land'.

Which brings me to something I've been meaning to ask you about. To write that essay I reached out to our colleagues on the boards of the International David Foster Wallace Society and *The Journal of David Foster Wallace Studies*, as well as the community on the wallace-l, the email listserv and earliest iteration of the fan community, and many people, you included, wrote back to me about your relationship to Wallace and to each other. I used those stories in my essay, framed by my commentary and scholarship on fandom to, I hope, shift our attention from Wallace to something more outward-looking, something generative and valuable that has come from readers of his work, despite his problematic status. I know my relationship to Wallace has greatly changed, or come into sharper focus, over the course of writing the essays, and I'm curious to know what it was like for you to reflect on your own relationship to him and the community. How did you feel about my representation of Wallace fans, and the community, and you?

Grace

Dear Grace,

I do not yearn for the nostalgic image of 'Saint Dave', but I do wish he were still alive and publishing fiction. Those were exciting times. When a new story was published, a collective rush to read it was followed by a strong sense of bonding over the experience. I don't really get that feeling from any other authors alive and publishing right now, to be honest. But would we, as a fan community, have grappled with Wallace's personal life and flaws then? Certainly not—he kept it as private as possible—and that would just delay the moment the fandom would have to reckon with his abuses.

I've been a little stuck on this word 'problematic'. Donald Judd says you have to 'pay attention when someone talks about "problems", because problems in art are not like problems in science; their definition isn't as precise' (Judd and Murray 2019). My main issue is that it sounds too academic or mealy-mouthed, though I admit it is an easy shorthand or categorisation. Is it the teaching of Wallace that is problematic or the man himself? There are certainly some problems in Wallace's work and problems in his personal life, but shouldn't that make for better teaching material? I believe we approach art from several perspectives at once: aesthetically, emotionally, morally, and intellectually. In my experience, academia privileges the intellectual and aesthetic response above the moral and emotional response. And I get that plenty of readers or students won't bother to understand the details of Wallace's behaviour if he is written off as 'problematic'. I don't have a solution to any of this, just that I question the stories we tell around it—and I am glad to be here for the conversation around it which, as I said, would probably not be happening if Wallace were alive and publishing (now there's a double bind).

And there is power in the collective. This is one of the great lessons of *Infinite Jest*: community—as an antidote to isolation and solipsism—is integral to the development of some kind of faith, or what a more secular person like myself might term Truth or authenticity. We are interconnected, and we have an obligation to each other. Matthew Mullins argues that 'Wallace's faith is not concerned with a particular set of doctrines but with a generalized belief in something larger than oneself. The "something larger" in this case is community itself' (2018, 200). I never consciously realised I was joining a DFW fandom, by the way. At some point in 2000 I realised that the emails from this one group energised me more than anything. As I got to know this group of people, I grew to value them as a community—and I grew to value the concept of community in every way. So if we have faith in something larger than ourselves, what exactly are we being saved from? Mullins says: 'We are saved, not for our own sake, but for others, for the sake of a community in which we are each a piece rather than the point' (201).

You ask how it feels to read an essay in which the DFW community (self included) is portrayed and examined and my immediate response is that it feels good! I've always been particularly proud of the self-organised, autonomous nature of the wallace-l listserv, always felt like it's a hidden gem of the internet. Here is an incredibly erudite group of folks, some of them semi-famous, some of them students, many of them entirely anonymous, lurkers, all united by their shared love of a book and a writer's work. And, unlike a lot of fan communities, wallace-l isn't a Tumblr or blog that I can link you to where you can go scan the history of the fandom in a few minutes. There are 24 years of text-only archives, conference papers detailing its history, monograph chapters to read. Maria Bustillos (herself now a big-time publisher and writer), wrote an appreciation for 2009s Infinite Summer called 'The Wonder of Wallace-l' where she called the list 'a gathering of people who value intellectual curiosity, humanity, candour and humility, like a mirror of Wallace's own qualities, and in that way is keeping something of him alive' (Bustillos 2009). Isn't that better than a statue?

Matt

Dear Matt:

I don't have a precise definition, I guess, for 'problematic'. I think it's one of those words that gets thrown around, the gist being gotten through context clues. When I hear or deploy the word in my writing about Wallace, I take it to refer to a person of prominence, anyone in the public eye, whose behaviour, past or present, is unethical, harmful, or outside the bounds of what we consider appropriate or acceptable. Obviously that lacks nuance; lumping Wallace and Harvey Weinstein and Kanye West (and so on, and on, and on) together simply because they've all been cancelled or labelled 'problematic' conflates a whole lot of distinct acts and issues that aren't benefitted by broad strokes condemnation.

I think when it comes to art 'problematic fave' denotes the cognitive dissonance between enjoying an artist's work but disliking them as a person on the grounds of their politics or behaviour. This gets even stickier when you come up against the scholarly argument for separating the artist from the art. Which leads me to your question about whether it's the teaching of Wallace that's problematic or the man himself; it's both, depending on who you ask. I mean, Amy Hungerford's article in *The Chronicle of Higher Education*, later a chapter in her book, on refusing to read and teach DFW is in part based on the assumption that Wallace's problematic behaviour towards women may be reproduced in his relationship with his reader (that, and she doesn't think *Infinite Jest* is worth the time it takes to read, in comparison to what else she might get through in the same amount of time).[10]

Then there are other refusals that are less anything to do with the work itself and more based on objections to his behaviour and biography.[11] I think in academia we're trained to focus on and give our aesthetic and intellectual arguments about works, and we need to start learning how to talk in an informed and articulate way about our emotional and moral responses—learning to do this better would probably have some nice corollary effects outside academia, too.

The thing that's bothered me about Wallace being considered problematic is, as we've talked around in our earlier letters, that this label seems to have been transferred from him to his fans. And it's one thing to decide whether or not to keep loving an artist, but what happens then to the relationships you've built with people because of your shared connection to that artist? This is when I think it's worth looking closer at why people like the things they do, maybe less for what the thing says about those people and more about what those people can say about the thing, if that makes sense. I think you hit on this with your connecting the importance of community in *Infinite Jest* with Wallace fandom more broadly.

Henry Jenkins describes fandom as a participatory culture, a space where members feel their contributions matter, and where they 'feel some degree of social connection with one another' (2017, 18). Nicolle Lamerichs writes that '[b]eing a fan is an experience that is grounded in a feeling' (2018, 18–19), and it is this 'affective orientation' of fandom that 'help[s] to form bonds between individuals that sustain a sense of community' (Dean 2017, 413). This sense of community is 'associated with greater social support, … life satisfaction, … quality of life, … and social and subjective well-being' (Chadborn, Edwards, and Reysen 2018, 242), and is often a significant and cherished component of fandom. Joli Jensen believes that 'what it means to be a fan should be explored in relation to the larger question of what it means to desire, cherish, seek, long, admire, envy, celebrate, protect, ally with others' (1992, 26–27). Fandom, Jensen argues, is one part of 'how we make sense of the world, in relation to mass media, and in relation to our historical, social, cultural location. Thinking well about fans and fandom can help us think more fully and respectfully about what it means today to be alive and to be human' (1992, 26–27). Thinking about fans as allies, as protecting each other, as examples that can give insight into what it means to be human and how we make sense of the world—all of this feels important, especially in relation to movements like #MeToo and cancel culture and all the connecting issues. I'm not sure if I'm making myself clear here. I think it just seems like a missing part of the stories we tell about our problematic faves. A part that's missing but that might be precisely what's needed in these conversations.

I don't think we can (and as fans, I don't think we do) overestimate the value of finding somewhere we belong. In a study that investigated the relationship between fan identity and well-being, evidence suggested that 'overall fan identity predicted overall well-being' (Vinney et al. 2019, 1). Additionally, 'social fan identity', that is, the identity we gain over time through interacting with other fans as part of a community, 'predicted relational well-being and marginally predicted physical well-being' (Vinney et al. 2019, 1). For over 24 years, Wallace has brought (and still brings) together complete strangers to talk about their shared love of him and his work, and the benefits of this go beyond appreciation of an artist.

And yes, this legacy is way better than a statue.

Grace

Dear Grace,

That Jenkins quote about the participatory nature of fandom has helped me understand an issue related to our shared moral obligations as consumers of art, as readers and watchers, and as fans.

Do we have a responsibility to research the personal politics and behaviour and moral failings of the creators of everything we consume? For example, if I watch *The Crown* on Netflix should I pause when it says 'Directed by Stephen Daldry' and then pull up Wikipedia and make sure Daldry isn't a known rapist or abuser? Or maybe I switch over to watch *The Queen's Gambit* and stop to research who directed each episode and check them out, or do I have to research all the actors and crew as well? This is an absurd example to say that the problematic fave is usually sorted out well before someone consumes the art. What the culture is doing with #MeToo, and by extension, DFW, is creating a shorthand that spares you the effort of researching anything. And in a lot of ways, that's super helpful. I don't follow Johnny Depp's personal life and don't care much for whatever films he is making these days, but when my teenage son casually mentions that a woman is trying to 'take him down' in the press, I have to pause and say, no, let's go look at this story more in depth together. These stories live in a very shallow zone where they are transmitted too simply—and they can be completely turned around. Maybe the shorthand for DFW is that he was a bad person, maybe a rapist or abuser, but then maybe the narrative shifts to 'he was thought to be bad but it's complicated and he's worth reading and teaching' and then, who knows, maybe the narrative shifts again in another direction.

But by Jenkins' definition, I'm not really a fan of any of those Netflix shows or Johnny Depp's movies. I don't participate in the culture around them or try to meet other fans—I'm just a consumer. It'd be easy to give up my appreciation for Johnny Depp's work or *The Cosby Show* because I wasn't emotionally invested in them. Whatever surface-level obligation I have to boycotting their work pales in comparison to the obligations of those who have actively built fandoms around them. And I do think *fans* have a moral obligation to the thing they are fanatical about.

Embarrassed by too much enthusiasm, the cool, collected intellectual regards passion as ultimately naïve. And this presumption of the fan's naïveté, of the fan as 'other', can also free the critic and the scholar from any such moral obligations. I am reminded of that Felski quote in your first letter to me: the detachment of the critic also prevents the study of one's own irrational attachment, what Matt Luter called referred to as the way art and, I'd argue, fandom 'operates fruitfully in the everyday emotional and intellectual lives of actual readers' (2017, 2).

So if I'm admitting I have a moral obligation as a fan, why stick around? Why do I do keep doing this, knowing what I know about David Foster Wallace now? In that Abdur-raqib interview you mentioned, he cautions against nostalgia—let's call it my nostalgia for when it was cool to be a DFW or *Infinite Jest* fan, when it was easier to love DFW because we didn't know about his flaws and abuses. So I will resolve to challenge any of that nostalgia that looks backward toward a time when women did not feel safe to name their famous abusers, a time when a great male artist could be forgiven for practically all sins. But I stick around for something even more personal. It should be clear by now, but I don't know if I've said this directly before: I love the community of people I have met through this work, people I expect to know and grow with for the rest of my life, more than I could possibly love any one book or writer. And I hope these letters are some evidence to you that I care less about my own 'social fan identity' and more about those interpersonal connections that bind us together.

Matt

Notes

1. See, as one example: Gondelman, Josh and Will Schwalbe. "Comedian Josh Gondelman Talks Empathy and Infinite Jest." https://lithub.com/comedian-josh-gondelman-talks-empathy-and-infinite-jest/.

2. For more on this, a good starting point would be Lisa Ruddick's article for *The Point* magazine, 'When Nothing is Cool,' which later appeared in *The Future of Scholarly Writing: Critical Interventions*, published by Palgrave.
3. At least, there have been examples of scholars, especially in feminist and cultural studies, exploring different affective modes of critique before Felski's *Uses of Literature*, published in 2008, but the whole postcritical school of thought in literary studies is often introduced alongside Felski and her work.
4. https://twitter.com/marykarrlit/status/992545700004139008?lang=en
5. See any or all of these examples: Breslaw, Anna. '6 Ways to Judge Him by His Lit-Bro Idol', *Elle,* (2015) https://www.elle.com/culture/books/a27230/6-lit-bros-you-can-totally-judge-guys-for-worshipping/; Boswell, Marshall. *The Wallace Effect: David Foster Wallace and the Contemporary Literary Imagination.* New York, NY: Bloomsbury Academic, 2019; Clark, Jonathan Russell. "Reclaiming David Foster Wallace from the Lit-Bros." https://lithub.com/reclaiming-david-foster-wallace-from-the-lit-bros/; Fischer, Molly. "Why Literary Chauvinists Love David Foster Wallace." *The Cut*, 2015, https://www.thecut.com/2015/08/david-foster-wallace-beloved-author-of-bros.html; Paulson, Steve. "David Foster Wallace in the #Metoo Era: A Conversation with Clare Hayes-Brady." *Los Angeles Review of Books*, 2018, https://lareviewofbooks.org/article/david-foster-wallace-in-the-metoo-era-a-conversation-with-clare-hayes-brady/; Perper, Em. "The Cult Could Become a Church: On David Foster Wallace." *Longreads*, 2015, https://longreads.com/2015/07/01/the-cult-could-become-a-church-on-david-foster-wallace/; Rowan, Nic. "Let Us Now Praise Famous Lit Bros." *Washington Examiner*, 2019, https://www.washingtonexaminer.com/opinion/in-defense-of-david-foster-wallace-jonathan-franzen-and-the-lit-bro-canon; Shephard, Alex. "Neil Gorsuch Will Be Our First Lit Bro Supreme Court Justice." *The New Republic*, 2017, https://newrepublic.com/minutes/141498/neil-gorsuch-will-first-lit-bro-supreme-court-justice; Timberg, Scott. "David Foster Wallace Was Not a Bro: Let's Not Paint the Writer with the Same Brush as His Fans." https://www.salon.com/2015/08/13/david_foster_wallace_was_not_a_bro_lets_not_paint_the_writer_with_the_same_brush_as_his_fans/; Williams, Brett. "We Need to Lay Off the Overzealous Hero-Worship of Elon Musk." *Mashable Australia*, 2017, https://mashable.com/2017/12/15/the-dangerous-cult-of-elon-musk-david-foster-wallace/
6. See, for example: Alsup, Benjamin. "Saint David Foster Wallace." Esquire https://classic.esquire.com/article/2011/4/1/saint-david-foster-wallace.
7. Coyle, Deirdre. "Men Recommend David Foster Wallace to Me." *Electric Literature*, 2017, https://electricliterature.com/men-recommend-david-foster-wallace-to-me.
8. Some Wallace fans have written about this process. See, for example: Taranto, Julius. "On Outgrowing David Foster Wallace." LA Review of Books https://lareviewofbooks.org/article/on-outgrowing-david-foster-wallace/; Moreau, Nathan. "Describing the Surface: David Foster Wallace and Postcritical Reading." *New Critique*, 2020, https://newcritique.co.uk/2020/08/01/essay-describing-the-surface-david-foster-wallace-and-postcritical-reading-nathan-moreau/
9. Abdurraqib is the author of *Go Ahead in the Rain: Notes to A Tribe Called Quest*, a 2019 essay collection about his love of the hip hop group.
10. See: Hungerford, Amy. *Making Literature Now.* Palo Alto: Stanford University Press, 2016.
11. One example is Megan Garber's "David Foster Wallace and the Dangerous Romance of Male Genius." *The Atlantic.* Accessed 4 Jan 2020. https://www.theatlantic.com/entertainment/archive/2018/05/the-world-still-spins-around-male-genius/559925/.

Disclosure statement

No potential conflict of interest was reported by the author(s).

References

Abdurraqib, Hanif. 2019. "How to Be Critical of the Things You Love." https://www.thenation.com/article/archive/hanif-abdurraqib-tribe-called-quest-book-interview/.

Bustillos, Maria. 2009. "The Wonder of Wallace-L." http://infinitesummer.org/archives/1606.

Chadborn, Daniel, Patrick Edwards, and Stephen Reysen. 2018. "Reexamining Differences between Fandom and Local Sense of Community." *Psychology of Popular Media Culture* 7 (3): 241–249. doi:10.1037/ppm0000125.

Dean, Jonathan. 2017. "Politicising Fandom." *The British Journal of Politics and International Relations* 19 (2): 408–424. doi:10.1177/1369148117701754.

Felski, Rita. 2015. *The Limits of Critique*. Chicago: The University of Chicago Press.

Hardwick, Courtney. 2020. "J.K. Rowling's History of Transphobia." Accessed 12 November 2020. http://inmagazine.ca/2020/06/j-k-rowlings-history-of-transphobia/.

Jenkins, Henry. 2017. "Fandom, Negotiation, and Participatory Culture." In *The Routledge Companion to Media Fandom*, edited by Melissa A. Click, and Suzanne Scott, 13–27. Milton: Routledge.

Jensen, Joli. 1992. "Fandom as Pathology: The Consequences of Characterization." In *The Adoring Audience: Fan Culture and Popular Media*, edited by Lisa A. Lewis, 9–30. New York: Routledge.

Judd, Flavin, and Caitlin Murray. 2019. "Donald Judd Interviews." Judd Foundation/David Zwirner Books.

Lamerichs, Nicolle. 2018. *Productive Fandom: Intermediality and Affective Reception in Fan Cultures*. Amsterdam: Amsterdam University Press.

Luter, Matthew. 2017. "Me and Wallace's Shadow: Creating Space for the Personal in Writing About Wallace." Paper presented at the Third Annual International David Foster Wallace Conference.

Mullins, Matthew. , 2018. "Wallace, Spirituality, and Religion." In *Cambridge Companions to Literature*, edited by Ralph Clare, 190–203. Cambridge: Cambridge University Press.

Vinney, Cynthia, Karen E. Dill-Shackleford, Courtney N. Plante, and Anne Bartsch. 2019. "Development and Validation of a Measure of Popular Media Fan Identity and Its Relationship to Well-Being." *Psychology of Popular Media Culture* 8 (3): 296–307. doi:10.1037/ppm0000188.

Letter Writing and Space for Women's Self-expression in Janet Frame's *Owls Do Cry* and Jane Campion's *An Angel at My Table*

Hannah Matthews

ABSTRACT

This essay engages with life writing in Janet Frame's 1957 novel, *Owls Do Cry* and Jane Campion's 1990 film biopic of Frame's autobiographies, *An Angel At My Table*. It aims to consider the physical and socio-political constraints on women's writing, and how these may be deconstructed through non-conventional forms of intellectual exploration. Communication between women is explored in the formats used in both Frame's novel and Campion's film. With a primary focus on letter writing, this essay also considers diary entries, published literary work, the film text, and silence as areas of interest. This essay employs the form of letter writing in attempt to explore the medium used by Frame and the characters in *Owls Do Cry* as an alternative form of intellectual scholarly practice. In doing so, it aims to consider Frame's literary legacy as a paradigm for academic study, in which women's varied creative practices can be considered for academic exploration. The letter form also signifies an attempt to recontextualise the letter form, in order to compare the constraints on women's writing in 1940s and 1950s New Zealand with twenty-first-century concerns about gender equality in academia and creative writing.

Dear Janet Frame,

Help, help, help (Frame 2002, 102).[1] The day is early on the morning of my twenty-fifth birthday and it seems as good a time as any to search for answers. Therein, I am searching for you, Miss Frame. For in the year 2020, some thirty-six years after you wrote that society's expectations made you feel as though 'there were no place on earth' for you, I cannot help but question the place of the contemporary female author (Ash 1988, 182). I am troubled by the notion that my writing may always be confined by the boxes in which I reside; the structures, the households, the hierarchies. This letter has already been interrupted in duty to a washing machine drum that required spinning. If you were to assure me that writing has the power to create a free space for women, then I would know to keep writing. However, if enclosure is all that exists, then I would reconsider my options. For when it comes to domestic duties, 'unless a woman knows she is another Virginia Woolf or Jane Austen, how can she say no ... ?' (Russ

2018, 9). In aspects of your writing you seem to condemn yourself to textual, if not physical enclosure, and in other aspects, it liberates you.

In writing letters to your multitude of literary personas, I hope to discover whether you reside in freedom or in oppression. Why letters? Letters feature prominently in your fiction. In *Owls Do Cry*, your first published fiction novel, letters written by women provide great insight into their thoughts. The character Chicks is portrayed only through life writing—via diary entries and letters alike. They create paths through institutions that allow women to connect with one another in a separate space. The act of letter writing has historically played an integral role in 'the process of identity formation for women' who sought to exchange ideas and discuss their reading (Hannan 2016, 10). Though this practice fosters a somewhat artificial construction of selfhood, that construction allows women to reimagine their roles and their relationships with other women. In such times when identities are so constructed by social institutions, the opportunity to curate one's own intellectual identity through dedicated letter-writing seems preferable.

Moreover, letters provide a means of confounding time and space in the name of personal connection. Perhaps the most personal form of writing between two people, letters bridge spatial differences. Leonie Hannan comments on seventeenth- and eighteenth-century letter writing which brought women closer to their friends via 'mental proximity', which was viewed as the next best thing to physical closeness (Hannan 2016, 21). I use epistolary writing as a means of inquiry and intellectual exploration, but I also use it to feel closer to you and your literary personas, as well as Jane Campion, the Director of *An Angel At My Table*, the biopic of your autobiographies. Defying the boundaries of time and space, I hope to retrospectively connect myself to you all in a chain of communication that both acknowledges the differences in our milieus and the timelessness of our situation as female writers and intellectual explorers. I explore the letter form as an alternative form of scholarly writing, that may defy the limits of domestic life-writing. If I can deconstruct the differences between us, and bolster our situational similarities, I might find hope as a young female writer, as you did.

Letter writing deconstructs time and space in two primary ways. Firstly, by the material's passage through space—often great international distances, at speed. A person in Europe could easily send a message to a person in New Zealand via letter form. Relaying the message in person would require much more personal time and expense, and would be a far less viable option for most people. Secondly, letters have historically survived well throughout time. James Daybell notes that letter collections form the 'most copious body of sixteenth-century English women's surviving writing' (Daybell 2006, 5). At a time when the literary canon was rendered through patriarchal notions of genius, even more so than it is today, female life-writing still occupied a space in literary history.[2] When institutional ideals omit women from the literary canon, life writing remains a means for women to 'shape a literary legacy' and 'contribute to the collective memories and historical narratives of the age' (Cook and Culley 2012, 2). Letter writing and the general practice of life writing permit the addition of different and varied narratives to the historical and cultural archive.

Letters also take on a variety of forms that are all equally valid. They can be personal or informative, domestic or professional, or an intersection of all these attributes. Writing in this way allows me to write freely, without pressure to conform to the institutional way of doing things; the normal way. God, normality is oppressive. Formally, 2020 Britain is unlike 1930s New Zealand, in which time, the *Thomas Report* considered gender when grouping students into educational pathways (Middleton 1998, 53). However, as a woman, it still feels inherent to meekly wander the halls of my university, adorned with busts of male academics, questioning whether this is my place. There is a fixed form for writing intellectually and it is prescribed as the precursor to academic success.

As I tend to my washing machine, I think of Walter Nash, Minister of Finance and Marketing, who argued 'women's work, though still hard, is easier than ever before' in 1940s New Zealand (Brickell 2006, 144). 'Women's work', as he so puts it, involved domestic chores, which were made easier by new consumer goods that cluttered family homes. Consumption came to define the social aspirations of New Zealanders, during a pivotal decade in your life. During the years in which you attended university, attempted suicide and began living in Seacliff Lunatic Asylum, social identities became defined 'much more by their relationships to consumption than to production' (143). I would like to explore the ways in which your writing defies this political observation, and creates space for production.

Through your autobiographical and fictional works, you have created personas that act as versions of the writer, Janet Frame. You have also been recreated by Jane Campion, in her biopic *An Angel at My Table*, an adaptation of your autobiographies. Considering this film and your novel, *Owls Do Cry*, I will attempt to uncover the liberating power of female writing in a series of letters to women in confined spaces. I hope to make sense of your process, and thereby make sense of the true power of women's life writing. I hope that I too may be able to escape to an inner world, in creating this pathway back to you, through exploring your novel as a space in which readers and writers can explore an imaginative connection.

Yours faithfully,

Reader

Dear Chicks,

I write in hope of discovering the power of women's writing, for I'm searching for a way to escape the confines of patriarchal structures. As a character in Janet Frame's *Owls Do Cry*, you wrote for some time in a diary, but I'm not sure these entries can be read at face value. Kate Wilhelm writes of how domestic tasks are expected to take precedence: 'the children, the house, school functions, husband's needs, yard, etc. all come first' (Russ 2018, 9). I fear that domestic life completely dictated your writing process. You confess that you may likely pause your writing if you had not found the time, adding 'after all, I am a housewife' (Frame 2002, 96). This calls into question whether the act of writing functioned, for you, as a retreat from the oppression of home life, or embedded you deeper within it; encouraging you into a tighter space within the marital home. Your diaries position you firmly within domesticity. Going to great lengths to describe your chores and daily routines in the home, you negate the idea that there may be more to a woman's life than 'scientific housework' (98; Brickell 2006, 139). Centred around consumer culture, scientific housework was a popular metaphor for individual and social prosperity in 1940s New Zealand, and aligns heavily with your description of your quotidian life.

A diary is typically a personal account of one's innermost thoughts, away from quotidian existence. Janet Frame describes in one of her autobiographical works, *The Envoy from Mirror City*, of how her writing creates this 'Mirror City', where everything 'known or seen or dreamed of is bathed in the light of another world' (Ash 1988, 183). This notion allows the woman writer to escape from places within patriarchal structures, such as the marital home, to a sphere that she has created. Conversely, you use the personal space of your diary to muse 'What if I have *no inner life*?' (Frame 2002, 104). This suggests that your existence is dictated by your outward role as housewife; negating your inner role as a writer. It also suggests the absence of your personality. This is a complex notion, for it would be right to say you place high value on personality. When your sister Daphne writes you a very strange letter, you note of her needing the kind of brain operation that changes one's personality, and observe that it would be terrible to 'be deprived of one's personality' (108). Daphne, you think, requires curing. However, if you have no *inner life*, and are thus devoid of your own personality, have you already been cured of your own abnormalities? Were you once also a madwoman? To claim you may have no inner life suggests you have already been lobotomised.

If this were true, it may account for your quibbling over which symphony you should be listening to. It seems that you are trying to furnish a personality for yourself in the proper way. You have been re-born as a product of new consumer culture. You confess that whilst you played the *Fifth Symphony* to the Bessicks, you hoped you had 'an intelligent expression' on your face (Frame 2002, 106). You read culture through a lens defined by your social aspirations, seeking Prime Minister, Peter Fraser's approval in digesting his 'culture to the masses' (Brickell 2006, 133).[3] This diminishes your position as writer, as you form your observations rigidly, in the prescribed way. Your diary therefore acts as reinforcement of your new constructed self, post-lobotomy. Instead of creating a space separate from your domestic life, your diary expands this domestic space, conforming to political expectations.

I know what you're thinking. You suppose that I am the mad one for suggesting you've been lobotomised? After all, Frame's writing is characteristic in its ability to describe normal people who misrecognise themselves as sane, as noted in Susan Schwartz's (1996, 125) 'Dancing in the Asylum'. Though you mightn't have had an operation, you were lobotomised through marriage. Writing about incarcerated women, Yannick Ripa (1990, 57–58) notes that without a husband, women were traditionally still thought of as children and so, 'getting married was a way for young women to gain access to womanhood and to begin to exist in their own right', though she notes that they would exist solely in relation to the husband.[4] It makes sense then, that your diaries describe your new life as Teresa—your new grown up identity, illustrating only the domestic space, other than in dreams or in letters to your family. Your new identity is something you seem anxious to affirm, asserting that if people from you childhood home in Waimaru were to refer to you as 'Chicks', you would 'refuse to answer'. Perhaps your dissatisfaction with your childhood nickname, which reduced you to the little dark chicken 'trying to catch up with people', therefore forced you to reidentify in your role as wife (Frame 2002, 97). Susan Ash (1988, 171) writes of how the wife, mother or unmarried daughter is taught to 'subvert their essential selves' in order to nurture others, and is therefore only able to identify herself in relation to others. You echo this in the introduction to your diary, 'Perhaps I shall refer to my childhood and the members of my family' (98). In one way or another, as the lobotomised diary writer, you must position yourself only in relation to an authoritative space; that of the family or marital home.

Your definitions of normality hinge upon marital life. Much like her doctors, you confess your concerns of Daphne never getting better and 'living a normal life', like yourself (Frame 2002, 101). This normal life that you lead aligns with Schwartz's (1996, 125) analysis of Frame's characters, who misjudge their own sanity. Whilst your diary writing could provide space for you to solidify your own truths, it destabilises your own version of normality. You describe a life so detached from your childhood, scorning it on many occasions, and yet you hint at yearnings for it. Though you credit your marital life, expecting your childhood neighbours to respect your beautiful home for its commodities, you write 'Oh, I am tired and unhappy' (113). This snippet of true emotion is parenthesised within references of domesticity, and yet seemingly disconnected from them. It is almost as if you conceal your true diary intentions, so that one could miss them if they weren't paying close enough attention. This is not the only reference you make to unhappiness. After you wake up from a startling dream about a little Arab girl, you confess 'for one second apart from all other time, I wanted to be a little girl [...] sitting in the rubbish dump' (117). This suggests that the commodity and fancy you boast of in your writing is inconsequential to your happiness. Perhaps most pertinently of all, you sign a letter to Daphne 'Love, Chicks' (155). In the moments in between, you declare your true feelings. In dreams, between living and not living, and in letters that pass through and occupy the space in between institutions, you become Chicks again.

Diaries, like dreams, act as liminal spaces, in their ability to transfer thoughts and feelings into physical space. Your diary may well have provided some reprieve, had you kept it private from your husband. When you began writing, you noted that Tim was amused at the prospect, threatening to read it (Frame 2002, 96). If one is aware that her husband may judge her, she may knowingly or unknowingly filter her most private thoughts in order to appease his views, particularly if he holds the balance of power within the household. Elaine Reuben (1972, 43) comments on writing as an asset of femininity, noting 'women should not only dress to be attractive to men; they must write to be attractive to them'. Self-admittedly a housewife, I wonder whether your prescribed roles inhibit your true written expression. Ash (1988, 171) writes of the destructive social conventions that afflict the life of the mother and wife. She describes the heroine, who 'presents a mask to the world'. Your mask of Teresa, who occupies the domestic space, is characteristic of the heroine who waits for a male rescuer to change her circumstances. Ironically, Ash notes 'the rescuer would not free the female but capture her into society's enclosures'. By writing Teresa's diary to appease Tim's patriarchal requirements, you continue to ask him for rescue, and continue to be engulfed into his world; a world that you must occupy after your former self is destructed. This disparate selfhood is characteristic of madness stereotypes, which Ripa (1990, 20) notes as 'people who fantasized that they were someone else'. In this way, your diary writing marks you as a woman who would like to create an inner space, a fuller character, but is too affixed within domesticity and consumerism to be able to write transgressive narratives.

That said, I don't wish to entirely undermine the act of life writing you practice so conscientiously. Though I'm troubled by the way in which you write your diary entries to appease Tim's gaze, I must acknowledge the significance of your writing. Your diary entries act as accounts of your quotidian life. You describe your domestic surroundings in detail and are meticulous in noting your reading behaviours. This behaviour evokes Leonie Hannan's (2016, 10) description of letter writing, that traditionally functioned as a form of correspondence in which women could 'discuss their reading and exchange ideas'. Though these are personal accounts and are not being posted for someone else to read, they do provide a means for you to discuss your reading habits and note your thoughts on social customs. In this way, your diary entries act as a form of correspondence between your mind and physical self. Your writing transports your thoughts into the material world you inhabit, bridging the space between the two. The very practice of your writing suggests evidence of your inner world, or surely, the pages would be blank? This acknowledgement of an inner self through diary writing may act as a liberating device. It creates an alternate existence outside of domesticity. Plus, perhaps I should be more tolerant of your descriptions of consumer appliances if they free your time for writing. For me, my washing machine is merely a source of annoyance, as I neglect to acknowledge how time-consuming domestic duties were for women before the invention of such appliances. Hannan (123) reminds me that private writing space was no use to a woman 'without the time to spend in that space'.

Additionally, though your writing is dictated by your domestic life, these domestic descriptions permit the act of writing. They act as content for your diarising and provoke commentary. Summit and Wolley (2004, 202) suggest that letter writing was traditionally 'the defining genre of the household', permitting the coexistence of domestic life with intellectual exploration. It is often frustrating to read snippets of intellectual concepts crowded with mundane descriptions of the washing machine leaking over the floor and the shame of having to 'undo the cellophane' off packs of shop-bought biscuits (Frame 2002, 97, 99). However, women are not always free to write down intellectual thoughts, exclusively. This is maybe best evidenced during Frame's university experience, during which her psychology professor, John Forrest made assumptions about her mental health after reading her short story. Frame's writing provoked Forrest's line of inquiry which led to her wrongful schizophrenia diagnosis and admission to hospital. Diary writing, permitted from the safety of domestic life has often been used in women's life writing to 'deflect criticism', as there are inherent risks for women who wish to put 'the personal on public display' (Cook and Culley 2012, 4). If you are using the domestic commentary as an intentional strategy to preserve your intellectual exploration, you acknowledge the construction of the domestic space. This may explain why you offer snippets of your true emotions in parenthesis of household descriptions.

Though traditionally academic writing and publishing act as powerful means of escape from institutional structures, all female writing provides insight into the female position. By writing about your home life, whether as a decoy or otherwise, you log your experience in a social history. Miriam Wallace (2016, 63) argues that biographical writing operates as a 'fluid' form that links the personal with the historical, thereby 'expanding both the content and the kinds of subjects represented in the historical'. Though I question whether you felt liberated by your writing at the time of writing, your diarising has survived the passing of time. In a metaphorical sense, your writing has transported your ideas into 2020 time. However, this was possible only in its addition to a published novel—a public and more highly prized form of writing. The novel has created a space in which we can be in close 'mental proximity' to one another, and so your writing has had the power to liberate female ideas from your domestic space, if not your body from it, when allowed to participate in the culturally-credited body of work.

I hope that you will keep this letter private, and allow this mental proximity to remain as a pathway between us two women.
Yours faithfully,
Reader

Dear Daphne,

I hope you are well in your new, normal life. I write in search of help from Janet Frame. You know her intimately, for the gap between autobiography and fiction proves only to be the difference in discursive positions (Baisnée 1997, 95). I am seeking to find out whether the act of writing has the potential to liberate women from patriarchal spaces. One of these spaces is the confines of the asylum. I hope not to evoke any painful memories, but I do hope to evoke memory. For Daphne, in your role as Janet Frame's alternate ending, you eventually free yourself by doing what was instructed of you. Unlike Frame, who avoided lobotomy, freeing herself from mental observation by publishing an award-winning novel, you remained in the asylum, and did undergo lobotomisation. I hope to uncover what your options may have been as a woman in an asylum, who didn't write, but for letters. I notice that you and your sister, Chicks shared a practice of letter writing. Whereas Chicks's writing marked her desire to obtain an inner world, your writing was your only form of communication outside of your own thoughts. You refused to speak to those around you. Nevertheless, these varied forms of communication serve to reinforce both of your definitions of normality, but from opposite discursive positions.

Unlike Frame, you weren't freed from the hospital by your published works. You didn't write, but demonstrated your own form of agency in refusing to speak to your keepers. Your doctor addresses you in a manner of superiority, 'Now now, Daphne, speak to me, like a good little girl' (Frame 2002, 134). Your refusal to respond demonstrates your own authority to do what you please. This bolstered your transgressive role, for in your silence, your keepers became more certain of your madness, noting 'she is too ill to understand what you say'. In playing the role of the schizophrenic woman, Frame positions you as the superior person, knowing more than your doctors and nurses in the asylum. For you had inside knowledge, thinking to yourself 'there is nothing in the world the matter with me' (130). Arthur W. Frank (2004, 179) writes that life writing

> breaks with the epistemology of the ill or disabled person as the object of knowledge ... and asserts such persons' claim to be knowing subjects.

In this way, your internal dialogue acts as a form of life writing that marks you as a person of superior knowledge. Just as Chicks uses the guise of domestic descriptions to provide a safe space for intellectual discussion, may you be allowing your keepers to assume your madness in order to create a personal space of freedom? Elaine Showalter (1987, 204) notes modernist literary movements that have 'appropriated the schizophrenic woman as the symbol of linguistic, religious, and sexual breakdown and rebellion'. In refusing to abide by your doctors' linguistic boundaries, you place yourself outside of patriarchal order. You observe the other girls in the yard, who are 'laughing and screaming and fighting and dead' (136). In their audibility, they enter the numbed reality of women in the hospital. You, however, have an inner world, as Frame does. You think inside yourself, 'They are mad. They are frauds' (134). In *Madness and Civilization*, Michel Foucault (1967, 250) writes that 'madness is responsible only for that part of itself which is visible. All the rest is reduced to silence'. I would like to extend the visibility of madness to audibility, too. Your silence marks you as all knowing, in an institution that marks you as mad. You are able to journey therefore, to your Mirror City within you, by refusing to actualise your interpretations.

Laingian theory interprets schizophrenia as 'a form of protest against the female role', expanding that madness became 'a form of communication in response to the contradictory messages and demands about femininity women faced in patriarchal society' (Foucault 1967, 250). This is a complex stance, for whilst your roleplaying may have provided a means of protest, your lack of verbal protest ultimately condemned you to lobotomy. In your own way, you may have perceived this as an heroic act. Though Frame doesn't advocate any psychological theories, she tolerated Carl Jung's psychology (Ash 1988, 172). Jung's 'animus' is the unconscious masculine side of the woman, and vice versa. Through his 'latent masculine principle', he notes that women must 'know' but not exercise this masculine knowledge (Fordham 1976, 55–57). You therefore find yourself in the heroine's position, who has sacrificed her 'masculine' knowledge in favour of escaping her role within patriarchal society, but is simultaneously confined, as she now requires a man to save her from heroinism (Ash).[5] Thus, in a matter of interpretation, you've merely prolonged your condemnation into a patriarchal space of 'normality'. Of course, this theory supposes that you were in control. In such patriarchal times, it may be presumptuous to assume this. Nevertheless, Frame writes in *An Angel at My Table* that she 'consciously played the role of schizophrenic' to win the attention of John Forrest, her professor (Showalter 1987, 215). By writing your story as an alternate ending, Frame takes back control as the female author. In writing your madness, she is able to detach herself from the position of the woman in the asylum, and become the observer, rather than the observed. Under observation 'madness is constantly required' (Foucault). Frame rids herself of her madness by letting you play that role instead.

However, whilst distancing herself from a personal identity as the madwoman in the asylum, Frame also uses your madness to preserve the association. Frame is clear about the fact that she is not you, Daphne, but your stories follow the same trajectory until lobotomy. Frame admits in her autobiography that within the growing literary community of New Zealand 'her madness continued to be seen as essential to her literary personality' (Wood 2013, 174). Moreover, Ruth Brown (2003, 126) argues that Frame's association with madness may have 'formed the basis for her literary fame'. Whilst Frame frees herself of mental illness by writing about your story, she also fosters a self-association with madness. In this way, your superior internal dialogue may be seen as futile. For although you and Frame are both in on a secret higher understanding, your ultimate condemnation to lobotomy sacrifices you to the wills of the New Zealand literary establishment, thereby freeing Frame from the madness it requires. And so, although you free yourself from Foucault's definition of madness by refusing to audibly defend your sanity, your lack of protest condemns you to act as Frame's mad symbiotic presence that ties you both into a public spectacle.

Alas, this symbiotic link works both ways. Frame ties you into a duplicity to invoke and free herself from associations with madness, which simultaneously ties you, Daphne, into associations with the successful author, Janet Frame. One cannot read your madness as a counter-narrative to Frame's story without also considering Frame's talent as something you are capable of and entitled to. Though your lobotomy is tragic and upsetting, I can't help but acknowledge your alternate ending as a renowned author. Thus, by using you as a means of controlling her own public persona, Frame entitles you to a piece of her success, too. The inside knowledge shared by you and Frame, as a letter between the two of you, acts as a pathway between Janet Frame the observer and Daphne the observed, allowing a mutual permeation of the mind. In this way, Frame frees you from the confines of the institution, always protecting you by way of her creation.

Ultimately, I believe you would have escaped this role, if you could have. Whilst Frank (2004, 179) credits Frame's writing as a break in the standard cultural narrative about being the object of knowledge, she is quite evidently a knowing subject, and endeavouring to be otherwise problematises her authority. Do you feel oppressed by your position as the mentally ill alternate persona? You write to Chicks and close with the words 'Help help help' (Frame 2002, 101). This may have been a warning to Chicks, about her own afflictions, but I suspect this was also a plea for rescue; an attempt to send a message through a tunnel you wish to crawl through, to the other side. After all, Frame's sister is the one who rescues her from the hospital, by publishing her writing on her behalf. Do you resent the success that's attributed to Janet, in place of yourself?

Now that you have crawled through to Chicks's side, I hope that normality is treating you better than it is treating her.

Yours faithfully,

Reader

Dear Jane Campion,

I write to you as an aspiring female writer. I am trying to discover the potential of female writing to free women from patriarchal spaces. Your depiction of Janet Frame in *An Angel at My Table* inspires me to pursue the difficult act of writing, for Kerry Fox's portrayal of the grown up Janet in parts two and three of the biopic illustrates not only Frame's afflictions, but also the power of overcoming them. The Frame you present has anxieties about social interactions, troubling reactions to 'normal' occurrences and facial expressions that would make any viewer squirm. Her uncomfortable response to John Forrest playing classical music in the lecture theatre, depicted by her wriggling in her seat and biting her nails, and lack of social awareness when approaching Colin in Ibiza exemplify this. Simultaneously, she is courageous, confident in her own ability and triumphant against patriarchal expectations. One need only reference the scenes in London to observe a role reversal of domestic gender norms. Patrick, a man who lives at her residence, who has taken a fancy to her, is the one who waits up for Janet at night. Though he attempts to deter her from her craft, Janet asserts 'I'm a writer, Patrick'. In its varied and intriguing portrayals of Frame, your biopic thus aligns with Cixous and Khun's (1981, 53) description of the female text that takes the 'metaphorical form of wandering' and 'can't be predicted, isn't predictable, isn't knowable and is therefore very disturbing'. As a product of the film as a text, Janet disturbs traditional expectations of both the woman in society and the film heroine. In her pursuit of experience she metaphorically and physically wanders through the film. The use of tracking shots portray this wandering. This is perhaps most notable when Janet returns home after learning her father has died. The camera tracks Janet as she walks along the bay, overlooking the sea that she once sang to with her sisters, evoking a sense of the long journey taken (Campion 2002).

Janet's return is provoked by a letter noting her father's death. In the film, letters create pivotal moments in Janet's journey. Belén Vidal (2006, 419) considers the letter as 'a formal device in the film text' which provides a 'visual inscription of the various manifestations of an utterance ... deferred through time and space'. Letters have the authority to shift the time and setting in the film. After returning home from hospital, Janet brings with her a doctor's letter, confirming her schizophrenia. Janet thrusts the letter over the table to her mother. The camera focuses in on the letter and out again to the scene that receives it. This emphasises a purposeful interchange between two women. It may then be said that Janet values her mother's authority more than her father's. Or simply, that she wants to show her mother the tunnel to the rest of the world, albeit one in which she will suffer, in the short term. Frame writes that she had a strong feeling that her mother was never permitted to enter the 'life within', as she was. The next letter comes to the mailbox outside Frank's house. This letter informs Janet that a publisher has accepted her book, and is her ticket to the wider world. This allows her to travel to London, a place in which Frame herself began 'living the life of a writer' (Ash 1988, 183). The final letter informs her of her father's death. Janet returns to her family home in a scene that is symbolic of her emancipation. With the camera focusing on Janet's feet in her own shoes, stood in a two-shoe queue behind her father's boots, she steps into his shoes metaphorically and physically, as head of the household (Campion 2002). Janet's journey to this point is by no means linear. Cixous and Khun (1981, 43) write of the *Little Red Riding Hood* theory, by which the female goes 'from one house to another by the shortest route possible [...], from the mother to the other'. The complex journey you illustrate shows Janet's comfort in lingering in the forest. On several occasions, she triumphs over the Big Bad Wolf, the superego who 'threatens all the little female red riding hoods who try to go out and explore their forest without the psychoanalyst's permission' (44). Though letters are the tickets that confirm the next parts of her complex journey, each letter is provoked by Janet's writing.

Janet escapes Seacliff Lunatic Asylum after winning the Hubert Church Memorial award for her first novel. The order of scenes creates a protest, in which Janet demands, through her passion, to be let free. In the scene before, Janet is framed by a high angle shot in a room by herself. The mise en scène is blank, apart from Janet and the door to freedom. The camera moves to extreme close up as she fiercely begins writing on the wall. In the following scene, the doctor enters the ward to inform Janet she has won the prize (Campion 2002). Hilary Neroni (2012, 291) notes of your films, 'As Campion depicts it, passion is a formal expression of the psyche, not just what one thinks but also how one thinks'. Janet's insistence on writing defines her psychological state, beyond any objections. Moreover, Neroni asserts that you revolutionise cinema by forcing viewers to change how we look at revolution, noting 'Revolution is a passionate engagement within the everyday, not an escape from it' (306–307). In this way, Janet's passion locates her within the comfort of her Mirror City; her inner world.

Her writing has the power to overthrow the Big Bad Wolf and enter the wilderness by herself. This is exemplified in Janet's moments of success. When she receives the publisher's letter, Janet is stood in the garden of Frank's modest home in the woods. Notably, she starts in the wrong direction to tell him the news. You emphasise Janet's zig-zag path here, that is rooted in nature, not within patriarchal spaces. This is a space unlike the Labour Party's suburb in their *An Era of Plenty* pamphlet, this is rural life (Brickell 2006, 140). Moreover, when Janet returns to her family home, she is sought after by journalists who wish to tell her story. The camera position here evokes a cyclical journey. As the journalists call from the bottom of the hill 'can we come up?', Janet stands at the top in a back view shot. The journalists then crawl to reach her. This camera position mirrors that of Janet's first university scene at the start of Part Two. The camera sits at the top of the lecture theatre, with a back view of the boys at the top. Most of the women, including Janet, sit on the stalls below. This is followed by Janet chatting to a group of girls at the door of the lecture theatre. They remark how 'fun' college is, and ask her to come for a coffee. As she leaves with them, Janet looks longingly back into the lecture theatre at the men who remain sitting amongst the stalls. Finally, through her writing, Janet takes the place of the person sitting at the top, and inverts the political expectation that *Women of the Future*[6] belong in the kitchen, surrounded by consumer goods (142).[6] Moreover, as one final kick in the teeth to the oppressive psychoanalyst, Janet is pictured burning unwanted things from her family home (Campion 2002). This negates psychiatrist Otto Rank's assertion that, 'to create it is necessary to destroy. Women cannot destroy (Russ 2018, 15). Janet's destruction and success here emancipates her from consumerist culture, in which she is expected to seek fulfilment through consuming, rather than by hard work and creativity (Brickell, 144).

As Janet is freed from socially constructed norms by her creativity, I believe that something similar could be said of your own experience, Jane. Letters are a powerful means of female expression in *An Angel At My Table*, but their power is not limited to the film. Your Director's Commentary of the film acts as a letter to Janet Frame, in that it creates a space of close mental proximity between the two of you. You make it clear that you are both united in thought, as intimately as Janet and Daphne may be, for example. In the behind the scenes DVD feature, you confess that when reading Frame's autobiographies, you loved the 'intimacy and the openness' expressed, and felt 'quite capable of understanding it and wanted to communicate it further. In making this connection, you mark yourself as a female writer of letters and create a shared safe space for the intellectual conversation between you and Frame. Your creative direction to Kerry Fox in the behind the scenes footage of the film shows a dedication to detail. Fox recalls how you were always determined to 'go deeper' into Frame's character, with you directing her voiceover recording with 'you're coming clean, not hiding anything from anybody' (Campion 2002). Your craft establishes a connection between you and Frame through your reproduction of her story, in which you use your own understanding of her life and work to create a close mental proximity between Frame and Fox, as well as between Frame and yourself. You confess that you were a fan of Frame's work before you embarked upon the project. This categorises you into what Barbara Brookes (2006, 210) describes as 'young women in the 1970s' who were 'eager to read about women's (imagined unitary) past'. Whilst you mark yourself as Frame's intellectual equal, your fan letter of a Director's Commentary also unites you with the women who read Frame's fiction. In this way, the letter acts as a discussion of what you're reading between yourself, Frame and Frame's readers. This, in turn, encourages Frame's readers into your intellectual discussion, providing a safe space for contemporary women to express their opinions.

This has an emancipatory effect for the community of Frame fans, which includes your younger self. You note that you first read *Owls Do Cry* at thirteen-years-old (Campion 2002). Your letter to Frame's readers thus becomes a letter to your younger self, one which provides a pathway between time. This pathway informs your younger self of a direction to fulfilment and success within the film industry. I assume you acknowledge your success, as a prominent player in the redefinition of New Zealand's film industry, one that reformed the previously 'predominantly testosterone fuelled' film culture (Conrich 2009, 27). In any case, your letter liberates your younger self from your contemporary struggles, and provides sanction from the difficulties of your youth. In the Director's Commentary, you remark that you could really 'see yourself' in Frame's story, noting 'we all feel vulnerable and unchosen' (Campion 2002). In intertwining your personal experiences with intellectual discussion, you protect the space of both, so as to diminish the inherent risk in putting the personal on public display (Cook and Culley 2012, 4). This tactic makes both emotional and professional exploration viable, and models how to do so for readers.

In an interview with the *Otago Daily Times*, your sister Anna comments on the potential for creativity to save women from mental and situational difficulties. Anna recalls that you 'got on to the idea of projects to save' yourself (Mackenzie 1999, 70). This suggests that the film itself may act as a safe space. This is echoed in critics' responses to your work. Observers note that *An Angel At My Table* carefully considers the position of women in New Zealand's social history. Just as letters act as devices that historicise the social and domestic positions of women, your film broadens the scope for women's experience in social history; a letter in itself. Hilary Radner (2011, 259) reaffirms this by describing *An Angel At My Table* as 'screen narratives that consider the place of New Zealand women in the nation's history'. Your film broadens the scope for what can be recorded and considered as women's history, as a piece of lifewriting that re-frames the past in a way relevant to a contemporary audiences. In this way, *An Angel At My Table* defies the confines of space and time to unite us female viewers in a collective emancipatory experience.

Thank you for encouraging me into your intellectual discussion. I wonder, would you advise your younger self, the girl who felt vulnerable and unchosen, and indeed women like me who feel downtrodden by our institutional settings, to pursue our crafts?
Yours Faithfully,
Viewer

Dear Writer,
Thank you for your letters. I have received them all, in one way or another. In your quest to discover the liberating power of women's writing, I see you have drawn some clear conclusions. In certain situations, writing's liberating powers seem futile. If one writes under the watchful eye of their oppressor, their writing merely forms a declaration of their obedience to the programme. Chicks, for example, writes to appease Tim; as a consumer first, and a creator second. Similarly, Daphne is unable to write under the

observation of her doctors. Her only other form of protest is silence. Though heroic, this ultimately leads her to lobotomy. However, you have noted the power of these women's letters. This is where we find some exceptions. In this format, these women write to convey a message; to transfer meaning from one person to another. Though these letters do not save them in the end, they open up a liminal space in which these women can be free of their environments. Their words break through the confines of their walls. In this transition, Chicks and Daphne can briefly escape to their inner spaces.

Though Chicks's diary entries comply with Tim's, and indeed, society's ideal of what a woman should say and be, her intermittent derogatory remarks convey a secret message. Chicks is more aware of the construction of domesticity than one may think when reading the entries at face value. Thus, her higher knowledge acts as a free space. By conceptualising domestic constructions on paper, her mind is freed of these confines. She creates a safer personal space; a Mirror City that is hers, alone. Similarly, Daphne's internal dialogue proves to be all-knowing. She plays the role of the schizophrenic to satisfy her keepers of their authority, and protect herself from audible assertions of madness. The life writing of these two women preserves their inner selves, keeping their inner spaces disparate from exterior confines. Patricia Spacks (2003, 8) explores psychological privacy as a 'privacy of the mind and heart' which provided 'breathing space from the rest of life's demands'.

This life writing cannot be undermined. Throughout your letters, I got the impression that you were trying to apply your own modern privileges to theorise the practices of women writers of another time. Though the passing of time allows us to extend the spectrum of liberation through time and space, it does not diminish the liberating effects of creative works in their own time. Women have not always been free to share their intellectual and creative thoughts openly, and indeed, oppression still remains today. Make no mistake that all female writing is powerful when accepted for its individuality. The beauty of life writing is that there is no culturally correct form. Try not to assume the same institutional practices that trouble you so. If you strive to respect women's life writing for its individuality and non-conformity, perhaps the women who proceed you shall not wander the halls of your university so meekly. Diversity in form illuminates the 'individualised nature of the life of the mind', which creates each author's individual Mirror City (Hannan 2012, 590).

The act of writing allowed me to reside in my Mirror City. Whilst personal satisfaction is always valuable, this may not have been sufficient in my liberation. For if this work had not been published, I may likely have remained in hospital, and lobotomised, like Daphne. Publishing grants an altogether new potential. My published work acted as a ticket to the outside world in Campion's *An Angel at My Table*, and indeed, my own life. Without this, I would have held my inferior position as the observed, rather than the observer. I urge you to write as if you weren't expected to tend to the washing machine's whims. For if it serves only as an unpublished account of your experience, its presence may allow your cultural experience to live on. Or, if you publish work, you may write letters to other women, to create pathways of safety for them, as I and Campion have done.

I must say, there is a certain discomfort to your analyses and to the duplicity of my literary representations. After all, I am now, once again, under observation, where 'madness is constantly required' (Foucault 1967, 250). Thank goodness that these observations reside in the private spaces of letters between women. I fear that I would otherwise be reduced to the fictional character. I would cease to be creator and would once again be forced into the 'nowhereness' of observed existence (Ash 1988, 82).[7] Assumptions would be made that as the observed subject, I become a commodity of literary interpretation … if there were anyone in the world to make them.

Hush, hush, hush,[8]

Janet.

Notes

1. 'Help help help' is a reference from Daphne's letter to Chicks, written in the asylum. All further references are to this edition and will be cited parenthetically within the main body of the essay.
2. In light of this, my letter-writing to Frame and others assumes a pseudo-historic approach to communication. Given the displacement of letter-writing with email, letter-writing here serves to bolster my connection to an acknowledged past, hence creating a direct line of intellectual inquiry.
3. Peter Fraser was elected as Prime Minister of New Zealand in 1940 and notably commented on the 'new-fangled gramophone' which could bring culture to the masses.
4. Ripa comments on incarceration in Nineteenth Century France. Though indirectly related to Chicks' lobotomy, her inability to speak French but attempt to make appropriate 'French' gestures likens her further to Ripa's observation of the locked up women who could not access the world of their keepers.
5. This refers to Ash's understanding of what it means to abide by the 'latent masculine principle', and her description of the heroine as a woman who waits passively for a male rescuer to change her circumstances.
6. *Women of the Future* is a 1949 pamphlet from New Zealand's National Party.
7. Ash (1988, 182). 'Nowhereness' is in reference to Frame's assertion that society's expectations made her feel as though 'there were no place on earth' for her.
8. The final spoken words of Campion's *An Angel at My Table*, and the end of the female text.

Disclosure statement

No potential conflict of interest was reported by the author(s).

References

Ash, Susan. 1988. "Janet Frame: The Female Artist as Hero." *Journal of New Zealand Literature: JNZL* (6): 170–189. www.jstor.org/stable/20764059.

Baisnée, Valerie. 1997. *Gendered Resistance: The Autobiographies of Simone de Beauvoir, Maya Angelou, Janet Frame and Marguerite Duras*. Amsterdam, Atlanta: Rodopi.

Brickell, Chris. 2006. "The Politics of Post-War Consumer Culture." *New Zealand Journal of History* 40 (2): 133–155. http://www.nzjh.auckland.ac.nz/docs/2006/NZJH_40_2_01b.pdf.

Brookes, Barbara. 2006. "A Germaine Moment: Style, Language, and Audience." In *Disputed Histories: Imagining New Zealand's Pasts*, edited by Tony Ballantyne, and Brian Moloughney, 191–203. Dunedin: University of Otago Press.

Brown, Ruth. 2003. "Beyond the Myth: Janet Frame Unframed." *Journal of New Zealand Literature* 21: 122–139. https://www.jstor.org/stable/20112359.

Campion, Jane, dir. *An Angel at my Table*, 1990. UK: Fox Video, 2002. DVD.

Cixous, Hélène, and Annette Khun. 1981. "Castration or Decapitation?" *Signs: Journal of Women in Culture and Society* 7 (1): 41–55. www.jstor.org/stable/3173505.

Conrich, Ian. 2009. *Studies in New Zealand Cinema*. London: Kakopo Books.

Cook, Daniel, and Amy Culley. 2012. *Women's Life Writing, 1700–1850: Gender, Genre and Authorship*. Basingstoke: Palgrave Macmillan.

Daybell, James. 2006. *Women Letter-Writers in Tudor England*. Oxford: Oxford University Press.

Fordham, Frieda. 1976. *An Introduction to Jung's Psychology*. Harmondsworth: Penguin.

Foucault, Michel. 1967. *Madness and Civilization: A History of Insanity in the Age of Reason*. London: Tavistock Publications Ltd.

Frame, Janet. 2002. *Owls Do Cry*. London: The Women's Press Ltd.

Frank, A. W. 2004. "Moral Non-fiction: Life Writing and Children's Disability." In *The Ethics of Life Writing*, edited by Paul John Eakin, 174–194. Ithaca, NY: Cornell University Press.

Hannan, Leonie. 2012. "Making Space: English Women, Letter-Writing, and the Life of the Mind, c.1650–1750." *Women's History Review: Space, Place and Gendered Identities: Feminist History and the Spatial Turn* 21 (4): 589–604. doi-org.abc.cardiff.ac.uk/10.1080/09612025.2012.658173.

Hannan, Leonie. 2016. *Women of Letters: Gender, Writing and the Life of the Mind in Early Modern England*. Manchester: Manchester University Press.

Mackenzie, Suzie. 1999. "Campions Enjoy a Rich Friendship." *Otago Daily Times*, October 2. https://natlib.govt.nz/records/21179240?search%5Bi%5D%5Bprimary_collection%5D=findNZarticles&search%5Bi%5D%5Bsubject_text%5D=Campion%2C(Jane&search%5Bpath%5D=items.

Middleton, Sue. 1998. "Schools at War: A Life-History Analysis of Learning and Teaching in New Zealand, 1939-1949." *Discourse: Studies in the Cultural Politics of Education* 19 (1): 53–74. doi:10.1080/0159630980190104.

Neroni, Hilary. 2012. "Following the Impossible Road to Female Passion: Psychoanalysis, the Mundane, and the Films of Jane Campion." *Discourse* 34 (2): 290–310. https://www-muse-jhu-edu.abc.cardiff.ac.uk/article/522515.

Radner, Hilary. 2011. "Screening Women's Histories: Jane Campion and the New Zealand Heritage Film, from the Biopic to the Female Gothic." In *New Zealand Cinema Interpreting the Past*, edited by Alistair Fox, Barry Keith Grant, and Hilary Radner, 257–276. Bristol, Chicago: Intellect

Reuben, Elaine. 1972. "Can a Young Girl from a Small Mining Town Find Happiness Writing Criticism for *The New York Review of Books?*" *College English* 34 (1): 40–43. doi:10.2307/375217.

Ripa, Yannick. 1990. *Women and Madness*. Cambridge: Polity Press.

Russ, Joanna. 2018. *How to Suppress Women's Writing*. Austin: University of Texas Press.

Schwartz, Susan. 1996. "Dancing in the Asylum: The Uncanny Truth of the Madwoman in Janet Frame's Fiction." *Ariel: A Review of International English Literature* 27 (4): 113–127. https://journalhosting.ucalgary.ca/index.php/ariel/article/view/33806.

Showalter, Elaine. 1987. *The Female Malady: Women, Madness and English Culture 1830–1980*. London: Virago Press.

Spacks, Patricia. 2003. *Privacy: Concealing the Eighteenth-Century Self*. Chicago: University of Chicago Press.

Summit, Jennifer. 2004. "Writing Home: Hannah Wolley, The Oxinden Letters and Household Epistolary Practice." In *Women, Property, and the Letters of the Law in Early Modern*

England, edited by N. E. Wright, M. W. Ferguson, and A. R. Buck, 201–208. Toronto: University of Toronto Press.

Vidal, Belén. 2006. "Labyrinths of Loss: The Letter as Figure of Desire and Deferral in the Literary Film." *Journal of European Studies* 36 (4): 418–436. doi:10.1177/0047244106071071.

Wallace, Miriam. 2016. "Writing Lives and Gendering History in Mary Hays's Female Biography (1803)." In *Romantic Autobiography in England*, edited by Eugene Stelzig, 63–78. London: Routledge.

Wood, Mary Elene. 2013. *Life Writing and Schizophrenia: Encounters at the Edge of Meaning*. Amsterdam, New York: Rodopi.

In Parallel With My Actual Diary: On Re-writing an Exile

Chris Campanioni ⓘ

ABSTRACT

How can the production of migratory texts provide social and political agency for migrants? My starting point for investigating connections between literary acts of resistance and literal acts of resistance is in fact multiple: the discontinuous pathways of exile. In re-drafting Walter Benjamin's seven-year exile from Paris to Lourdes, Lourdes to Marseilles, Marseilles to Port-Vendres, Port-Vendres to Portbou, 'In Parallel With My Actual Diary' also re-evaluates the xenophobic culture of the European cities that we each traverse, bridging gaps between 1940 and today to shed light on the often undocumented microhistories of migration and the dead end of diaspora: the largest human displacement since the Second World War. In my endeavour to converge past and present, I collage letters written by Benjamin during his exile; scenes of departure culled from interviews, photographic evidence, and testimonies; reportage of political and social upheaval in Europe in the summer of 2017; and finally, my own letters, written to Walter as I read him back. The goal of re-writing Benjamin's exile as epistolary essay is to engender empathy, while forming parallels between his piecemeal, processual, itinerant (and unfinished) *Arcades Project* and the migratory – collaborative, anonymous, transmedial – texts produced by displaced persons today.

The composition of this essay and its research that began, officially, in the summer of 2017 but which I've reckoned with since my birth, has been marked by experiences of thrilling discovery, the continuous exchange between anxiety and urgency, and a pulsating sense of home that I've carried with me my whole life, a sense of home that I've been carried by, that I've internalised and imagined. These are obligatory preconditions for most children of migrants, especially the children born to two exiles: those persons, perhaps now adults, perhaps now with children of their own, who can only remember the places where they've come from in stories. And I guess that is the point, of all of this, the research and the work itself, what the research found, if it found anything besides the fact of moving, of being moved by a necessary lack. I learned, from such an early age, a common narrative, which was in fact the absence of it. The self-silencing I became accustomed to as a child, from my mother and father, turned me from a reader into a writer, a writer into an instructor, an instructor into a researcher, who could only theorise a migratory text by looking, first, at my own life, where so much of the personal has been deferred or dislocated through the institutionalised agenda of objectivity and distance, of specialisation and separation and the cultured language of the intellectual. Everything I wish to theorise first goes through the body, what it can and cannot say, or more specifically, the trauma which is both unspeakable and transmittable, inchoate and yet undeniably passed down. What else have I inherited but each of my parent's desires to change, and so to change the present means to alter the outcome, but also the trajectory. How we got here. And where were we, or: how do we begin?

The discourse of migration is fraught with academic, literary, and political spokespeople, conditions which leave little room for self-representation and pathways for self-determination. What I want is to pay careful attention to the moments that contradict these regular and regulative state and cultural practices, moments in which the partial, piecemeal, and processual personal texts produced by migrants, stateless, and displaced persons have been able to enact the possibilities of something else, beyond being spoken about and spoken for and otherwise self-silenced. And I began, in the summer of 2017, or rather, I continued, in June of that same year, by walking in the footsteps of Walter Benjamin, traversing the numerous sites of his seven-year exile while reading the letters he wrote at each waypoint, while writing him letters when I arrived. The occasion for meeting, for convergence, takes time, and specifically, a time that is not ordered and uniform, that is not linear, that does not separate the *before* and the *after*, that does not repeat this violence (which is all separation) through monumentalisation (which is history), a time that is not about closure but about the opening up of another narrative, neither public nor hidden, but nascent: the certain uncertainty of the ways in which our lives are unfolding in relation to each other. I am looking for the moment a past becomes a post. Or rather, when past and post become part of the same transmission, belonging to the same space, the same breath, a moment to read and be read in all its dimensions – awaited and remembered and hallucinated and hypostatised – this thin paper surface as Möbius strip.

•

This story starts on a train, or the moment one exits one. To become another.

Walter Benjamin walks the last few craggy passes of a makeshift trail in the Pyrenees and sets foot on Spanish soil. He's breathing heavily, one hand on his walking stick, the other holding his briefcase. A 'leather briefcase like those used by businessmen', according to official court documents. He already sees the small custom house to which he'd been directed upon arrival.

It's a momentary pause. The cessation between two worlds and two words, the passage between escape and true freedom, the perpetual exile of breathing in a body that has been condemned to the ritual of arriving and departing, an unceasing search that is also misguided. The point was to get lost. All this untellable time. A train whistles. Wind sweeps down the mountains. Then the sea was calm. Then the water rose and fell. Then the white foam burst against the rocks. Another train rattles over, from the opposite direction. I'm on this one. From the future of the present or the yesterday of today, I arrive. Too late, I would have thought, in earlier moments. Except I know time is only ever now.

Benjamin takes a look at the Franco-Spanish frontier and sighs, wipes his eyeglasses, directs his worn eyes toward the bombed-out buildings and scattered rubble – another casualty of fascism, the Spanish Civil War. A deluge of refugees fled toward France.

Then refugees in France fled toward Spain. The promise of movement, of striving onward. If only to keep striving, or to keep straddling, but without borders. Like the sea, that always exceeds the limits of the frame in the eye of a camera.

Picture it.

Picture it again.

Better.

Picture yourself there. Engender empathy.

Benjamin, together with Lisa Fittko, Henny Gurland, and her son, Joseph, reach the custom house on foot, wait three hours for acknowledgement of their travel documents, are told they will be escorted back to Nazi-occupied France the following day, spared the afternoon in Portbou because of Walter's ailing heart, the long, slow march through the Pyrenees. A clerical error, a technicality, an accident, or coincidence.

What's the difference between a coincidence and something written as fate? Years later, Lisa Fittko describes Walter Benjamin as 'most remarkable. Born to attract misfortune' (Heinemann 1993, 140).

To be mistaken or to be mistaken for someone else.

He checks into room 4 on the Hotel Francia's second floor. He orders five lemonades. He places four phone calls during the evening.

Then he dies.

'The story is by now so well known that it barely needs to be retold,' apologises novelist J.M. Coetzee in 2001, in an essay for *The New York Review of Books* to herald the long-awaited English-language publication of the *Arcades Project*.

Except there's truth in the retelling. Just as Benjamin painstakingly copied out the aphorisms and observations of what others had already said to produce a text that is almost authorless – a collaborative, citational work of so many voices – the same sound heard again is always heard differently. When I exit this train, I will always be in a new place, as a new person.

It is precisely because this story is so well known that it needs to be retold.

I will not apologise.

Everything in this story depends on playing back the scene or site of original trauma, and as Édouard Glissant reminds us, 'while one can communicate through errantry's imaginary vision, the experiences of exiles are incommunicable' (1997, 20).

So to move, and to allow another to move inside me.

And every passage carries its own impasse within it – what Giorgio Agamben calls the 'non-coincidence between facts and truth, between verification and comprehension', a relationship that makes something like a testimony possible, even if *and especially because* the author can only testify on behalf of someone else, a witness, the one who has been subjected to silence (1999, 12). There are events, there are moments, there is a violence that remain unassimilable; there are testimonies that necessarily stand outside the continuum of narrative.

How, then, do we re-write an exile?

We begin by seeking alternate sources of evidence – notebooks, diaries, journals, letters, ephemeral embraces – forms too often dismissed by academia, voices too often absent from the archive, amid the heteronormative, racialised, cultural, and state processes that have only produced exclusion under the auspices of forming a national identity. We begin through collective refusal and collaborative self-expression, the sharing of migratory passages, the co-creation of testimony, the dissolution between subject and object, story-teller and listener, the intimacy of anonymous encounters. We begin with recitation and citation, a procedure that is not concerned with writing out but taking in, so as to mix without merging, retrieve without replacing.

Why does the work of critical writing so often abandon the personal for the posture of distance and detachment? I want to pursue a mode of criticism that is harnessed to the body – inextricable and intimate, a critical work that is sensitive to its own makeup, carried by and yet carrying the personal into something not clearly understood, marked out, measured in advance. In advance of nothing if not the desire to fold *inward*, toward tenuous beginnings. The aporia of critical engagement is that we can afford to be objective and neutral, that we can afford to erase the fact of our own place and position within and without our institutions, that we can afford to disregard the relationship between our role as subjects and the subjects of our critical inquiries. The aporia of critical engagement is that there is no difference between the history of the public and the history of the individual, that personal events are not entangled in larger, more legible stories that the public calls the past. But the critical – from the Late Latin criticus *at a turning point*, borrowed from the Greek kritikós, a derivative of krísis – also suggests abrupt change, a point at which some quality, property, or phenomenon undergoes a definite deviation. To pretend otherwise ignores the uncomfortable reality of the power structures we work in and on, the reproduction of knowledge reserved – that is placed, stored, kept, and, etymologically, *kept back*. To pretend otherwise is to not look, or: to pretend not to see, to turn from acknowledging the agony and impossibility of telling our stories and yet, despite or exactly because of this, understanding the necessity of doing so.

It is difficult to pretend to be anyone but myself when I encounter photographs of children at a primary school in 1950s Warsaw at the DDR Museum in Berlin, and I ask my mom, over text and a series of images, if she remembers the school, if she can make out any of the faces; children soaked in sepia and arranged for the flash. What came first, the preservation of history or its presentation? It is difficult to pretend to be objective, distanced, neutral – to not have a stake in what it is I'm researching – when I'm reminded by my own notes, as I continue to pursue convergences between the interwar period and today, and the different hemispheric legacies of the Cold War, that when my dad left Cuba as a child, Operación Pedro Pan would go on, and go on to become the largest migration of unaccompanied minors in the history of human passage.

I am looking for a correspondence between events. Between then and now, there and here, imagination and memory, and the actuality of this transcription. In the gap between occurrence and its remembering there is a residue, not an excess but an absence, to the extent that it opens up or indexes something beyond us. Our role is to keep looking, at everything we can't see.

Spivak (1993) says sometimes the details of an author's life are not enough. What the text begs of us, what we beg of the text, is more than biographical details but the history of the author's moment, the history of the language-in-and-as-translation, the history of authorial detours, reverses, addendums, redactions. I would like to make a book with as many errors as exits; I would like to remind myself that it is the breakdown of language that offers the opportunity for its reappraisal; the breakdown of the subject which gives rise to the opportunity for the subject to become, once again, sovereign – limitless and liquid, neither raised nor arisen but *rising*.

I write to you; I write you. In French – je t'écris – it's only ever the same, understanding that correspondence is always a form of visitation, but also an act of metempsychosis, in which I become the subject I am writing about, the person to whom I am writing.

If the original manuscript for the *Arcades Project* was indeed the version entrusted to Georges Bataille at the Bibliothèque Nationale, and no one knows which manuscript went missing in Benjamin's briefcase, I'd like to think of this text as the copy: Side B. A perversion or inversion of the original. Walter Benjamin as Benjamin Walter. *Side B.*

When he was buried, on 28 September 1940, no one at the ceremony knew who he was. The registry office's record reads, 'Señor Benjamin Walter, 48 years old, born in Berlin, passing through' (Ferrer-Cussó 1993, 157). On 28 September 1940, a funeral was held for someone who did not exist.

I often imagine another Benjamin, not a Benjamin Walter but another Walter Benjamin, someone carved from the same revised historical materialism as his life's work, so slow of foot and ailing in heart that he arrives in Portbou *one day later.*

•

29 June 2017, 10:10pm
somewhere over the Atlantic

Dear Walter,

I am writing to you from the air. I am following you, at least as far as the Franco-Spanish station of the cross. The edge of the world, according to Walter. Das Passagen-Werk. There is no better subject to begin with. I am searching for the social urgency in the mobile text. Your *Arcades Project* is an assemblage of thoughts and images, a shutter roll of film developed from the negatives. A starting point for producing an equality out of history's least common denominators. In each of these endeavours, I think we both asked a similar question: How do we write about something that remains undocumented?

Dear Walter, today we can track a collective, unconscious mood through the marking of the mundane, flow that relies on the redundancy of every day and everyday redundancies. And what's more, this ambient awareness has the tendency to alight upon the moments where the ordinary shifts into emergency, an indexical activism that becomes itself and also its own record or trace.

Dear Walter, I want to make a point about the counterpublics cultivated by the migratory text, and how a greater engagement with such personal letters and journals can provoke questions necessary to a re-evaluation of our current norms and rules within a Post Internet culture, the post that comes before and comes after, etymologically behind but also toward, to, near, late, close by, but also away from – all of these. To signal *post* is to entertain the multiple singularities of correspondence – *I am writing to you* – the addressee and the event of address, and when I write to you *I keep you close at hand,* a coinciding of proximity and distance. Post thus reflects the implications for the future and also the mode of self-publication and circulation, the ways in which media is exchanged and capital is produced. At once noun, verb, and prefix, post – set aside, divested of hyphen – calls attention, in this essay, to the binary between historical time and personal time that is problematised by the migratory text. Historical and personal: it is a mistake to think that one is shared and one is solitary.

We live, each of us, before and after history. Fin-de-siècle modernity and Post Internet culture are strikingly similar, the way Paris in the nineteenth century follows New York in the twenty-first after a brief break in continuity, like the delay in a dubbed film, where the words come a moment after the mouth moves. I am speaking now of the residue of our past. And let the rubble pile up. If I don't wake up in Paris tomorrow morning, I'd prefer to suffocate on it.

•

30 June 2017, 9:35am
Paris

Dear Walter,

Which Paris will I write about when I revisit your life? Will it be the city of Baudelaire and Proust, whom you read and fell in love with during your days as a student, or the city that preoccupied you from the 1920s, and in which you wrote, tirelessly, at 5 Rue Vivienne? The Paris of a nineteenth-century artificial paradise, the arcades of preserved consumerism, idealised microcosms of modernity, its own precursor to the panorama of cinema: a self-contained world.

Or will it be the Paris of your exile? The Paris of fourteen governments in six years, the Paris of political destabilisation, economic ruin, and xenophobia, the Paris you feared as you retreated, in 1933, to Ibiza, desperate, the Paris of the popular slogan, 'Les émigrés sont pires que les boches' (the immigrants are worse than the German soldiers)?

When you returned, you changed addresses about eighteen times. I will be staying at the same studio apartment until I leave, voluntarily, for a high-speed train to Lourdes.

Dear Walter, Paris is still branding itself as the cosmopolis par excellence, the twenty-first century's global city of hospitality, while outside the city limits, unwanted persons starve in detention centers we call 'shelters.'

•

3 July 2017, 12:26pm
Paris

Dear Walter,

I wait in line to be let in at the BnF and receive a slip that says DEMANDE D' ACCRÉDITATION 017. The attendant says that the photograph on my T-shirt was taken inside, a few steps away, or so I imagine, if I'm permitted to enter the sliding door. Your lithographed face repeated nine times across the chest and down the torso, stopping at my navel, almost where my belt is, or where my belt would be if I was wearing one.

Dear Walter, who shot you here? And where are the outtakes?

•

3 July 2017, 1:26pm
Paris

Dear Walter,

Now the time stamp on the Dell PC from which I type says 13:26. The room where you researched is now the art history library. Today other scholars crowd around me on their devices: tablets, smart phones, laptops. Google says people typically spend four hours here. The sun is coming through the skylight and half my face is in shade. My search returns one manuscript: a microfilm of one of your letters. It's three pages and costs 5 euro to access.

Dear Walter, where is everything else?

•

4 July 2017, 4:34pm
in between Paris ᵕᵕᵕᵕᵕ

Dear Walter,

I take my phone out to videotape the French countryside from my seat near the window, in the second class. I would like to message L these videos so she could see what I am seeing, or not seeing, as I ride south. I would like you to see me in the act of videotaping the French countryside and I would like to watch it for myself, but later. With a song I've selected, because everything is better with music. Dear Walter, so much of your work presents an image bank or the archive of lost and found memories, a pastiche of masterworks alongside the ads in a travel magazine, like the *High Life* I pilfered from British Airways before I deplaned. You knew that coincidence and concentration could both contribute to the formation of ideas, that even accidents render and reframe our production of knowledge, that what we delete from the search field after typing it into a digital database is more informative to our gatekeepers than anything we've actually published. But how did you know?

Dear Walter, consider the role of language in shaping social consciousness.

•

5 July 2017, 11:33am
Lourdes

Dear Walter,

When I take a photo of the Hotel de Nevers, which is a block south from my own hotel, I am reminded by your internment at Nièvre, inside a completely empty estate building transformed into a work camp, where you were transported following two agonising weeks in the Stade de Colombes: an unroofed cycling arena with no chair, no bed, tens of thousands of other men. Everyone under fifty. Then, everyone under fifty-five. On 4 September 1939, notices began to appear everywhere in Paris. 'Hostile foreigners' would be required to assemble at specific camps. Immigrants were recommended to bring a blanket, soap, and food. But for how many days?

Dear Walter, I want to tell you about the testimonies of those men with whom you waited, those men with whom you did anything but wait, and all the memories that have lasted within them, the Walter Benjamin that lives on when they think of their own internment. Hans Sahl speaks of a course you held at Nièvre. 'At this point something rather ironic occurred,' he writes, 'about which very little has been written: the organisational genius of the prisoners [...] won out over the French disorganisation. [...] A wandervogel spirit behind barbed wires swept rooms with straw brooms, hung wash out to dry, organised lectures comparing Freud and Jung, Lenin and Trotsky. A community that began to function was soon fashioned from the void; from chaos and helplessness emerged a society' (1988, 348–349).

ESSAYS IN LIFE WRITING 99

Dear Walter, I want to tell you that even while waiting you were not biding your time.

•

5 July 2017, 12:45pm
Lourdes

Dear Walter,

The dream you had some time ago[1] still fills me with hope. In it, you describe being examined, a fear that the results of your handwriting will reveal who you really are, your 'personal characteristics.' You move closer, you see a piece of cloth covered with images, but the only thing you can distinguish is the top half of the letter *d*. Was it lowercase or capitalised? You never say. You say, instead, 'its elongation revealed an extreme aspiration to achieve spirituality.' Your handwriting becomes a topic of interest for everyone present; it's the only topic of discussion. You are unable to recall the opinions expressed. But you recall very well the only thing you ever say, at some point, before you wake. 'It was a matter of turning a poem into a fichu' (Benjamin 2012, 615).

What else could that mean but that poetry could be anything, could be anywhere, and that it is only a matter of re-training our eyes to consider the power of transforming one thing into another – imagination, memory, and the call for inclusivity, to include everything, to stick in, throw on, fichu, from Vulgar Latin, figicāre. Dear Walter, it is always the hybrid form that has the most power, that attracts the most disgust, the most fear and consternation; that which is unexplainable because it warrants no explanation. It only demands more space to ask the question, to fill the space, to leave it open.

•

6 July 2017, 4:33pm
Marseilles

Dear Walter,

I'd like to write these notes out in a notebook, by hand, so you can see what my handwriting looks like, not just how it feels when I read it out loud.

I'd like to mimic your own minuscule handwriting, an attempt to fit up to one hundred lines on a page in an octavo notebook, an act that mirrors the ambition of concentrating on the smallest details. Gershom Scholem says you once told him: 'A philosophy that is unable to incorporate and elucidate the possibility of prophesying from coffee grounds cannot be a true philosophy' (Llovet 1993, 206).

Small things interested you the most because the more closely you look at a word, the more distantly it looks back – and how things withstand the gaze. The point was resistance and concentration, and the point itself, not the whole. Like any good method of resurrection or reactivation, servicing marginalia is a way to breathe life into dead forms. And anyway – isn't it true Walter? – that it's not just words, but people too; that the most distant people could be the ones closest to us.

And there's something I want to say about copying things out, about the slippage of writer and reader, and the writing of a composite text passed along from every person who has been here and who remains here in the here-after. It is a mistake to ignore the exigency of the anecdotal; incidental situations have a spiritual weight that intervenes in the stack or stockpile of history.

6 July 2017, 7:25pm
Marseilles

Dear Walter,

The first time you ever saw Marseilles, you wrote to Scholem, urging him to see it with you, in spirit or in substance, 'in order to look at this unspeakably beautiful city that has been frozen in time' (Benjamin 2012, 307). When you returned, much later, desperate, disguised as a sailor, Marseilles was just a port of call in your exile; you didn't write about it, you didn't write about anything to anyone while you were in Marseilles, slipping in between the Vichy militia and the Gestapo, looking for a way out. Even in the unoccupied zone, there were French patrols dedicated to tracking down refugees and handing them over to the Nazis.

When you left Marseilles, you left without receiving an exit visa, recently declared necessary for leaving France. Dear Walter, if the country in which you were living and working refused to see you as one of its citizens, why did its government force you to stay?

•

8 July 2017, 11:12am
Port-Vendres

Dear Walter,

All roads lead to la gare de Port-Vendres and to the Auberge Béar, a building that looks, maybe, unchanged from when you arrived on your own train. You had to have seen it; it's the last thing anyone sees when they leave, the first thing anyone sees when they arrive. I'm on the third floor, in the tenth room. I am writing this from a small white balcony. It's the one with the terrace, and the blue shorts and the green shirt hanging in between two pots of red flowers, each of them a different shade. You came here with Henny and Joseph, two people you met during your internment at Nevers, in the Château de Vernuche. Hans Fittko, whom you also befriended at Nevers, told you to come; he was always doling out favours on behalf of his wife. Lisa, too, was on the run. And so you sought her help, the way I sought help, too, not knowing how I'll reach Portbou tomorrow, if I'll reach Portbou at all.

Dear Walter, the train station is just a terminal. No one works there. There is no lobby. Only two benches sit, unsat upon, outside. The mountains that look majestic if I only turn around are oppressive from this angle.

When I ask the hotel manager about transportation, she laughs and shakes her head. It's a dead station, she says. Unless she says: It's a dead end. I can't be sure and anyway, I'm writing this from the future. I can't remember everything exactly as it occurred.

The point anyway – isn't it Walter? – is to make you feel it.

•

8 July 2017, 7:06pm
Port-Vendres

Dear Walter,

During the forty-eight hours prior to my departure from New York City last week, twelve-thousand refugees arrived on Italian shores. Yesterday's report from Amnesty International stated that in these first five months of 2017, more than 2,000 refugees had died en route (see 'Central Mediterranean 2017). The European Union is turning a blind eye, the report said, to abuses in Libyan detention centers. Instead of aiding migrants, EU officials have been making deals with the governments from which these migrants are fleeing, to prevent them from entering European territory. Undermined by legal gridlock, sub-Saharan migrants are attempting an even more dangerous route into Spain's southern coast. The ones that have made it to France have already been abandoned by French authorities, an asylum process that involves evading riot police equipped with batons and tear gas, a system of hospitality that involves no access to running water in the sand dunes outside Calais, where the Jungle once stood, before it was demolished by the government last October. Yesterday, Paris police evicted almost three thousand migrants from city streets, loading everyone, including unaccompanied children, into vans and coaches at dawn (Chrisafis 2017).

Dear Walter, it's the largest human displacement since the Second World War.

Dear Walter, your discontinuous migration becomes another eddy in the whirlpool you often speak of, swirling back to meet us in the very sites we both traverse.

•

9 July 2017, 11:17am
in between Port-Vendres ৫৫৫৫৫

Dear Walter,

And this is where the story starts to get sideways. And this is where it swerves and turns, where it folds over endlessly … where I lose my place as if stepping backstage for a cigarette, a glass of water, everything looks the same except for my face, which looks blurry at the window.

I count the stops – first comes Banyuls-sur-Mer, where you begin your ascent, another small coastal port whose mayor, Vincent Azéma, is sympathetic to the resistance. Later, Azéma and Lisa Fittko will create a network of communication, a part of Varian Fry's 'border project' to help so many other émigrés like you. Now we are at Cerbère. A minute passes. At some point, another. During the third minute we pull in slowly to Portbou, the final stop, the only place left in which to exit, or enter.

The passage from France to Spain takes seventeen minutes and there's no one waiting to check my identity, stamp my papers, permit my passage. Your crossing, instead, takes two days. First, the practice run; the night comes, you don't turn back with the others, you stay right where you've stopped, sleeping in the mountains, alone, accounting for your poor heart, the exhaustion of carrying the briefcase everywhere, of never letting it out of your sight. Dear Walter, didn't you know that your briefcase limits your ability to disappear? In the mountains, of course, from the Vichy militia and the Gestapo patrols, but also in the minds of everyone who will come after you, searching for a manuscript that's absent from all records. Dear Walter, what is a briefcase anyway except a deferred proposal? A receptacle that promises material even as it prevents the possibility of it being read – holding or hiding the text so as to transport it *somewhere else*.

Dear Walter, perhaps it is time to state what has been on both of our minds for a while now: the briefcase archive demands we substitute our own text for what remains missing, staging a scenario that is less hypothetical – What if? – and more hypostatic – I am – the charged possibility of its continuance. Dear Walter, I care little about conspiracy theories. Dear Walter, I want to reach a point where theory falls silent, into the generous redemption of what it means to tell a story, and what it means to listen. Dear Walter, the noise of chronology and discursive structure and academic discourse is so overrated.

•

9 July 2017, 11:55am
Portbou

Dear Walter,

So much bare life to move so barely. But you moved, at the limits of your strength, you continued your passage, and now I'm also thinking of your itinerant *Passagen-Werk* and your movable library, how you described it when you expressed your concern to Theodor Adorno, in a letter dated October 4, 1938, when you were already expecting, any day now, to flee the city of light despite already preparing several hundred books for transportation to an address in Paris. So many people are forced to live this way, to give themselves up or over to a world in which the authorities decide the law in a single stamp, checkmark, checkpoint – a world in which life is delivered and denigrated by a piece of paper.

'I was in a race against the war,' you had written to Adorno, from Svendborg. 'And in spite of all my choking fear, I felt a feeling of triumph on the day I wrapped up the "flaneur," which had been almost fifteen years in the planning, before the end of the world (the fragility of a manuscript!)' (Benjamin 2012, 576). In another translation, you say: *before the world went under.*

•

9 July 2017, 12:42pm
Portbou

Dear Walter,

I drop my bag in the lobby of the Hotel Comodoro and follow the numerous signs pointing toward your memorial. The path is similar to the one I'd trodden in Port-Vendres; I'm always either ascending or descending, then curving up again to meet a tablet in your name, signs pointing toward *Passages* – a monument constructed by Israeli artist Dani Karavan, commissioned by the governments of Catalonia and Germany in 1989 – before the Walls collapsed, before mothers were reunited with their daughters and their sons – and completed five years later.

In the Cementiri Municipal, I find your grave one flight up from the entrance. There's no one here but me, and three children sitting on the steps where I've just ascended. Before your grave is another monument, an obelisk with words etched in four languages: Spanish on one side, French on another, Catalan, English. Dear Walter, a letter from Walter Benjamin to Henny Gurland and Theodor W. Adorno: 'In a situation with no way out, I have no other choice but to make an end of it. It is in a small village in the Pyrenees, where no one knows me, that my life will come to a close. I ask you to give my regards to my friend Adorno and to explain to him the situation in which I find myself placed. There is not enough time to write all the letters I should have wished to write.'

Dear Walter, you never signed your last letter. Dear Walter, I would like to sign it for you; I would like to tell you about the small village in the Pyrenees you had no way of knowing, the small village in the Pyrenees where no one knew you. Dear Walter, I would like to write all the letters I should have wished for you to write.

ESSAYS IN LIFE WRITING

103

•

9 July 2017, 1:15pm
Portbou

Dear Walter,

Originally you were buried elsewhere. Even in death, you continue to drift, wander, flicker in and out of focus, below the vanishing point of the mountains which can't be unseen or ignored; when one looks up, any view from the village includes the Pyrenees. And I am reminded of something that Baudrillard said, unless it was only me reading Baudrillard – 'Astral America'? – and wishing he'd said it; and in his place I will: if you take the signs away, there is no place. So I continue to transmit messages along the route, an itinerary that was already made for me through your passage; and I am thinking right now about translations, how you thought of it as a mode, how it requires one to *go back to the original* (see: Benjamin 1968a) – how I know it has less to do with reading the lines than reading in between them, seeing and hearing and most of all, feeling the echoes of its author, who is not original but multiple. Dear Walter, isn't any translation more like a remix than a faithful rendering? And now I am thinking less about language and more about thought. Earlier, in Marseilles, I wrote to you on a napkin, explaining or describing my thoughts on reading; how learning what another is reading is the most intimate thing you could ever learn about them. The way you absorbed Jean François Paul de Gondi, Cardinal de Retz, in your letter to Hannah, the way we inevitably absorb each other if the contact is made and it's made to last. Dear Walter, isn't the goal of life to escape into our counterpart?

Perhaps the most faithful rereading of any text is the one in which the reader walks in the footsteps of its author. Dear Walter, my endeavour isn't language, it's experience.

•

9 July 2017, 1:31pm
Portbou

Dear Walter,

From the outside, overlooking the mountains and the bay of Portbou, Dani Karavan's *Passages* looks like a darkened chute or slide, my favourite kind as a child, in which I could stay, stuck, somewhere in the middle, and pretend I was nowhere or *not yet*, and if I closed my eyes or ignored the brilliant bright light at the very bottom, I believed it.

I lower my head and descend the steps, one at a time, haltingly, as if reaching the bottom would mean reaching the end of our correspondence, whatever we've shared and everything we haven't; I only want exits, lines or lines of flight. Even in the darkness of the passageway I can see the foam rising to meet my feet if not for the glass separating passerby and sea, the rocks and waves that rise up over the surface.

Up, down. Down, up. A third time, and on this occasion, I begin to count.

Seventy narrow steps cut into the cliff, and all walks, whether or not we retrace them, lead to the dead end of diaspora.

Dear Walter, did I tell you what's been written into or onto the glass that blocks the ultimate passage into the depths of water, a dizzying plummet if not for the protection or direction of your monument – only one way out and it leads to a hedge of bricks. 'It is more arduous to honour the memory of the nameless than that of the renowned.

Historical construction is devoted to the memory of the nameless.' Your own words, from your 'Theses on the Philosophy of History' (see: Benjamin 1968b) ... the text written earlier, in 1940, the text that stirred up so much trouble for you, the text you mailed to Hannah Arendt, with the expressed wish that it remain unpublished. Arendt brought it in her baggage when she herself passed through Portbou, months after you did.

I walk back out, once more, into the too-bright sun, into the midday glare and the mountains, which, finally, I can't see. The grave and the monument. Dear Walter, what is a monument but another grave? And when we look at graves, or monuments, do they force us to remember people, the named and also the nameless? Or are they an excuse to forget to engage with the life left behind?

Maybe Dani Karavan knew this too. Maybe that's why, like your *Arcades*, he didn't resort to a signature or symbol to compromise or compose the (w)hole. Dear Walter, you only cared about the variations on a singular theme, which was concentration and the complex relationships between the particles of a body – to brush up against it, to edge it onward, to leave at the height of contact, and now I also feel like coming, or coming back to what's already there. Here. Here –

Karavan told Ingrid and Konrad Scheurmann in an interview, 'the sea tells the entire tragedy of this man. The work is already there. I can't do better. I only have to make people see that' (Karavan 1993, 255).

Dear Walter, nature creates forms the same way writers do. You and I both know that we need only lie back and let it happen; cultural phenomena bring forth meaning by its arrangement – and rearrangement – with all the others in the text. Look, these points laid out in a constellation are right now overlapping. And when I say look, I also mean *listen*. You had been working on the *Arcades Project* for over thirteen years; even if you were alive today, it would be unfinished. The point of true progression is for the work to remain, always, a work in progress. Dear Walter, any time I write anything, I want it to be read as if it were being written at the moment one reads it, and another's contact constitutes a marker or waypoint on the map that expands and also contracts, to meet each gaze.

•

10 July 2017, 1:47pm
Portbou

Dear Walter,

In your unfinished notebook entries, the one that interest me the most is the one dated 'August 7, 1931, to the Day of My Death.'

'This diary,' you wrote, 'does not promise to become very long. Today I received a negative response from Anton Kippenberg, and this gives my plan the relevance that only futility can guarantee. I need to discover "a method that is just as convenient but somewhat less definitive," I said to I, today' (Benjamin 1999a, 501).

Dear Walter, you had only ever played with the idea of suicide. But you know as well as I (I said to I, today) that in every performance is the genuine awareness of the real. Only those of us with the most secure grasp on the real can perform, can really be good at the performance. And by staging the real, we can hold up its inherent fictions.

Dear Walter, in another entry, titled 'In Parallel With My Actual Diary,' you say that certain things have 'the peculiar ability to take on bodily forms as the need arises, so that fingers or nose, flippers or tail, can be formed from the same cells. In the same way, great passions have the ability to stand in vicariously for quite different forms of life' (Benjamin 1999b, 413).

Dear Walter, I sometimes believe that reading your notes and writing my own has become a substitute for every passing glance on the street. And what's more, it's as if you've touched me more than if we had passed, on Odéon or the Cannebière or somewhere among the hills of Lourdes, among the mountain passes bridging France and Spain. It's as if we had shaken hands, or you had reached yours out, to help me on my way.

•

11 July 2017, 12:24pm
Portbou

Dear Walter,

I've always been bad with good-byes. Maybe it's because I don't believe in them; not that I don't think I'll ever be here again – I know I won't and it's the fact of a moment's unreturnability that makes each one so beautiful – but I don't believe in walls or doors or closing them, and I like windows all right if I can let the air through.

Dear Walter, my favourite story about you is the one where you're escaping the Nazis, sloping down the Pyrenees toward liberation, rest, the pause in the changeover: to replace the reel or real with something else. You're carrying your big leather briefcase and counting the steps that you allow yourself to take before you require rest. You've always been so detailed, so methodical, understanding in advance the limits of your exertion. During your escape, amid bare mountains and imaginable tragedy, you turn to Lisa Fittko to begin a discussion about tomatoes (Heinemann 1993, 142).

•

11 July 2017, 4:46pm
Barcelona

Dear Walter,

You never made it out of Portbou. I left there just under four hours ago, to arrive in Barcelona. After I find my hotel, I drop my bags and walk to the beach. It's four blocks from where I've checked in, on Marquès De L'Argentera, and I've brought your letters with me, the ones you wrote to others, friends and admirers. They kept you from disintegrating. At times, writing to you has kept me present too, while presenting me with another task: locating the political and social agency of the personal text produced in transit – a migratory poetics.

You sought a form that would allow you to forage *for* mystery, to be at home in such marginal spaces (see Benjamin 1999c). Fragmentation and drift is a testament to the fate of so many other people on the move, those who left and those who were left behind. The exile narrative is always a body in migration, incapable of being placed. And if placeless, its domain is everywhere. When I sink my head far enough into the sea, when I come up for air and reach my arms above me, I can feel it too.

•

11 July 2017, 5:36pm
Barcelona

Dear Walter,

I'd forgotten to mention a funny thing that happened, back in Paris. We were in Pigalle, a name that I wouldn't recognise until I wrote it down just now. The miracle of Facebook materialised a reading for me, at Bar Angora, on the second floor, in the afternoon, with all the lights off and the windows open and so much pastis being passed around, and the joy of company and poetry, and the promise of friendship. Hannah Arendt suggested, in her introduction to your *Illuminations*, that the reason you fell in love with Paris at the very beginning was because of how gracious the city was, how it offered itself to all homeless people as a second home. Dear Walter, on a single day, I felt it too. People read, passed around their books, bartered them for drinks, exchanged contacts and addresses.

I've left these letters in Portbou, at the Hotel Comodoro. Room 110, in the nightstand with the small pink lamp, beside the sliding glass doors. For the one who came before me. And the one who walks in your footsteps next.

I've laid everything out for you. Everything you need is already here.

•

I had promised myself that I would return, when I was on the verge of completing my dissertation, the genesis of which can be traced here, the nearness of being in parallel with another's diary, the composition of another's life. I had envisioned returning to these addresses, a journey that involves rereading this correspondence but also re-treading its itinerary.

We know that acts of remembering *take place* in specific locations, in particular circumstances. Remembering, and the inscribing of memory in any method of life writing, is associative and occasional. These letters, thus, are an occasion to remember, a reminder to remember the material reality of deportation and exile, and of the correspondences that can now *take the place of* more conventional, historical, and objective repositories of the past. The work of life writing, then, begs not only the question of the presentation of life but of a *living* present.

In my living present, much of the world's population is in quarantine. Even before shelter in place orders, however, the rise of nationalism in the Americas and throughout Europe – alongside normalised racism, right-wing immigration policies, anti-globalism discourse, and increasing practices of securitisation – had already cast a threatening cloud over the future of mobility. Politicians across the European Union have begun to exploit the virus by directing blame at migrants, targeting specific nationalities on the pretext of containing the spread of disease. I am writing this, right now, from my one-bedroom apartment in Brooklyn, in a neighbourhood where more than sixty-five percent of the residents who have been tested for COVID-19 have tested positive,[2] a number that now includes me. The future of mobility is at stake in any vision of a post-pandemic worldview, and it will have to involve questions that require us to think not only about the displacement and forced migration that follows climate change as well as military and economic violence, but also the internal exclusion and systemic inequalities brought about by our political and social structures, the unequal access that citizenship elides.

Another ambulance barrels down the street; I try to picture its path from my window, which is open. Sunlight, a bare breeze. I think about a story that starts or ends: *at a time when women and men were asked to play God,*[3] *and when God – or at least the public celebration of faith – had already disappeared.*

ESSAYS IN LIFE WRITING

If acts of personal remembering are fundamentally social and collective, as Sidonie Smith and Julia Watson (2001) propose, then the inscription of these personal memories in a form of autobiography is also collective, belonging not only to the author but to all those persons who have shaped it, and in this sense, as aggregation and anticipation, to all those persons who will be shaped by it. The names here, the places, the sites of retrieval – Paris, Lourdes, Marseilles, Port-Vendres, Portbou – suggest that the story of one's exile cannot be told without first imagining an address, and moreover, an addressee. I write you, and when I write you, dear Walter, I write, also, (to) myself. 'Life narrative,' Smith and Watson contend, 'inextricably links memory, subjectivity, and the materiality of the body' (2001, 37). I want to go further, and insist that life narrative, through this link, commingles the boundaries of individual identity and experience so as to destabilise them. In this correspondence, we become both less and more – less than what we are and more than what we will ever be. It is this moment – not of remembrance, but of forgetting – that authorises this letter, that stamps the envelope, that provides for its dispersal. And by forgetting the border between then and now, between there and here, I can remember the gift of the text, which is a hospitality that exceeds all temporal and spatial conditions: the invitation to enter into each other's interiority.

Notes

1. See the letter dated December 14, 1939, from the concentration camp in Nevers, to Gretel Adorno, in Benjamin (2012, 614–616).
2. As of 17 April 2020, based on information provided by the New York City Department of Health and Mental Hygiene.
3. The current shortage of medical resources, such as ventilators, has forced healthcare workers in New York City and elsewhere to weigh ethical questions about who should have the chance to live.

Disclosure statement

No potential conflict of interest was reported by the author(s).

ORCID

Chris Campanioni ⓘ http://orcid.org/0000-0002-1146-8931

References

Agamben, Giorgio. 1999. *Remnants of Auschwitz: The Witness and the Archive*. Translated by Daniel Heller-Roazen. New York: Zone Books.

Benjamin, Walter. 1968a. "The Task of the Translator." Translated by Harry Zohn. In *Illuminations*, edited by Hannah Arendt, 69–82. New York: Schocken Books.

Benjamin, Walter. 1968b. "Theses on the Philosophy of History." Translated by Harry Zohn. In *Illuminations*, edited by Hannah Arendt, 153–164. New York: Schocken Books.

Benjamin, Walter. 1999a. "Diary from August 7, 1931, to the Day of My Death." Translated by Rodney Livingstone. In *Walter Benjamin: Selected Writings (Volume 2, Part 2, 1931–1934)*, edited by Michael W. Jennings, Marcus Bullock, Howard Eiland, and Gary Smith, 501–506. Cambridge: Harvard University Press.

Benjamin, Walter. 1999b. "'In Parallel With My Actual Diary." Translated by Rodney Livingstone. In *Walter Benjamin: Selected Writings (Volume 2, Part 2, 1931–1934)*, edited by Michael W. Jennings, Marcus Bullock, Howard Eiland, and Gary Smith, 413–414. Cambridge: Harvard University Press.

Benjamin, Walter. 1999c. "Notes From Svendborg, Summer 1934." Translated by Rodney Livingstone. In *Walter Benjamin: Selected Writings (Volume 2, Part 2, 1931–1934)*, edited by Michael W. Jennings, Marcus Bullock, Howard Eiland, and Gary Smith, 783–791. Cambridge: Harvard University Press.

Benjamin, Walter. 2012. *The Correspondence of Walter Benjamin, 1910–1940*. Edited by Gershom Scholem and Theodor W. Adorno. Chicago, IL: University Of Chicago Press.

"Central Mediterranean: Death Toll Soars as EU Turns Its Back on Refugees and Migrants." 2017. *Amnesty International*, July 6. https://www.amnesty.org/en/latest/news/2017/07/central-mediterranean-death-toll-soars-as-eu-turns-its-back-on-refugees-and-migrants/.

Chrisafis, Angelique. 2017. "Police Remove 2,000 Refugees and Migrants Sleeping Rough in Paris." *The Guardian*, July 7. https://www.theguardian.com/world/2017/jul/07/french-police-evict-2000-refugees-and-migrants-sleeping-rough-in-paris.

Coetzee, J. M. 2001. "The Marvels of Walter Benjamin." *The New York Review of Books*, January 11. https://www.nybooks.com/articles/2001/01/11/the-marvels-of-walter-benjamin/.

Ferrer-Cussó, Manuel. 1993. "Walter Benjamin's Last Frontier: Sequences of an Approach." In *For Walter Benjamin*, edited by Ingrid Scheurmann and Konrad Scheurmann, 154–161. Bonn: AsKI.

Glissant, Édouard. 1997. *Poetics of Relation*. Translated by Betsy Wing. Ann Arbor: University of Michigan.

Heinemann, Richard. 1993. "Lisa Fittko on Walter Benjamin's Flight." In *For Walter Benjamin*, edited by Ingrid Scheurmann and Konrad Scheurmann, 139–153. Bonn: AsKI.

Karavan, Dani. 1993. "Dani Karavan on the 'Passages' Memorial to Walter Benjamin: An Interview with Ingrid and Konrad Scheurmann." In *For Walter Benjamin*, edited by Ingrid Scheurmann and Konrad Scheurmann, 255–264. Bonn: AsKI.

Llovet, Jordi. 1993. "Benjamin Flâneur: The Arcades Project." In *For Walter Benjamin*, edited by Ingrid Scheurmann and Konrad Scheurmann, 205–218. Bonn: AsKI.

Sahl, Hans. 1988. "Walter Benjamin in the Internment Camp." Translated by Deborah Johnson. In *On Walter Benjamin*, edited by Gary Smith, 346–352. Cambridge: The MIT Press.

Smith, Sidonie, and Julia Watson. 2001. *Reading Autobiography: A Guide for Interpreting Life Narratives*. Minneapolis: University of Minnesota Press.

Spivak, Gayatri Chakravorty. 1993. *Outside in the Teaching Machine*. New York: Routledge.

Metaphor and Neonatal Death: How Stories Can Help When a Baby Dies at Birth

Tamarin Norwood ⓘ

ABSTRACT
The death of a baby at birth is uniquely unsupported by the rituals and cultural scripts we depend upon to make sense of death. Left out of these shared narratives, the grief of parents bereaved at birth is often minimised and unassimilated into the parents' social world, leading to isolation and disenfranchisement that contributes to a higher rate of pathological grief patterns in this group. Building on the insights of narrative palliative therapy, material culture in death studies, and my own maternal experience of neonatal loss, this autobiographical essay identifies strategies from life writing – specifically esoteric meaning-making through metaphor – that can redress this lack of narrative on an individual level. It makes a case for metaphor as a precision instrument for probing, magnifying and capturing the precious and fleeting sensations, thoughts and experiences of parenthood cut short, and making these tiny moments robust enough to withstand being brought out into the social world. Finally, it argues that the stories we tell ourselves when a baby dies can be a first step towards a re-enfranchised experience of mourning, which continues rather than relinquishes bonds after death, and contributes to the wider project of releasing neonatal death from social taboo.

My twelve-week ultrasound revealed an ambiguous shadow in the region of the baby's abdomen, long and sharp like a spear but soft like a smudge, as though it might be part of the greyscale image of the baby but not part of the baby itself. I gladly overlooked the caution in the sonographer's voice when she said it might be nothing. We went home happy enough, the only catch to the festivity being another scan the following week. There was indeed another scan, and another and another. The shadow ceased to be nothing, nor a smudge, nor a spear. It established a form of its own, with outlines firm and clear, and then settled among the organs of the abdomen and began to fill them. Before long only the ambiguity of that original scan remained. The mass had density and detailed measurements captured with cursor on screen, but each scan presented new contradictions. For two weeks or more it was thought to be a teratoma, a tumorous region of growth named after the Greek for *monster* for the full range of human cells it might contain from hair to nail to tooth to part of eye. Such a monster would have ended the baby's life long before it was due to be born, yet the next scan told a story with no monsters but other threats; the next, another story again.

So we passed the summer. We slept very little, saving conversations until our three-year-old son was asleep, then spending the nights looking up new words, probabilities, local provision for social care, advice on bereavement in young children. The thought of the monster had infected me, grey and pale and silent. I had a university library account, we remembered, and we made nightmarish use of it, reading articles in medical journals we hoped would not come true. Everything we learned we learned provisionally. We did not know which ocean we would drown in, but we would drown.

So began my second pregnancy and the life of our beloved son Gabriel, who died peacefully in my arms when he was 72 min old. This paper draws upon the unexpected collision of two domains of my own experience – the neonatal loss of our son and a research specialism in metaphors of liminality – to explore how strategies from life writing and palliative narrative therapy can re-enfranchise bereaved parents by helping to articulate a loss that is uniquely under-served by the stories and cultural scripts we usually depend upon to make sense of death.

Creating narrative bonds as death approaches

Outside the context of pregnancy, it is well-documented that a terminal diagnosis changes loving relationships long before the event of death. Anticipatory grief can be overwhelming (Nielsen et al. 2016), and the so-called social death of the dying individual effectively hastens them along the pathway towards the end of life as their social identity is increasingly linked to death and the dead rather than life and the living (Borgstrom 2017). In grief studies, as more prominence comes to fall upon the value of continuing rather than relinquishing bonds with loved ones after death (Klass, Silverman, and Nickman 1996), so interest grows in forms of life writing that offer ways to prepare the emotional landscapes of loved ones as pathways diverge and death draws near. For example, narrative therapy and narrative palliative care tend to background medical language that emphasises the physical body, beginning instead from the premise that the self is made up of stories, and that you can have some hand in the construction of those stories even when life presents you with circumstances that seem uncontrollable. For adults nearing the end of life, narrative therapeutic interventions can be very structured, for instance supporting the effort of authoring and sharing with loved ones a life review, rather like writing a memoir or a eulogy for yourself; or they can be unstructured and as informal as initiating reflective conversations at the bedside. Often it is a process of finding a narrative arc or constructing one where there seems to be none, and then crafting new meaning within such an arc – even deviating from reality to express a more rewarding or coherent version of yourself and your relationships (Fivush and Haden 2003). This is creative work.

When a terminal foetal diagnosis is made during pregnancy, the exceptionally entwined pathways of a mother and a baby – who has no voice and socially little or no personhood – offer a unique perspective of the role life writing can play when shared pathways are forced apart too soon.

Neonatal death: a loss without a narrative

During pregnancy, the life paths of mother and baby are temporarily aligned. They are a single 'psychobiological organism', and in significant ways, this symbiotic togetherness continues even after the cutting of the cord in a period now protected by many hospitals as the 'sacred hour' of uninterrupted skin-to-skin contact immediately after birth (Phillips 2013, 68). Such contact has been found to regulate and stabilise the new-born's respiration, oxygenation, glucose levels, temperature and blood pressure as the mother's body responds to its needs: for instance, the temperature of her chest increases or decreases to regulate the baby's stable body temperature (68). Mother and baby will share this pathway for some months to come. A baby's need for the environment of its mother's body comes alive in the following very striking interpretation:

> Mother and offspring live in a biological state that has much in common with addiction. When they are parted, the infant does not just miss its mother. It experiences a physical and psychological withdrawal from a host of her sensory stimuli not unlike the plight of a heroin addict who goes 'cold turkey'. (Gallagher 1992, 13; cited in Phillips 2013, 89)

If Gallagher's words are true of the infant, then given the symbiotic interdependence of mother and baby, I wonder if the bereaved mother of a deceased new-born feels something of this too? Anecdotally, even though I wasn't dependent on my new-born baby for survival, the day after his death I noticed that holding the bundle of his blanket to my chest provoked a wonderful all-over feeling of physical relief, as though my body's demands were being answered by embracing something of his size and weight.

Of course, there is only so far a blanket can go – although it does go quite far, and I will come back to the materialities of neonatal death in due course. To come to terms with grief people need more than blankets, they need narratives that make sense of death in terms of the society they are part of rituals of funeral, burial, condolence and mourning, expectations of how people behave around death, of how people speak of the dead, of the spectrum of grief experiences.

But when it comes to neonatal loss we are uniquely short on such 'cultural scripts', be they formal or informal (Murphy and Cacciatore 2017, 133). Perinatal loss, which encapsulates miscarriage, induced abortion, stillbirth and neonatal death, is 'the *only* type of loss in Western society for which there are no culturally sanctioned rituals or traditions to help the bereaved say good-bye' (Markin and Zilcha-Mano 2018, 21). Depending on the weeks of gestation, formal acknowledgements such as death certificate and funeral may or may not be available, and whether or not they are, informal acknowledgements may minimise and invalidate parents' grief. In the well-meaning reassurances of family, friends and medical professionals, we can discern 'an active culture of denial and intellectualization that discourages parents from grieving' as they are reassured that the death was, for instance, for the best, that it happens all the time, that they can always have another baby (21).

Such responses, though well-meaning, can deny the unique personhood of the baby and contribute to an experience of disenfranchised grief: loss 'that is not or cannot be openly acknowledged, publicly mourned, or socially supported' (Doka 1989, 4). Compounding this wider sociocultural disenfranchisement is the fact that the baby was itself unknown to its parents, who will often report psychological confusion within themselves, not knowing 'who or what they have lost' (Bleyen 2010, 69), and this contributes still further to an overall 'sense of unreality' (Murphy and Cacciatore 2017, 130). This absence of cultural scripts, with families struggling to 'make meaning from loss' (132) contributes to the fact that the pattern of neonatal and perinatal grief often fails to show the typical linear decline associated with other types of grief, and is more likely to become pathological over time (Lin and Lasker 1996). Thus it is clear that bereaved parents sorely need a framework within which to understand, describe and integrate the unique nature of their loss.

Stumbling upon a narrative

These findings are repeated in my own experience as a recently bereaved mother. Just under two years ago our second child died very peacefully in my arms when he was 72 min old. Midway through the pregnancy we had learned that his lungs were not developing normally, and by the end of the pregnancy there was almost no amniotic fluid left. Because amniotic fluid plays an essential role in preparing foetal lungs to breathe at birth, we knew that although he was stable where he was, once brought out into the light – as birth is described in some languages – he would not survive long at all.

While I was preparing for our baby's birth and death I was also preparing for my doctoral viva, defending a thesis I had submitted before I knew any of this was going to happen. What makes my situation unusual is that during these anxious months I began to see a great many connections between the subject of my thesis and the story unfolding within me, and these connections became central to way I understood that story.

My DPhil was not health- or bereavement-related but in Fine Art, and specifically on liminality in representation: those marshy borderlands between the thoughts and feelings and ideas that are too far beneath the surface to get your hands on and really grasp, and those ideas you do manage to dredge up to the surface, make sense of, and pin down on the page in words or image. What emerged through my research was the extent to which metaphors of water and its correlates pervade the way we imagine liminality. A wide-ranging landscape can be imagined comprising two distinct worlds: the dark, underwater, night-time world of the ungraspable and unknown, and above the surface of the water the lucid, breathable, daylight world, home to clear sight, perspective, and the firm ground of rational thought. And at the water's surface: this is where all of life's transitions play out: where life becomes death, wakefulness becomes sleep and dream, the unknown is dredged up into the light. Virginia Woolf imagined this landscape in vivid detail. She imagined thought letting its line down into a stream, swaying, lifting, sinking, until there's a 'little tug' on the line (Woolf 1928, 5). She imagines cautiously beginning to haul in that small and infinitely promising little slip of an idea, then carefully laying it out on the grass where, alas, it is suddenly small, insignificant, almost lifeless (5–6).

As Woolf's image makes plain, crossing the threshold between these two worlds is no mean feat; almost as impossible as waking from a dream with its imaginary treasure still in your hands. This cautious struggle has been rehearsed over and over in many traditions through world history in the trope of the night sea journey – think of the classical stories of the Odyssey, the Iliad, the Metamorphosis, the biblical story of Jonah in the belly of the whale, of Moby Dick. The heroes of these stories do not send lines down into the stream as Woolf imagined, but bodily journey down into the depths themselves, hoping to bring back up some hard-won insight, victory or treasure of some value to life in the upper world. And where water is used to express liminality, very often it is to reflect upon the struggle of making it though that liminal transition, and profound and threatening changes it brings.

You can hear, in the following passage from my own writing, how this imagery took root in my imagination and grew and grew during the pregnancy, unfurling into a series of confused images that tried to find a way out of my inescapable situation:

> Now five months into the pregnancy, we could see without ambiguity that Gabriel would not survive his brief cresting into the light of the world.
>
> But by night, the clarity of day was shot through with possibility. In these months the nights were long and wakeful and dark, and full of invention. My body was the whole of his world, I thought, so surely I had within me the means to save him. I would do anything. In the dark my mind turned over and over the same dilemma, searching for a way out. As long as he did not surface he was safe, I thought, like a sort of fish, who would drown in air. I imagined his developing lungs like gills: systems of paper-thin folds held apart by the water that flows between them and so delicate they collapse if brought up into the air. It is as dangerous for a fish to rise to the surface of the water as it is for a person to dive beneath it, and the effort no less great. Here was a possibility. If the effort and the threat were alike for him and me, then I could reverse it, and take on the effort myself. I could learn to dive, to open my eyes and hold my breath underwater, and when he was born he would never need try his lungs, only his gills, and we could dwell together. I knew he could swim; I had seen it in the first of his ultrasound scans, when the grainy dark smudge in his abdomen was yet to be seen and all was still well. I heard a radio report around this time of train carriages felled, at the end of their lives, to the bed of the ocean where they become new reefs, their weltered metal walls coralline and pink and suckled by the gaping mouths of fish, doors and windows wide to boneless squid that dart and hide and I thought there, we could live there, I could swim down and down and down never come up, and there you would be, and there we would be safe.
>
> On sleepless nights I sent out thoughts like these to probe the furthest depths of hope, of poetry, of science: emergency beacons that one by one returned without news. Whatever outbound route they took there was only one way back, to me, my baby, as close and distant as it was possible to be. He doesn't have gills, he has lungs. All the oxygen in his blood is from my breath. The fluid in my womb is gone. And I have a living son, who needs me on dry land.
>
> These nights revealed me to myself as two distinct terrains: inside, in the dark, rosy and rounded, warm and safe, a pool, an underground lake—and this was where he lived; hemmed all around by the impenetrable bank that is the surface of me—and this was where I lived. I had never so keenly felt that I live on the surface of myself, that my body is shaped to meet what is outside itself and not within. How ill-judged it seemed that my arms, my mouth, my eyes should be out here with me, how poorly planned, when there is such fullness, such lively richness, such possibility, within.

You can hear how I am making the metaphor of water my own to help me shape the conceptually very complicated reality that there is someone as close to me as possible – actually inside me – whom I know completely yet do not know at all, and who will cease to exist as soon as I can finally hold him. This metaphor helped me to pin down the topology of the situation and its emotional stakes in a way that was not factually accurate, but was very precisely accurate in another way, enlarging subtleties of feeling and indulging nuances of emotion in such a way as to make them real and give them space. During the pregnancy I was aware of the limits of these images. I knew they were not real but they would do for now, until there was the real comfort of his birth. I wrote:

As his birth approached, these furthest depths of hope and poetry and science offered little consolation for what was to come. None of it was certain. All that was fixed and sure was the slender promise that I would, I certainly would, one day soon hold him in my arms and kiss him every inch—

In these lines you can see I had the metaphors in their place. They were just stories and images, and once I held him in my arms and could kiss him, I would no longer need the stories because I would have real life. But I was wrong. As it turned out, it was not until after the birth that these images of water really began to show their worth. The sentence above actually ends like this:

I would, I certainly would, one day soon hold him in my arms and kiss him every inch— although in the end, when it was time, I forgot to grant these kisses.

Through metaphor, a shared landscape for birthing mother and dying baby

In the days after the birth these failures of connection were intolerable to me. And so it was with pleasure and relief that I recalled, not long after his death, that when we talk about labour and childbirth we talk about mothers labouring in the dark, shielded from the bright light of day. Not only from daylight, in fact, but from what we might call diurnal patterns of thought: clarity, lucidity, rationality, decision-making, the subtleties of social interaction: all of this daytime activity tends to inhibit the secretion of hormones needed for a smooth labour (Buckley 2015). Natural childbirth is supported, on the other hand, by darkness, quiet, privacy, and the kinds of intellectual and social expectations you would have for somebody trying to fall asleep (Croft 2011, 28). Indeed, labour most often takes hold at night, and when it takes hold during the day labouring women often close or cover their eyes and, looking back afterwards, recall being 'in the zone [...] somewhere akin to meditation, a concentrated turning inwards, a place where language fails' (McKinnon 2020, 42) which displaces '"rational" thought from its position of privilege' to make space 'for the alter-rationality that belongs to embodied or instinctive thought' (51). This trance-like state does not dissipate immediately after birth but rather sprawls out into that dozy, hormone-heavy 'sacred hour' of post-partum bonding with the baby. Recalling all this, with pleasure and relief I ventured the thought that all the time Gabriel was in my arms I was underwater, on my own strange night sea journey.

And it was with something like delight that I remembered the idea of oceanic feeling: the sense of limitless oneness with the world a very new-born baby is meant to feel, all at sea in the ocean of its mothers arms, both physiologically and psychologically at one not only with the mother but with the world, not yet able to conceive of itself as distinct. This feeling of ecstatic limitlessness has been explored as the root of religious feeling (Parsons 1998): that the longing to be one with God is a longing to return to this first oceanic state, before language, before anything can be isolated and grasped in the watery flux of existence.

Water imagery is also common in stories that explore the liminal period surrounding death, especially where life's end is imagined as the beginning of a new life. The challenges of the night sea journey involve a descent into the deep followed by a triumphant surfacing often imagined as a kind of rebirth. When mortal life came to an end for the ancient Greeks, passing across water was seen to mark their transition from one life to the next, each river cleansing them of their old lives: Lethe for forgetfulness, Archeron for woe, Cocytus for lamentation. The Old Testament flood plunged all of creation into a languageless sea before new life could rise again, a story frequently recalled in the pervasive Biblical metaphor of water as purity and the source of new life (DiFransico 2015).

Thus in the weeks and months after Gabriel's birth and death, shattered by his loss, mind swimming with the strangely distant memories of my very recent doctoral research, I sank into the realisation that these metaphors of water could serve me even more powerfully now than they had during pregnancy, offering me a thickly reinforced narrative that he and I had shared a common geography for those moments of his birth and death.

These metaphors were enough to let me believe Gabriel never really surfaced from his underwater home in the womb and the oceanic daze of birth before the waters of death submerged him – and that although I was not dying, nor being born, by an incredible stroke of luck I was one of those unlikely people who make it into that place where it's dark, where there's no language or logical thought. In my postnatal doziness, in his new-born daze, in the light-headedness, perhaps, of approaching death and fused by rivers of hormonal love, we dwelled together for the 72 min between his birth and death, down where it's dark and unknowable, where things aren't gathered into the lucidity of a thought, or differentiated into subject and object, and there is only flux. Of course I never kissed him. We were too undifferentiated from one another to be separate enough to come together in a kiss. I know it's just a story. But I live by it.

Metaphor: a precision instrument

Stepping back from the story I tell myself, what really happened over the course of Gabriel's life and death? In practical terms, very much less than all this. His was a life that took place on a very small scale, upon a very small stage, and a hidden stage at that. Most of what happened was inside my body and Gabriel's body, and what wasn't happening there was happening, really, inside my mind, hidden even to the instruments of medicine which at least were able to probe, scan, magnify, capture and meticulously examine the secrets unfolding in my womb.

But looked at another way, these stories, with their scale and grandeur and significance far in excess of the facts on the ground, really work as instruments in their own right. They gave me a way to probe and magnify the tiny fleeting sensations, thoughts and feelings I was experiencing: the tiny grains of experience too odd and esoteric to make much sense on their own. They gave me a way to set these grains in poetry and metaphor as if set in hard, translucent amber, where they could be held in the mind's eye, turned, magnified and meticulously examined. For example, one moment set in metaphorical amber is the split second when my son was lying in my arms and very briefly opened one eye. I wrote about it like this:

> By now I am sleepy. I have fused into a kind of dream with our baby, if a dream can be made of body as much as mind. His little breaths rise and fall on the waves of my lungs as though we are sealed together, as though you could press a sonographer's wand against the surface of our dream and find a single shared interior, our organs mixed, outlines transparent, a miracle of synchrony.

Then all of a sudden, to my great surprise and wonder, he crumpled one eyelid open –

and with this crumpling, a little black crescent of sight breaches the surface of our dream. Almost as soon as it opens it closes again, and I am left in wonder.

This image of his briefly visible eye as a little black crescent of sight just breaching the surface of our dream reveals more and more and more about what his life and death mean to me, as I magnify and examine it in detail. Here's one way I looked at it:

What did he make of it, this sip of sight? Perhaps this was the furthest reach of his excursion into the world, his greatest adventure in defiance of death. Perhaps to him, it felt like the opening up of his whole self, opening the floodgates onto all the world, onto a great tumbling and crashing of world without end. And I hope he sipped of it before his eyes were sealed.

In this way the metaphors of water and surfacing serve to elaborate that tiny and brief but possibly momentous moment in his life. But there is more to this moment. I turned the metaphor around in my mind and found all these other ways to look at it:

I imagine the crescent of his eye the furthest leap of a fish, the gleaming curve of its back above the waves just enough to let slip a darting swooping secret life beneath. Perhaps it was his fullest exertion into the world, a glimpse of effort and pleasure and something like the joy of being alive. Perhaps, and more likely, there was nothing like joy or pleasure or feeling. If the opening of an eye is an involuntary new-born checking of the system, then to this dying infant perhaps the opening of an eye meant nothing. The prow of a stricken ship indifferently keeling, breaking the surface upended by the blind luck of physics and beginning its roll to the depths of the ocean floor. And where does it leave me. And I imagine the crescent of his eye the black peak of an underwater mountain, cavernous and vast, unmoving, always there, but only for a moment showing. Only for a moment, but long enough to draw me to it; the crag of a rock I rush to splinter myself against.

Spending time turning this image in my mind's eye and examining every tiny grain of feeling that accompanies it allows me to acknowledge the powerful ambivalence of my strong feelings towards a baby for whom the more love I feel, the more pain I can expect to endure. My love for him can only end in loss, like the siren's song that lures sailors to their death and yet, even knowing it will drown them, sailors still follow that song it is so lovely.

Gabriel was not a vast ship keeling, nor was I an Argonaut embarked on an epic quest that would end in my death. Nothing this big was happening. And yet in a very real way, the powerful operatic scale of these images is a more accurate description of the experience than a straightforward account of the facts.

Metaphor is a very powerful instrument in the face of death. Experience that is mysterious, unfamiliar, frightening, lacking in stories, can be made sense of if parsed through the terms of something familiar, safe, known and validated. The analogy of death to sleep, for instance, shows how the familiar can be recruited to make the unknown known, not only in phrases like 'he fell asleep' but in the bed-like design of the traditional coffin and the custom of being quiet or silent around the time of death: if we treat death like sleep, perhaps we needn't be so afraid of its mysteries (Hockey 2010, 9).

The hidden grief practices of bereaved parents

With this in mind, let me return to the point that neonatal loss is under-served by stories and cultural scripts that should be helping to make sense of what is already a particularly disorienting death. In this context, material objects help, and can even be understood as physical metaphors that tangibly stand in for the lost child:

> the absent child could remain socially present *within* things and places. Objects such as pictures or clothes, and locations including the grave and the nursery, could become extensions of their absence. (Bleyen 2010, 75)

My experience of relief holding Gabriel's blanket might be seen not just in physiological terms but metaphorical ones, manifesting his absence through its presence (76). Such physical metaphors go some way to making the unknown knowable, in this case not just the unknown quantity of death, but the unknown quantity of the baby itself who died before its parents got to know it. Given that a new-born baby leaves very little behind in the way of material objects, it is accepted good practice in UK hospitals to help parents create tangible mementos when a baby dies. For instance Sands, a stillbirth and neonatal death charity, supplies hospitals with Memory Boxes containing a soft white blanket, teddies, a footprint and handprint kit and an unofficial certificate of birth, to 'produce physical evidence of their babies' lives and start forging a parental bond that will endure after saying goodbye' (Sands website).

In my personal experience, this is a deeply appreciated, meticulously choreographed intervention from very well-trained staff which is so private, so achingly painful and so unacceptably out of place as to almost be a secret. Parents might supplement these institutionally supported practices with their own private memorials, traditions, and archives, or might *only* have their own ad hoc memorials to draw upon where neonatal loss is not recognised at all, as was more commonly the case in the UK in the 1960s and earlier (Bleyen 2010, 71).

But when these practices make it out of institutions and into the home as ad hoc practices invented by parents themselves, they seem to stay secret, such that to share them might even be a source of embarrassment or shame, as the following example makes plain. Bleyen describes how one bereaved mother, Sarah, established a practice of photographing the memorial of her son, 'storing identical – yet evolving – images of the [memorial] in a small album' (77). She points out that

> the precious album of photos was something Sarah, at least in my interpretation, perceived as irrational and shameful—at first she didn't want to show it to me, just as she didn't show it to her friends or family members—and kept it hidden in a cupboard. (77)

For Sarah this practice is clearly effective, meaningful and effortful, but despite all of this she perceives it to be irrational and believes that in her social world it might be unacceptable and a source of shame. If meaning-making takes place on a social level, co-created, sanctioned and reinforced through continual shared use within a community, then these secret practices are not doing all they could to support the needs of bereaved parents. This is why, for instance, Sands not only provides Memory Boxes but campaigns to make neonatal loss part of the public conversation.

Releasing hidden grief practices into the social world

I believe this is also where certain narrative approaches to end-of-life and palliative care could supplement the institutionally-supported and ad hoc material grief practices of newly bereaved parents. As in narrative palliative care for adults, the effort of storytelling can rescue thoughts or events from oblivion and, as I have found in my own experience, can assimilate granular details of thoughts and feelings which, were they to remain unassimilated, might seem irrational and even shameful as Sarah's seemed to. Again, this is creative work.

For bereaved parents faced with the unreality and double disenfranchisement of socially unsupported grief for a baby even they did not know, the benefits of story-making are threefold. First, as we have seen, it can create a powerful personal narrative robust enough to hold esoteric and otherwise unsupported thoughts and practices, creating a narrative arc that can attenuate the divergence of pathways between parent and baby, binding them together for longer, and even preparing the landscape so that the pathway of the deceased can continue in step with those left behind, and bonds can continue after loss rather than being relinquished. Second, a greater sense of enfranchisement might be clawed back through this process when, by creating their own story, parents becomes an agent of their own narrative rather than its passive recipients (Guilfoyle 2015). Third, by releasing personal grief practices from feelings of irrationality and shame, these stories are more able to enter the social world, challenging the traditional 'womb to tomb' model to admit into the life course the social identities of both the unborn and the deceased. Such challenges will often occur within 'homely moments' (Hockey and Draper 2005, 42) among family members and close friends, those relationships we depend upon most of all to co-regulate and make sense of our experiences (Markin and Zilcha-Mano 2018, 22), as individuals navigate quandaries such as how to answer the question 'how many children do you have?', whether words of comfort are chosen to acknowledge or deny the unique personhood of the baby, whether or not to bring out the photo album of near-identical photos of a headstone as a way of prompting a conversation about a lost baby. These moments in turn stand to contribute to the wider project of releasing neonatal death from the social taboo that stands to jeopardise the grief narratives of bereaved parents of the future.

With mental health resources as stretched as they are, small and relatively inexpensive interventions might support parents to begin this journey on their own. For instance, the Sands Memory Box contains a book of poetry written by bereaved parents. In a similar way, might a dedicated booklet be made available to write in, perhaps guided by prompts to capture those first fleeting impressions, give them weight and space on the page; writing that might be shared within close relationships and further strengthened in these interactions?

I have my son's blanket and I hold it close, but I hold our story closer. I know that both, in their own way, are metaphors for something else, and this does not diminish their worth. The finely tuned instruments of poetry, metaphor and creative narrative thought – underwater thought – can access and probe and magnify the lived experience of grief, can make unknown known and the unspeakable speakable. If we can find ways to do the creative work of bringing these dreams up into the light of day and giving them a place in everyday discourse, we can create sense where there seems to be none.

Acknowledgements

This essay develops a presentation ('Rivers of Forgetfulness: articulating neonatal bereavement through metaphor') delivered at the Death and Culture III Conference, York St John University UK, on 4 September 2020, and a paper ('Something from Nothing? Constructing a narrative when a baby dies at birth') delivered at the Contemporary Women's Writing and the Medical Humanities seminar series, School of Advanced Study, University of London UK, on 20 October 2020. The life writing cited in the essay is from the author's forthcoming book, of which extracts were published online under the title 'Creating bonds with a baby expected to die at birth' at thepolyphony.org, the Durham University Institute for Medical Humanities blog, on 14 October 2020.

Disclosure statement

No potential conflict of interest was reported by the author(s).

ORCID

Tamarin Norwood ⓘ http://orcid.org/0000-0002-2142-3307

References

Bleyen, Jan. 2010. "The Materialities of Absence After Stillbirth: Historical Perspectives." In *The Matter of Death: Space, Place and Materiality*, edited by Jenny Hockey, Carol Komaromy, and Kate Woodthorpe, 69–84. Basingstoke: Palgrave Macmillan.

Borgstrom, Erica. 2017. "Social Death." *QJM: An International Journal of Medicine* 110 (1): 5–7. doi:10.1093/qjmed/hcw183.

Buckley, Sarah J. 2015. *Hormonal Physiology of Childbearing: Evidence and Implications for Women, Babies, and Maternity Care*. Washington, DC: Childbirth Connection Programs, National Partnership for Women & Families.

Croft, Nicole. 2011. *The Good Birth Companion*. London: Vermilion.

DiFransico, Lesley. 2015. "Identifying Inner-Biblical Allusion Through Metaphor: Washing Away Sin in Psalm 51." *Vetus Testamentum* 65 (4): 542–557. https://www.jstor.org/stable/43894313.

Doka, K. J. 1989. "Disenfranchised Grief." In *Disenfranchised Grief: Recognising Hidden Sorrow*, edited by K. J. Doka, 3–11. Lexington, MA: Lexington Books.

Fivush, R., and C. A. Haden. 2003. *Autobiographical Memory and the Construction of a Narrative Self: Developmental and Cultural Perspectives*. Hove, East Sussex: Psychology Press.

Gallagher, W. 1992. "Motherless Child." *The Sciences* 32 (4): 12–15. doi:10.1002/j.2326-1951.1992. tb02399.x.

Guilfoyle, Michael. 2015. "Listening in Narrative Therapy: Double Listening and Empathetic Positioning." *South African Journal of Psychology* 45 (1): 36–49. doi:10.1177/0081246314556711.

Hockey, Jenny, and Janet Draper. 2005. "Between the Womb and the Tomb: Identity, (Dis)Embodiment and the Life Course." *Body and Society* 11 (2): 41–57. doi:10.1177/1357034X05052461.

Hockey, Jenny, Carol Komaromy, and Kate Woodthorpe. 2010. "Materialising Absence." In *The Matter of Death: Space, Place and Materiality*, edited by Jenny Hockey, Carol Komaromy, and Kate Woodthorpe, 69–84. Basingstoke: Palgrave Macmillan.

Klass, D., P. R. Silverman, and S. L. Nickman. 1996. *Continuing Bonds: New Understandings of Grief.* Washington, DC: Taylor and Francis.

Lin, S. X., and J. N. Lasker. 1996. "Patterns of Grief Reaction After Pregnancy Loss." *American Journal of Orthopsychiatry* 66 (2): 262–271. doi:10.1037/h0080177.

Markin, Rayna D., and Sigal Zilcha-Mano. 2018. "Cultural Processes in Psychotherapy for Perinatal Loss: Breaking the Cultural Taboo Against Perinatal Grief." *Psychotherapy* 55 (1): 20–26. doi:10.1037/pst0000122.

McKinnon, Katharine. 2020. *Birthing Work: The Collective Labour of Childbirth.* Singapore: Palgrave Pivot.

Murphy, Samantha, and Joanne Cacciatore. 2017. "The Psychological, Social, and Economic Impact of Stillbirth on Families." *Seminars in Fetal and Neonatal Medicine* 22: 129–134. doi:10.1016/j.siny.2017.02.002.

Nielsen, Mette Kjaergaard, Mette Asbjoern Neergaard, Anders Bonde Jensen, Flemming Bro, and Mai-Britt Guldin. 2016. "Do We Need to Change our Understanding of Anticipatory Grief in Caregivers? A Systematic Review of Caregiver Studies During end-of-Life Caregiving and Bereavement." *Clinical Psychology Review* 44: 75–93. doi:10.1016/j.cpr.2016.01.002.

Parsons, William B. 1998. "The Oceanic Feeling Revisited." *The Journal of Religion* 78 (4): 501–523. https://www.jstor.org/stable/1206572.

Phillips, Raylene. 2013. "The Sacred Hour: Uninterrupted Skin-to-Skin Contact Immediately After Birth." *Newborn and Infant Nursing Reviews* 13: 67–72.

Sands: Stillbirth and Neonatal Death Society. https://www.sands.org.uk/support-you/how-we-offer-support/memory-box.

Woolf, Virginia. 1928. *A Room of One's Own.* London: Penguin Books.

Three Wheels on My Wagon: An Account of an Attempt to Use Life Writing to Access Shared Family Narratives After Bereavement

Jane Hughes ⓘ

ABSTRACT
The author encourages family members to write about their memories of shared events from the past in an attempt to foster a sense of connection after bereavement. When one impactful shared experience is remembered differently by different family members, the author has to come to terms with a resulting exacerbation of a sense of loss and disconnection.

To be sure, the events of courting and love, birth, generational conflict, sickness, and death present us with something to do; but more important, they also confront us with someone to be. They assault our identity. (May 1991, 4)

The loss of a close family member changes our perception of the world and our place in it. Especially when the death is sudden and unexpected, we are challenged to adjust to a new situation that can be difficult to understand or accept. As Arthur W. Frank (2013, 60) puts it in *The Wounded Storyteller*, the narrative of our lives has been fractured, and 'the present is not what the past was supposed to lead up to'.

We are meaning-making animals: this useful characteristic of the human mind has spurred us to investigate, learn, understand and develop as a species. But sometimes, at night, when we are plagued with circular thoughts, it can feel like a curse. The hardest problems to let go are the ones we can't make sense of, because we just keep trying to work it out. *But why? Why on earth did he say that? Why would she do that? How could this have happened?*

When happenings that we don't understand are coupled with the crashing finality of death, and we have to accept that we will *never* know the answer, grief can be complicated by anxiety, guilt or anger. We thrash around, trying to construct a new narrative that we can believe in. Finding oneself trapped in 'spirals' of thinking that are associated with distress, anxiety or sleeplessness is one reason why people make appointments to meet counsellors for 'talking therapies'. R.A. Neimeyer (1995, 227) points out that 'people can be construed as seeking therapy at points when their life stories become ineffective, necessitating editing, elaboration, or major "rebiographing"'. The peculiar process of converting a tangled woolly ball of thoughts into a series of sentences, and pushing them out through our mouths in the therapist's consulting room, somehow helps us to gain some perspective, to distance ourselves sufficiently from the incessant brain babble to be able to see more clearly what is going on. Hearing our thoughts spoken by our own voices, or mirrored by a therapist, can be highly illuminating, even shocking. There is something important about having our thoughts and feelings witnessed, especially when we are dealing with traumatic experience, and this is possible in a one-to-one conversation with a trusted and capable therapist.

Psychologist Kathleen R. Gilbert (2002, 236), whose studies focus upon grief, writes: 'We need to create stories to make order of disorder and to find meaning in the meaningless. This "drive to story" seems particularly strong when one is confronted with death, loss, and grief.' Only when we accept that the world has changed, irrevocably, do we start work on Worden's (1991, 16) fourth task of grieving: 'To emotionally relocate the deceased and move on with life.' Telling our stories is a powerful means of re-visioning our lives, and moving into a new version of life.

Talking therapies can allow us to tell our stories, and, in so doing, to find a way to impose some sense of order upon our inner chaos. But some stories are unspeakable. Psychology lecturer Susan Brison (2002) has written about the difficulty of speaking aloud about traumatic experiences. 'Survivors' may feel emotionally numbed; they may feel unable to share with anybody who has not 'been there'; they may also feel trapped between being unable to speak about their experience and a sense that doing anything else is pointless.

Susan Brison's memoir, *Aftermath: Violence and the Remaking of a Self*, is a personal account of ten years of post-traumatic psychological work which advocates writing as a therapeutic endeavour through which the storyteller can become their own witness.

> Psychologists writing about trauma stress that one has to tell one's trauma narrative to an empathic other in order for the telling to be therapeutic. But some survivors are helped by telling their stories to imagined others – to potential readers, for example, or to others kept alive in a photograph. [...] Simply writing in a journal can facilitate this, by temporarily splitting the self into an active – narrating – subject and a more passive – described – object. [...] It was only when I managed to write a narrative of my assault, several months after the attack, and then read it, that I realized, "My God, what a horrible thing to happen to someone!" (2002, 72–3)

Writing about experiences that are difficult to speak about offers much more than the opportunity to make a record of events, more than some special time to 'process' what has happened, more even than the therapeutic self-witnessing that Susan Brison describes. It allows us to use words in a way that might be unintelligible if spoken. By combining words in a fragmentary, poetic, evocative and provocative way, we might yet be able to convey something unspeakable to others. In *The Year of Magical Thinking*, Joan Didion uses fragmentary sentences, jerky transitions and looping repetition to create some feeling of the way grief breaks things, clatters things together, comes in waves. Dave Eggers (*A Heartbreaking Work of Staggering Genius*) and Max Porter (*Grief is the Thing With Feathers*) created innovative texts that somehow manage to convey the ineffable in a way that a straightforward narrative could not.

Unpredictable texts can reflect the breakage of the linear life story we imagine for ourselves, and seem to work well in stories of sudden loss. Having reviewed a selection of women's grief memoirs, Kathleen Fowler (2007) concludes that 'Despite diverse styles, types of losses, grief issues, and world views, one central theme regularly recurs in the grief memoir – the sense of finding oneself navigating uncharted territory'. Kathleen Vandenberg (2017, 42) describes Joan Didion being 'unmoored in the wake of her loss'. Arthur Frank (2013, 54–5) finds a similar sense of disorientation in narratives of illness:

> Almost every illness story I have read carries some sense of being shipwrecked by the storm of disease … The way out of the wreckage is telling stories

***

My mother died suddenly and unexpectedly, of a stroke, while she was sleeping. I was abroad at the time, and working on a collection of blackly comical short stories loosely based on my experience of working as a civil funeral celebrant. The sudden intrusion of real death, real loss and real grief unsurprisingly stopped me (dead). There is a smoking hole in my journal. But then I started to record my feelings. Perhaps memoirs of grief are like navigating uncharted territory, and memoirs of illness are like stories of shipwreck, but the jagged narrative that rushed out of me, fast and furious, as I processed the sudden loss of my mother, felt like a car crash.

> Three wheels on my wagon. I realise that me and Mum and Dad and Alan were the four corners of a square, very strong together. Even when we were apart we were still part of a group of four that would never change, even with the divorce and all of us finding partners, outriggers to support us, we were still a four. Now Mum has gone the whole thing has changed, me and Dad and Alan are having to shift closer together, a different shape, now a triangle will need to be made but right now, we are a square with a corner missing. We really miss that corner. We feel destabilised. Mum had Keith, but when she lost him she was weakened and maybe that's why she was the first to go. Everything has changed now, now that we are a three not a four. Me and Mum, Dad and Alan, everything was properly balanced. Now it's a triangle, the weight is unbalanced, we're not all balanced. Am I the odd bit now, the only woman? Or Dad, the only older one? Alan is part of two groups – the men and the kids. I've seen a couple of dogs around here that can't walk properly and they've been given a sort of trolley for their hind legs. I saw one with two hind wheels and its back legs still paddling away pointlessly in mid-air, and one still using one of its back legs but with a wheel for the other leg which was missing. We're like a three-legged dog without even a wheel. We're fatally destabilised. Now that one corner is gone, the balance has gone, we can get along but not forever, we're not built to stand this. The muscles and tendons aren't built for it. Before, nothing could knock us over. Now, until we regroup and even if we find a new balance, we're not right. There were four of us, four around the kitchen table, four in the car, each of us with a hand to hold.

Three Wheels on my Wagon is a strange little American popular song from the early 1960s that we used to sing in the family car, especially on long journeys. Or did we? I am squaring up to that memory and I don't believe it, I really don't think we ever sang together as a family. Perhaps we just enjoyed hearing it on the radio. I know it became a bit of a family motto – keep on keeping on, three wheels on my wagon but I'm still rolling along … but the song doesn't end well. '*I'm all in flames, at the reins, but I'm singing a happy tune!*'

The bleak stoicism and black humour of *Three Wheels on my Wagon*, the gut feeling of a rolling, tumbling car crash and the memory of a significant crash from my adolescence all rose up for me in the aftermath of my mother's death. Kathleen Pithouse-Morgan (Pithouse-Morgan et al. 2012) refers to an 'archaeology of emotions': 'once you start reflecting on an emotional experience, it leads to thinking about interconnections with previous emotionally significant experiences that you might not have thought about for a long time or even recognized as emotionally significant at the time.' I'm struck now by the strange interconnectedness of the song, my immediate sense of being fatally destabilised as a four-square family unit and the old car crash memory, which seemed to have little connection to losing Mum until I realised that that event was the closest I have come to losing Dad – and an unforgettable demonstration of what happens when one of the wheels comes off.

***

A few months later, my father, brother and I are in Covid-19 lockdown, trying like everybody else in the world to make sense of the unfathomable and communicating via WhatsApp from our three distanced corners of England: Manchester, London, Cornwall. In many ways we are closer than we once were, sharing our experiences and concerns every day now. In many ways, the old dynamic persists: we stay strong for each other, spare each other any major moments of fear or panic, talk about the weather, make stupid jokes, keep the politics light and the humour fairly dark.

I've been gently encouraging Dad to write about his life. It's partly to give him something to focus on, and partly because Mum disappeared so suddenly and took so much information about her life away with her. She was never keen to talk about her own past – once or twice I was persistent with my questions and she turned on me, demanding to know why I wanted to know. Dad is ready and willing to write, and he has an entertaining style. Given my sense of 'three wheels' and the car crash of losing Mum, it seemed surprisingly appropriate that he recently wrote and sent this snippet of memoir:

> The first time I rolled the MG was in a race at Brands Hatch. A rather unspectacular event in itself, not involving any kind of shunt with another car, I didn't need any help to give the spectators something to talk about.
>
> The saga of my self destruction started way back in the workshop where I was checking the underbody clearances after fitting a set of widened standard steel wheels. They were about 2 inches wider than normal and that plus fatter tyres meant clearances were minimal, in fact there were signs that the tyres had actually made contact and to measure the necessary gap for proper spacers to be made I temporarily inserted some steel washers on the wheel studs and refitted the wheels on top.
>
> Ok so you're ahead of me already …
>
> Modifying and preparing the car, kit, trailer, camper tow vehicle etc., necessarily had to take second place to running the business and so continuity was always patchy resulting into panic on the day before race days and I regularly trusted Zack my henchman to take care of the routine jobs such as putting the racer on the trailer.
>
> This time the racer happened to be raised on axle stands but Zack lowered it and loaded it.
>
> Race day came with the usual early start and hurried scrutineering before a couple of practice laps and unfortunately I had no reason to change the wheels before the race.
>
> Brands Hatch circuit is hilly and there is one particularly scary blind fast downhill bend, 'Paddock', where it feels like going over the edge of the world but it's ok once you know it as it has a wide sweep and plenty of space.
>
> During the race I was going well in the leading pack when leaning hard on the outside tyres descending Paddock the rear wheel came off resulting in the car instantly flipping over.

It slid on the fibreglass roof supported by the internal roll bar for what seemed an age, long enough for me to pray I had built things strong enough to take the punishment. I thought 'when the roof wears through the strain on the roll bar might be too much …'

And, 'can I release the fire extinguisher …'

When all went quiet I recall a marshal peering sideways at me as I hung suspended by my seat belt, he clearly expected me to be severely hurt.

After release I was carried away in the ambulance for standard medical checks where all was ok (they didn't do brain checks)

To my embarrassment it emerged that those spacing washers that I had played with in the workshop were still firmly bolted to the hub and the steel wheel having had no back support simply flexed to the point of breaking under the strain. I never intended driving with those washers in place. The failure was entirely my fault, it was not an accident.

It emerged that my little family team had seen a yellow car overturn but had no news whatsoever about me until I emerged from the medical facility and I could see the anxiety/relief in their faces when I came up behind them.

Later Alan said 'I saw a yellow car go over and my legs felt funny'

I realised at that point what I was doing to my gang.

The arrival of this piece in my email in-box was unexpected but very welcome. The tone is typical of Dad: funny, self-deprecatory, with a rueful comment at the end. Co-incidentally, I had written about the same incident a few months earlier, as part of my doctoral studies into memoir. I had needed a big dramatic memory to write about, and that was the one that sprang to mind.

I remember seeing something black bouncing across the curve of the track and wondering what it was. Sometimes it feels as if your mind moves very slowly. It must have been less than a second before Dad's car cartwheeled onto its back and skidded into the deep gravel trap on the bend. It all happened very fast and yet it seemed as if I was puzzling over that black bouncy thing for a while.

We were at Brands Hatch. There's a long, fast straight in front of the stands, and then the track curves uphill, still a fast stretch. When the 'Yellow Peril' came past, we must have checked the lap time and maybe I was making a note of it and eating a fish-paste sandwich when the bouncing wheel made me look again.

I remember the three of us trying to get down, through the stands, by climbing over the seats, they were just concrete pews with flat, blue plastic bench-tops and the stand was pretty empty but scrambling down to the trackside fence was nightmarish, it just took so long, grabbing not to fall, bashing our shins and we needed to watch what was happening on the track more than where we were going, so we were tripping and stumbling and maybe screaming.

Down below us, the pace car was out, red and black flags, the race was slowed, then stopped, and other drivers pulled over to help. And we were still trying to get there, and I knew, maybe I heard somebody say it, that the car might catch fire.

Then we were up against the high, wire fence by the pits, the place was noisy and blue with sweet, choking exhaust and confusion as MGs and Sprites braked and pulled off the track and all the while, the commentator was shouting with excitement through the loudspeakers, he thought it was a different yellow car! and another driver! and we were yelling across the engines, that's my dad! They still hadn't dragged him out of the wreck, the other drivers were trying to rock it back onto its three wheels when the ambulance came tearing past us and parked to obscure the view. I bet they do that deliberately.

I remember, on top of the fear and the shock, a rising sense of anger and disbelief, nobody knew what to do with us, we watched the ambulance drive away from the cars, blue lights flashing and we knew he must be in there but nobody seemed to know if he was OK or where the ambulance was going. It was hard to get information when people just wanted to calm us down. The not knowing wasn't the worst bit, the worst bit was seeing the other drivers trying to get him out and knowing that, upside down, petrol and oil running onto a hot engine could easily catch fire. But the not knowing was horrible and seemed to last a long time until somebody said the ambulance was in the paddock, and then we knew where to run to.

The weather must have been somewhere between fine and slippery, which accounts for a last-minute wheel-change ('Bob Luff's gone to slicks! What's Siddery-Smith up to? Kids, go and look!'). I don't entirely trust the memory I have of a sunburst illuminating the back doors of the ambulance as they flew open and there was Dad, standing there wild-eyed and grinning with his arms stretched wide like the resurrected Christ. I'm not sure I believe that he leapt from the back of the ambulance and hugged us all. I know the moment was brief, because they were towing the car in and everybody wanted to go and see the damage. What a write-off, the fibreglass top crushed around the roll-bar, the lights all smashed, the smell of scorched paint and hot oil on hot metal. Later, Dad retrieved a twisted lump of steel that was never supposed to be twistable and made it into a new trophy for the club. Best crash of the year.

What a story to tell, how grown-up and proud I felt as we towed the spectacularly wrecked car home that night, how fizzy pride took over from fear and we laughed ourselves silly over the holes that the leaking battery acid had made in Dad's underwear.

My version of the story seems so much more dramatic than Dad's. I was a bit surprised by his laid-back tone – it seemed as if my experience was more traumatic than his, and I felt a bit peeved that he could be so blasé about it when I was still pressed up against that high wire fence breathing in blue exhaust fumes and watching the ambulance scream past! Surely he must have been at least as terrified and shocked as me, but we both wrote about the same event some forty years later and perhaps I was playing it up and he was playing it down.

When Dad's contribution landed, I suddenly knew and understood a lot more of the story. Not surprisingly, my memory was wrong, the risen Christ in the ambulance was a strange bit of mythologising and the story about having to change the tyres because of a change in the weather was purely a means to explain why the wheel came off – even though the unreliable memory was lent some extra believability with added snippets of conversation that seem very real to me.

Having two contrasting points of view made it obvious that my memory wasn't entirely accurate. That shouldn't have been a great surprise – you don't have to study memoir in any great depth to realise that memory is fallible and that our stories are necessarily curated. I wasn't surprised that Dad hadn't emerged from the back of an ambulance like Lazarus rising from the dead, but I was surprised that my sense-making around the cause of the accident was so wrong. I can't see how I could have made up the story about the wheels having to be changed at the last minute. I suspect that there was an explanation needed at the time, and needed fast, and that somebody, almost certainly Dad, came up with it, and it made enough sense to settle us. I hadn't heard the story about the washers and the axle stands before, and it seems to me that Dad might have been unwilling to come clean about the real cause of the accident (or not accident) until now.

Dad's confession of his mistake shifts the arc of the story. He looks back in judgement upon his own behaviour – his casual lack of attention to his own safety, his belated realisation of the effect of that on his family. The old memory is pressed into service for a new story, one full of regret and self-blame which (I think) is closely connected with his feelings of guilt and loss around Mum's death.

As well as being surprised by the new narrative, I was a bit annoyed. Why did it take so long for me to get the truth? You might have told me.

Michael Hainey's memoir, *After Visiting Friends*, describes a search for truth partially driven by a childhood memory which is ultimately undermined. Hainey recalls that when their mother told her two young sons that their father was dead, his brother cried, and Michael laughed at him. It's a painful memory that haunts him. Towards the end of the book, the brothers have a conversation ...

> And I tell him the story I've carried with me all these years, and he listens and says, "Huh. No, I don't remember that."

> The thing I remember so vividly, he has no memory of. And vice versa. And part of me thinks, Did any of this happen? Or did we all black out so much of what we didn't want to remember? (2013, 96)

In *The Scent of Dried Roses*, Tim Lott (1996, 269) speaks of the familial story-making that arose after his mother's suicide: 'It is a point of view with which everyone who knew Jean seems to concur. Her life was a good life. Her mind was always healthy.' But his mother's patchy medical notes show that she was treated with strong drugs generally used in the management of epilepsy, schizophrenia and paranoia, for years and years. The story that everybody has agreed to tell is a lie. In 'Postcards, Ghosts, and Fathers', Barbara Jago (1996) writes about the gradual emergence of her family story, as told by her mother.

> My mother told me about my father and his disappearance gradually, doling out the details of her story in pieces, like Halloween candy, as she deemed me "old enough" to understand and cope with her version of the truth.

So, at nine, Barbara learned that her mother and father 'did not get along'. At thirteen, she learned that her father was alcoholic; at eighteen, that he was unfaithful; at 22, that he was verbally abusive. At 28, she learned that her father had had her mother confined to a mental institution for two years.

***

Reading Dad's story somehow made me feel quite alone. I felt unmoored, as if something important that I thought held us together as a family had been illusory. I had assumed that the memory of that day would be something that all three (all four) of us would have in common, a shared experience, a traumatic experience we all went through together, something we would all remember vividly. Perhaps I was hoping for a 'missing link' when I decided to email Alan, to see if I could get him to write about the crash from his perspective.

For dad crashing at Brands, sorry - I don't recall much at all. How old were we?

We were watching with mum in the stands, probably recording times with the orange stop-watch, as he would have just gone past us on the straight.

I really just remember seeing yellow/orange turn black from the corner of my eye as the car flipped and seeing the wheel.

Nobody was sure who it was, a lot of shock with the spectators, and more as they realised we were the family.

I don't recall reaction from you or mum or how we found out he was ok.

Was I gently shielded from looking as they got him out? Seems likely but I don't recall.

He had all those daft American bumper stickers on the car. They were scratched to bits.

Battery acid melted ate his overalls.

Any injury wasn't mentioned.

That's all - sorry. I was 10?

Three different stories. Dad's rueful, self-deprecatory, a piece of hindsight about his reckless behaviour and a sense of sadness around losing the family, felt strongly again after Mum's death. Mine, dramatic and emotional, with central themes of dislocation, fear and loss. My story is about losing Dad and nobody else in the world really understanding, of being a stranded family of three that nobody knew what to say to or how to deal with, of no longer belonging in that world by the racing track, a sudden loss of identity, happily rectified and laughed off when the four of us were back in the camper van with all four wheels, safe again. Alan is the only one of the three of us not attempting to craft a story that has a satisfying conclusion. His account doesn't make meaning of the event. 'I don't recall.' 'I was 10.' It looks and feels like a poem, a suitably fragmented style for his fragmentary childhood memory.

Ester Shapiro (1998, 99) speaks of grieving as a relational process, and of families being linked through 'unbreakable chains of memory and meaning': 'every family coping with grief needs to incorporate these collective memories in attempting to rebuild meaningful lives.' How am I to deal with the sense of loss and loneliness that comes from the realisation that a highly impactful shared family experience has not left us with a shared family memory? The idea that shared memories hold our fragmented family together is no more than a myth, and the idea that we might strengthen ourselves as a family unit by writing about our shared memories is all wrong – it just exposes our differences. Without Mum, the family is well and truly broken. The wheels are coming off this ride.

Dad messages me: in the past fortnight of lockdown (and strict self-isolation, so not much hope of a handyman ...) he has experienced blocked drains, a leaking roof and a kitchen fire. He writes 'Three wheels on my wagon ... ', and decorates his message with a treble clef and a frazzled-looking emoji. It amazes me that this snatch of song crops up so often in our lives. My experiment in bringing us together as a family around a shared memory has failed, but at least it has illuminated what we do have in common: we are self-deprecatory; we tend to minimise emotional stuff and hurry towards the positive (even when we are in flames at the reins); we have a dark sense of humour.

Dad messages me again: He has had an accident involving an experiment with a pressure cooker, and blown up his shed. He can't stop laughing.

> Narrative, I now think, facilitates the ability to go on by opening up possibilities for the future through retelling the stories of the past. It does this not by re-establishing the illusions of coherence of the past, control over the present, and predictability of the future, but by making it possible to carry on without these illusions. (Brison 2002, 104)

Disclosure statement

No potential conflict of interest was reported by the author(s).

ORCID

Jane Hughes ⓘ http://orcid.org/0000-0002-2934-3096

References

Brison, Susan. 2002. *Aftermath: Violence and the Remaking of a Self.* Princeton: Princeton University Press.

Fowler, Kathleen. 2007. "'So new, So New': Art and Heart in Women's Grief Memoirs." *Women's Studies* 36 (7): 525–549.

Frank, Arthur W. 2013. *The Wounded Storyteller: Body, Illness, and Ethics.* 2nd ed. Chicago: The University of Chicago Press.

Gilbert, Kathleen L. 2002. "Taking a Narrative Approach to Grief Research: Finding Meaning in Stories." *Death Studies* 26: 223–239.

Hainey, Michael. 2013. *After Visiting Friends.* New York: Scribner.

Jago, Barbara J. 1996. "Postcards, Ghosts, and Fathers: Revising Family Stories." *Qualitative Inquiry* 2 (4): 495–516.

Lott, Tim. 1996. *The Scent of Dried Roses.* London: Penguin.

May, William F. 1991. *The Patient's Ordeal.* Bloomington, IL: Indiana University Press.

Neimeyer, R. A. 1995. "Client-generated Narratives in Psychotherapy." In *Constructivism in Psychotherapy,* edited by R. A. Neimeyer, and M. J. Mahoney, 227. Washington, DC: American Psychological Association.

Pithouse-Morgan, Kathleen, Mathabo Khau, Lungile Masinga, and Catherine van de Ruit. 2012. "Letters to Those who Dare Feel: Using Reflective Letter-Writing to Explore the Emotionality of Research." *International Journal of Qualitative Methods* 11 (1): 40–56.

Shapiro, Ester. 1998. "The Healing Power of Culture Stories: What Writers can Teach Psychotherapists." *Cultural Diversity and Mental Health* 4 (2): 91–101.

Vandenberg, Kathleen M. 2017. "Joan Didion's Memoirs: Substance & Style." *Prose Studies* 39 (1): 39–60.

Worden, J. William. 1991. *Grief Counselling and Grief Therapy: A Handbook for the Mental Health Practitioner.* 2nd ed. London: Routledge.

🔓 OPEN ACCESS

Becoming a Traitor

Linus Hagström ⓘ

ABSTRACT
In this autobiographical essay, I narrate my experience of being positioned in public as naive in my profession and a traitor to my country after publishing an op-ed in Sweden's largest daily newspaper, in which I argued that Sweden should not join NATO — the transatlantic military alliance. Some of the negative reactions came from within my own workplace. I had just been promoted to Professor at the Swedish Defence University and colleagues thought I had also betrayed them and the university by publishing the piece. In this essay, I disclose some of the reactions I encountered but, more importantly, I try to understand the effect they had on me, recounting my own inner dialogue of shame and resistance. At times I worried that I lacked expertise or even secretly harboured an affinity with the country that is now seen to motivate a Swedish NATO membership — i.e. Russia. At other times, I tried to turn the tables on the stigmatisers, claiming that it was they who had to change. While I work in a highly militarised environment, I think the fear of social death and professional shame I explore in this essay has broader resonance.

I.

Standing in the middle of the schoolyard in the suburban community south of Stockholm where I live, I anxiously observe the large crowd of well-dressed parents and relatives. My kids' summer graduation ceremony is about to begin. The morning sun is blindingly bright, but that is not only why I regret having forgotten to bring my sunglasses. It would have felt so good to hide behind them right now. I may look myself, but my body is restless — hands and legs trembling imperceptibly, while the stomach is sending out signals of both uncontrollable hunger and profound nausea. I am not sure if she can sense that something is wrong, but my wife takes my hand.

We are approached by two neighbours, one of whom asks smilingly: 'Did you get much reaction to your NATO piece?' Based on what I think I know about his political views, I interpret the question as insinuating and perhaps scornful. But he might just be feeling uncomfortable about seeing me given that this very morning, editorials in two of Sweden's major dailies have accused me of toeing the Kremlin's line for arguing that

---

This is an Open Access article distributed under the terms of the Creative Commons Attribution-NonCommercial-NoDerivatives License (http://creativecommons.org/licenses/by-nc-nd/4.0/), which permits non-commercial re-use, distribution, and reproduction in any medium, provided the original work is properly cited, and is not altered, transformed, or built upon in any way.

Sweden should stay out of NATO, the transatlantic military alliance (*Dagens Nyheter 2015*; Johansson 2015; Johansson 2015a). We are surrounded by music. The ceremony is starting now so there is no time to ask what he meant, to try to defend myself or express disappointment at the apparent lack of moral support. I just nod defensively but moments later I can feel defiance rising up inside me. As the school choir starts to sing, I tell myself I do not need to hide; I have nothing to be ashamed of.

II.

Thirty-three hours earlier, I am lying in bed, scanning the Internet on my phone. I should have been able to fall asleep happily as my co-authored op-ed has just appeared online for the most prestigious page for political debate in Sweden. But my initial pride in having had the article published is already giving way to a growing sense of unease. As I update the newspaper's homepage time and again, waiting for readers' comments to appear, I scrutinise our argument: Swedish NATO membership risks aggravating the Russian sense of physical insecurity, a point University of Chicago professor John Mearsheimer (2014) has made about post-Cold War NATO enlargement. It might also deal a further blow to a fragile Russian great power identity — a topic explored by Norwegian international relations scholar Iver Neumann (2016a, 2016b). To prove beyond reasonable doubt that Russia *is* a great power, insulted Russian leaders might act even more as if the country were one. This would then make Sweden less, rather than more, physically secure (Hagström and Lundborg 2015a).

My co-author and I were convinced that our argument would fill a gap in the Swedish security debate. Since its annexation of Crimea the year before, Russia has been increasingly represented as a threat to the extent that joining NATO is now supported by a majority of the Swedish population. I think we may have been hoping to defeat Swedish NATO supporters using an argument drawn partly from their own preferred theory. But the first few comments are critical and demeaning, and I start to worry that those who want Sweden to join NATO will not yield so easily. Lying there wide-awake in the light of early dawn I am haunted by two disturbing thoughts: Am I unqualified to take part in this debate? Do I sympathise with Russia? I know that the answer to both questions is no, but cannot help also feel: 'well, maybe'.

Is it possible that I remain a child in my outlook, despite the fact that I have become a professor of political science specialising in security policy, let alone one working at the Swedish Defence University? One childhood friend at least tells me that to this day I fail to understand that states have to fend for themselves through armaments and alliance-building. He says my childish naivety is a luxury typical of both Swedes and academics. But is it *just* naivety or do I remain a child also in the sense of being anti-American? Some of my earliest childhood memories are of demonstrations against the US war in Vietnam and against Franco and Pinochet — the US supported dictators in Spain and Chile. Is it possible that being raised to be critical of US foreign and security policy has made me inadvertently sympathetic to Russia? Have I fallen into the tiresome trap of treating the enemy of my enemy as my friend?

I am highly alert now and sleep does not feel like an option. I hope my tossing and turning will wake my wife. I want to tell her I feel vulnerable and hope that she will rub my back and say that everything will be fine — but she just continues to sleep quietly next to me. After hours of agony over things I cannot control, I finally doze off after the blackbirds have already started to sing in our garden.

The following morning, I am riding the subway to work. Sitting there, sleep-deprived in the packed train, I remain anxious, but I also feel a tiny bit excited. My article has now appeared in the paper version of *Dagens Nyheter*, which several people on the train are reading on their way to work. I observe them and try to decipher from the looks on their faces if they might like our argument or if they, like some early readers last night, find it problematic and suspect. It is hard to tell, of course, and for now I decide to take it as a good sign that no one seems to recognise me.

In my briefcase, I have a red paper heart that my eight-year-old daughter gave me just as I was leaving for work, her sprawling letters say: 'Good luck today, Dad'. She and her older brother know I am under some pressure at work but have only a vague notion of why. As I finally got a chance over breakfast to ask my wife how to deal with the criticism I had received during the night, they interjected all sorts of questions: 'What is this NATO that some people want to join?'; 'Is the USA better or worse than Russia?', 'Is Putin crazy?', 'Why are they criticising you, Dad?' Not only did they constantly interrupt my private therapy session, but I was also unable to formulate any satisfactory answers. Perhaps there is less certainty than they think, and I need, but the heart in my bag at least provides me with a sense of comfort.

III.

As I arrive at work less than an hour later, I put up a shield as I walk the corridors filled with military memorabilia, and paintings and photographs of generations of Swedish officers. A few colleagues look up from their computers, smile and say 'good morning' as I rush by their open doors. We do this every day but one question — whether I am 'ready for the rough ride' — seems to confirm my suspicion that there is more than just curiosity in the air. I smile and respond with fake confidence, puffing myself up like a threatened frog. I do not want anyone to know that I am *not* ready.

Even the most mundane tasks prove challenging this morning. As my hand moves the mouse, the cursor circulates restlessly on the computer screen, but my mind does not quite follow. I jump at the ding of each new email, hoping to get some moral support at last, but there is just more scorn and contempt to process. One person asks, 'the simple question' whether we have 'considered what might happen if we let Russia decide what Sweden should and should not do'. A retired brigadier general, moreover, writes to share his criticism of the 'myth that Russia has been humiliated by the West'. Response op-eds from various politicians, pundits and scholars also start to appear in the online version of the newspaper — seven in two days, which is more than any op-ed on Sweden's relationship with NATO has received in the past few years. They are unanimously critical of us for 'lacking logical anchoring' (Albinsson 2015), 'presenting various excuses for Putin's violations of international law' (Askeljung et al. 2015) and, in essence, 'proposing 'Munich 2', the result [of which] ... was the Second World War' (Vinokuras 2015). The second biggest daily also publishes an editorial, saying that our op-ed is as unlikely as if two teachers at the Royal Institute of Technology were to argue that the earth is flat (Johansson 2015b).

The op-ed is shared on social media almost 4000 times in the first few days. On Twitter, the discussion explodes; my co-author and I are accused of 'losing our academic integrity' and 'whoring around for Putin' through our 'tendentious analysis'. One tweet represents the op-ed as 'shallow' and 'reflective of Russia's propaganda model'. Other tweets say we are surely on 'Putin's payroll' and express surprise that we are allowed to call ourselves 'researchers' and 'be paid a salary'. Yet others question our authority to debate Swedish NATO membership in the first place — but there is no consensus on whether we are just a joke reminiscent of the Marx Brothers, as suggested by one tweet, or 'traitors' 'for being officially used in Putin/the Kremlin's propaganda war', as argued by another.[1]

My fears from last night appear confirmed. We are indeed being accused of both naivety and treachery. I know these are not the same thing, but both allegations pull the rug from under my feet in similar ways. In the end, it does not really matter whether I am writing ludicrous things because I am colluding with the enemy or because I just happen to lack expertise. The little support we do get does not make things any easier, as it comes mostly from people and organisations I do not want in my corner. Apart from a few disenfranchised social democrats, it is a motley crew of left wing anti-imperialists so sceptical about everything American that they seem to support anything anti-American, including North Korea or indeed Vladimir Putin; the Russian news agency, Sputnik News; and the booming online alt-right media, which argues that the Swedish military should be strong enough to take care of national defence on its own (*Fria Tider 2015*; Frick 2015; Jinge 2015; Romelsjö 2015; Sandin 2015; *Sputnik News 2015*; Widegren 2015). It feels strange and unnerving that almost no legitimate actors are offering any encouragement (one exception is Bjereld 2015). I try to comfort myself that they are keeping quiet because public support for us would just add fuel to the fire, by mobilising opponents and friends that no one wants. But any sense of relief is highly transient. If our op-ed also just ended up energising the wrong people, was it a mistake to write it? Or are opponents of Swedish NATO membership keeping quiet because they too have *realised* that Sweden must change its security policy in the face of a rapidly changing strategic environment? Why am I unable to recognise what so many others have begun to take for granted?

Colleagues from the Swedish Defence University also publish two rejoinders in the major dailies. One criticises Mearsheimer's argument as 'reflecting ... ignorance about NATO enlargement and Russian behaviour in Ukraine, and a theoretically one-eyed position with problematic implications for defence and security policy practice' (Engelbrekt 2015). Under the headline, 'The War at the Swedish Defence University', the other 'seeks to nuance the image of the research that is conducted' at our university. It makes a distinction between the 'insights' it provides and our 'opinions', which 'lack objective support' (Edström et al. 2015). These articles are decidedly more academic in tone and content than some of the other criticism, but our colleagues seem equally annoyed by the op-ed.

'Part of the university is in uproar', a close confidante tells me in the late afternoon, 'I hear that some people are really mad and want to see you guys fired'. Are faculty members concerned that the op-ed might rub off on the university and undermine the reputation for expertise and legitimacy it has carefully sought to craft over the years? Do they worry that if the government were to listen to us, it might jeopardise the funding hikes we are expected to get thanks to the notion that Russia is becoming increasingly threatening? It feels like an abyss is opening up at the university, and I cannot even conceive of a way to bridge it by asking people in person. I try to understand them, but most of all I worry about how this might affect me.

On my way home from work my head continues to process different scenarios, as if on autopilot. There should be no legal grounds for my dismissal, but I am aware that employers have significant leeway in getting rid of employees they no longer want on the payroll. Being one of the newest political science faculty members might make it even easier for the university to get rid of me. Even if I am allowed to stay, I fear some colleagues might no longer take me seriously and I may have to change jobs anyway.

As this long day draws to an end, just before bedtime, I get an email from a superior with a lot of clout at the university — a commander on leave from the Swedish Navy. 'Have you seen these?' he writes, attaching links to various pieces of positive commentary on the op-ed, among them an article published by a neo-Nazi group (Nordfront 2015). When I seek her advice again, my wife gently chides me for checking my email at this late hour. She says I am usually too exhausted to handle what I get. But this is a rookie mistake I keep making, so the same procedure repeats itself the following night. I am not really sure what I hope to find in my inbox, but in his response to my reply, the commander now writes that debating NATO 'is not an academic armchair exercise but one of the most central matters for a state related to the survival of the nation — it engages many ... and you have completely pissed off a number of people'.

IV.

I recognise this feeling of being out of sync with other people from my childhood. Growing up in an apartment in Stockholm's northern suburbs, mainly inhabited by working class people, immigrants and young civil servants, I was not part of any significant in-group. I was seldom invited to play with the cool kids, but nor was I bullied. I think most people respected me, and I felt little pressure to conform. I did not pay much attention to the question of identity and difference until I was 13 years old, when my family moved to a house in a more affluent town further north of Stockholm, populated largely by private sector employees and owners of small businesses. From early on, I had the feeling that I was not going to be accepted here. Other kids made fun of my round glasses and red winter jacket and called me a communist. Verbal abuse was soon intertwined with mild physical bullying. Even though this was happening in the final years of the Cold War, being called a communist did not immediately make me a traitor. Many others suffered similar treatment and I do not know what — if anything — we had in common.

The changing rooms in the school gym were particularly violent in an arbitrary way, but I was initially more shocked and disgusted by what was going on there than concerned about my own safety. The other boys had discovered masturbation and engaged in various sexual games together. One day after gym class, they ran around the shower room urinating on each other. I tried my best to stay out of harm's way but became a target, nonetheless. Embarrassed and indignant I told my teacher about this but felt as if her disgusted grimace was directed at me as much as at the urination per se. I was an ambitious student, often more comfortable in the company of adults than with other kids, but my teacher did not seem to get me. She was more at ease among, and even charmed by, the boys who interfered with her teaching — the very same ones who had peed on my leg. I think I may have sought some redress, from both the urination and my teacher, and, encouraged by my parents, I proposed to bring up the changing room situation in a meeting of the whole class. My teacher reluctantly agreed.

Standing there in front of everyone, I tried my best to project clarity and confidence, but my shaky voice and stutter exposed me. The other boys behaved well, but their confident body language and amused exchanges of glances revealed what they were really thinking. Afterwards, they let me know in subtle ways that I was no longer just different but something worse. At times, I felt ashamed of having disclosed one of the secrets that seemed to glue the boys together. I tried to adapt or perhaps rather to become invisible. At other times I entertained heroic thoughts about how I would one day leave this town and prove my worth both to myself and to them. I remember clenching my fist in my pocket and thinking: 'one day I will show these assholes … '.

I have repeated this like a mantra ever since, but do not always know to whom 'these assholes' refers — or what it is exactly that I wish to 'show'. Nonetheless, 'they' keep making me feel as if I do not belong. I worry about this but do surprisingly little to adapt. Instead, I continue to shout out how the terms of the community must change so that I can finally become part of it without reservation. Then I worry even more.

V.

Nearly 30 years later, it is the spring of 2015. I have been working at the Swedish Defence University for less than a year and just weeks earlier been promoted to Professor. I am invited for the first time to a lunch meeting for full professors in the department and try to figure out this partly unknown form of social interaction. I feel at ease as long as the conversation revolves around gossip and departmental politics, but the exchange takes an unexpected turn when one colleague recalls having watched a debate about Sweden's relationship with NATO on television the night before. Someone says the female theatre director who spoke against Swedish NATO membership was naive and that her television appearance was embarrassing and inappropriate. No one dissents, including me, but by the time I get back to my office I am both puzzled and slightly agitated: Is this a university where professors can get away with making remarks that are theoretically and politically one-sided?

I run into a colleague who is also new to the university and tell him what happened at lunch. It turns out we are equally annoyed by the seeming lack of diversity of opinion among the professors. Perhaps both of us are also slightly uncomfortable in our new positions, being employed by a university that has an intimate relationship with the Swedish Armed Forces. It only takes us a few minutes to agree that international relations theory seems to provide a number of good arguments for why Sweden should not join NATO. When I call the editors in charge of the op-ed page to pitch our ideas, they seem excited about publishing an article opposed to Swedish NATO membership written by two faculty members at the Swedish Defence University. We are excited too as we start to smash the text back and forth between us.

VI.

As the graduation ceremony continues at my kids' school, my fist is again clenched in my pocket as shame starts to give way to defiance and resolve. After listening to songs and speeches and eating strawberry cake in the company of parents who may or may not find me suspect, I ride my bicycle home. I spend the rest of the day writing the first draft of a reply to all the expert rejoinders that have been published in the newspaper. I try to restore myself by asking: why does anti-NATO have to mean pro-Russia? (Hagström and Lundborg 2015b).

When the reply is published online a few days later, I circulate a link throughout the department, accompanied by a brief email that says I want the Swedish Defence University to become more inclusive, in the sense that researchers with opposite perspectives can coexist and be stimulated by lively internal debate. I invite people to come to my office to talk to me rather than about me. To my relief, a handful of people express their support — if not of my advocacy related to Sweden and NATO then at least of my right to take part in the national security debate.

An officer who is also a postdoc circulates a reply in which he explains that he 'was angry because it [the op-ed] was so naive... and because it represents the Swedish Defence University and thereby also me and all our colleagues'. He says he thinks the article 'runs errands for the enemy'. When I respond, also to the whole department, another postdoc angrily asks us 'to have this conversation outside of his mailbox'. Minutes later there is a knock on my office door and one of the faculty members who co-authored a public rejoinder comes into my room. His speech is loud and slightly forced, just like mine, but we agree at least that there should be more dialogue.

VII.

Despite all the brouhaha surrounding myself and the NATO op-ed a few years ago, I am still working at the Swedish Defence University. To my surprise, I have been given greater responsibilities and more power too. Most importantly perhaps, I have been elected representative of the faculty members on the university board. In that capacity I have a front-row seat to watch the ceremony in which the university is to commemorate 200 years as a military academy and 10 years as a more regular institution of higher learning. As I arrive at the hall where the celebration is about to take place, I am wearing my best suit. I seem to fit in relatively well, or do I? There is the king. There is the minister of defence. There is the commander-in-chief. The whole defence establishment is here too, including a number of current and former cabinet members, members of parliament, generals and admirals. People are standing in small groups. They seem happy to see each other and many of them engage in cheek kissing — a highly unusual form of social greeting in Sweden that I vaguely associate with the upper class. The other board members are too busy talking with dignitaries to take any notice of me. I tread a fine line between puffing up like a frog again and relishing my obvious invisibility. I try to meet the eyes of a general with whom I had some contact over East Asian security a few years before, but he seems keenly focused on ignoring me. The room is full of people, but I find my seat without speaking to anyone.

After the festivities, we all move to a room where there will be a standing lunch reception. On my way there, a director general who is a former cabinet member from the conservative party, as well as a former chairman of the board of my university sneaks up on me and introduces himself. He is clearly in high spirits after the celebration. We shake hands and he asks me who I am. When I tell him my name, he looks amused and says:

ESSAYS IN LIFE WRITING — 137

'Oh yes, I have heard about *you*'. He then turns away and starts to talk to someone else. I can feel my heart pounding but I keep on walking.

Note

1. Searches on http://twitter.com/.

Acknowledgements

For helpful comments on previous drafts of this article, I wish to thank Jessica Auchter, Kylie Cardell, Elizabeth Dauphinee, Håkan Edström, Anneli Silvén Hagström, Ulf Hagström, Arita Holmberg, Tom Lundborg, Andrew Mash and Jacob Stump. I am particularly grateful to Dan Öberg, who encouraged me to write the piece in the first place and provided thoughtful advice throughout. Where possible, I have tried my best not to reveal the identities of people who appear in the narrative.

Disclosure statement

No potential conflict of interest was reported by the author.

ORCID

Linus Hagström ⓘ http://orcid.org/0000-0001-7495-055X

References

Albinsson, Carl. 2015. "Ett fritt folks fria val är inte ett legitimt hot." [The Free Choice of a Free People Is Not a Legitimate Threat.] *Dagens Nyheter*, June 9. https://www.dn.se/debatt/repliker/ett-fritt-folks-fria-val-ar-inte-ett-legitimt-hot/.
Askeljung, Alfred, et al. 2015. "Sverige behöver reagera på utvecklingen." [Sweden Must React to the Development.] *Dagens Nyheter*, June 9. https://www.dn.se/debatt/repliker/sverige-behover-reagera-pa-utvecklingen/.
Bjereld, Ulf. 2015. "Skulle ett medlemskap i Nato försämra Sveriges säkerhet?" [Would Membership in NATO Impair Swedish Security?.] June 9. http://ulfbjereld.blogspot.se/2015/06/skulle-ett-medlemskap-i-Nato-forsamra.html.
Dagens Nyheter. 2015. "Kreml styr inte Sverige." [The Kremlin Does Not Govern Sweden.] June 9. https://www.dn.se/arkiv/ledare/kreml-styr-inte-sverige/.
Edström, Håkan, et al. 2015. "Kriget på Försvarshögskolan: Fem forskare svarar." [The War at the Swedish Defence University: Five Researchers Respond.] *Svenska Dagbladet*, June 11. https://www.svd.se/kriget-pa-forsvarshogskolan-fem-forskare-svarar.
Engelbrekt, Kjell. 2015. "Mearsheimer utelämnar viktiga sakförhållanden." [Mearsheimer Omits Important Circumstances.] *Dagens Nyheter*, June 10. https://www.dn.se/debatt/repliker/mearsheimer-utelamnar-viktiga-sakforhallanden/.

Fria Tider. 2015. "Forskare varnar för Natomedlemskap." [Researchers Warn About NATO Membership.] June 9. http://www.friatider.se/forskare-varnar-f-r-Natomedlemskap.

Frick, Chang. 2015. "Försvarshögskolans exporter rekommenderar: 'Gå inte med i Nato'." [Swedish Defence University's Experts: "Don't Join NATO".] *Nyheter idag*, June 9. https://nyheteridag.se/forsvarshogskolans-experter-rekommenderar-ga-inte-med-i-Nato/.

Hagström, Linus, and Tom Lundborg. 2015a. "Natomedlemskap gör Sverige mindre säkert." [NATO Membership Will Make Sweden Less Secure.] *Dagens Nyheter*, June 9, 2015. https://www.dn.se/debatt/Natomedlemskap-gor-sverige-mindre-sakert/.

Hagström, Linus, and Tom Lundborg. 2015b. "Nato-förespråkarnas argumentation alltför förenklad." [The NATO Supporters' Arguments Are Too Simplistic.] *Dagens Nyheter*, June 12. https://www.dn.se/debatt/repliker/nato-foresprakarnas-argumentation-alltfor-forenklad/.

Jinge. 2015. "Blir det riksrätt för Hagström och Lundborg nu?." [Will Hagström and Lundborg Be Impeached Now?] June 12. http://bilderblogg.se/politik/blir-det-riksratt-for-hagstrom-och-lundborg-nu.htm.

Johansson, Fredrik. 2015. "NATO och identitetspolitikens intåg på Försvarshögskolan." [NATO and the Entry of Identity Politics at the Swedish Defence University.] *Svenska Dagbladet*, June 9. https://www.svd.se/Nato-och-identitetspolitikens-intag-pa-forsvarshogskolan.

Johansson, Mats. 2015a. "Nu är vi närmare NATO än någonsin, bra." [No We're Closer to NATO Than Ever, Good.] *Svenska Dagbladet*, June 9. https://www.svd.se/nu-narmare-Nato-an-nagonsin-bra.

Johansson, Mats. 2015b. "Oklara budskap från Försvarshögskolan." [Unclear Messages from the Swedish Defence University.] *Svenska Dagbladet*, June 10. https://www.svd.se/oklara-budskap-fran-forsvarshogskolan.

Mearsheimer, John J. 2014. "Why the Ukraine Crisis is the West's Fault: The Liberal Delusions That Provoked Putin." *Foreign Affairs* 93 (5): 1–12.

Neumann, Iver B. 2016a. "Russia's Europe, 1991–2016: Inferiority to Superiority." *International Affairs* 92 (6): 1381–1399;

Neumann, Iver B. 2016b. "From Rome to Russia: Moscow's Byzantine Myth." *Foreign Affairs*, February 3. https://www.foreignaffairs.com/reviews/review-essay/2017-02-03/romerussia.

Nordfront. 2015. "Forskare: Svenskt Natomedlemskap gör Sverige osäkert." [Researchers: Swedish NATO Membership Will Make Sweden Insecure.] June 9, 2015. https://www.nordfront.se/svenskt-Nato-medlemskap-gor-sverige-osakert.smr.

Romelsjö, Anders. 2015. "Försvarsforskare: 'Nato-medlemskap gör Sverige mindre säkert'." [Defense Scholars: "NATO Membership Will Make Sweden Less Secure".] June 9. http://jinge.se/mediekritik/forsvarsforskare-Nato-medlemsskap-gor-sverige-mindre-sakert.htm.

Sandin, Åke. 2015. "Statsvetare emot Natomedlemskap." [Political Scientists Opposed to NATO Membership.] *Förbannad pacifist* [Angry Pacifist], June 10. http://tuffsandin.blogspot.se/2015/06/statsvetare-emot-Natomedlemskap.html.

Sputnik News. 2015. "Joining NATO Threatens Sweden's Security." June 14. https://sputniknews.com/europe/201506141023340685/.

Vinokuras, Arkadijus. 2015. "Icke-provokationspolitik mot Ryssland är kortsynt." [Non-Provocation Policy Vis-à-vis Russia Is Short-sighted.] *Dagens Nyheter*, June 10. https://www.dn.se/debatt/repliker/icke-provokationspolitik-mot-ryssland-ar-kortsynt/.

Widegren, Bo. 2015. "Hela DN går i gång när någon ifrågasätter svenskt NATO-medlemskap." [The Entire *Dagens Nyheter* Is Agitated when Someone Questions Swedish NATO Membership.] June 10. http://www.s-info.se/page/blogg.asp?id=1754&blogg=68268.

My Obscure Career as an Aspiring Poet

Eugene Stelzig

ABSTRACT
'My Obscure Career as an Aspiring Poet' is an account of my struggle and endless frustration, since my undergraduate days at the University of Pennsylvania, to get my poetry published. That struggle has been ongoing for nearly six decades now, with only some few and very intermittent successes.

I

A decade ago I gathered up my collection of poetry rejection slips accumulated over half a century and put them all in the trash. There were enough of these slips—some with scribbled notes on them ('sorry, not for us'), some even encouraging ('not this time, but try us again')—that I could have literally papered the walls of my study with them. And perhaps, if I were crazy or angry enough, that's what I should have done. But in the trash they went instead. I was also tempted to consign to the flames the growing pile of poetry stashed away in a desk drawer, but resisted that impulse because with my advancing years and grey hair that would have been far too jejune and melodramatic a gesture.

II

The urge to write poetry first surfaced during my adolescence. The only poem I specifically recall penning then was composed under the (in hindsight disastrous) influence of Edgar Allan Poe, whose sonorously haunting verse had captivated both my ear and my imagination. With his hypnotic incantations Poe was like bait that I swallowed hook, line, and sinker. I wallowed in his morbid mindscapes, 'down by the dank tarn of Auber,/ In the ghoul-haunted woodland of Weir,' and dreamed of his 'beautiful Annabel Lee' who lived in her 'kingdom by the sea' with her poet-lover lying (in necrophiliac bliss) beside her 'in her sepulcher'—where else than by that very same sea. My pubescent poetic debut was melodramatically inspired by and weakly imitative of 'The Raven': called 'The Loan,' it turned on the gothic motif of a man who has borrowed a large sum of money from a friend and never repaid it. The friend dies, and some time after that appears in the solitary debtor's chamber at midnight to dramatically demand repayment of 'the loan.' Fortunately the notebook in which I wrote this piece of adolescent poetic putrescence has long since vanished. There was some other beginner's verse in it as well, and I almost recall a very rhetorically and naively patriotic poem which fortunately has not even left the ghost of an impression in my brain.

The beginnings of a poetic career are in any case inevitably imitative, and perhaps the genuine poet is one who is able to work through a host of echoes and influences, conscious and chosen as well as unconscious and unsolicited, to find his or her own distinctive voice and poetic idiom. Those who remain imitators or echo-chambers or parrots, no matter how accomplished they become at the craft of poetry, will never be genuine poets. This, naturally, I did not fully realise until many years later.

The second and very intense stage of my poetic vocation or apprenticeship came during my undergraduate years. An English major, I also took a number of courses in French and German literature, as well as comparative literature offerings at the University of Pennsylvania. Thus I was exposed to a broad range of the Western canon, including a course on Greek literature in translation with an ample reading list that began with the beginnings of lyrical poetry (I still recall liking Archilochus), took us through Hesiod and then Homer (both *The Iliad* and *The Odyssey*), and ended with some leading later poets, including Pindar (whose odes were a challenge and a revelation). A course I took in Ancient Greek Philosophy also gave me a good grounding in a legendary world in which philosophy (the pre-Socratic fragments and the *Dialogues* of Plato, for instance) was not so far removed from poetry. This exposure to a wide spectrum of books from the Greeks to the twentieth century and in several national literatures opened my eyes to the staggering and near-infinite holdings of what Goethe famously championed as the ideal of World Literature.

Naturally, I had my favourites. In my sophomore year I took a course on nineteenth-century French poetry, and became quite infatuated with the verse of Lamartine (especially 'Le Lac'), Hugo (I loved his elegiac 'demain, dès l'aube'), Nerval (and his unforgettable lament of suicidal despair, 'El Desdichado'), Verlaine, and especially Rimbaud—that precocious (adolescent) prodigy who beat all the odds by writing dazzlingly original poetry at such a tender age under the polemical banner of the *poète maudit* as a *voyant* practicing a programme of the systematic derangement of all the senses. What an intoxicating but also mad and dangerous notion! The supreme master in this constellation is Baudelaire, of course, with his *Fleurs du Mal* probably still the greatest nineteenth-century virtuoso performance of verbal brilliance and supreme craftsmanship as well as bible of modern poetry with its unique blend of exquisite sensuality ('Le Balcon'), terminal disillusionment, and wonder ('Invitation au Voyage').

Although far from being my favourites, the classical tragedies of Racine and Corneille on which I also took a course taught me to appreciate the rational control of these poet-dramatists manifest in their highly artificial and stylised (in the best sense of the word) verse. I doubt that many undergraduates nowadays cross these poetic deserts. A German course on Goethe stands out for introducing me both to his lyrical poetry as well as to his verse dramas, especially *Faust*, and his philosophical Bildungsroman, *Wilhelm Meister's Apprenticeship*, and his enigmatic erotic arabesque, *Elective Affinities*. Some of the popular German Romantic poets, especially Eichendorff, strongly appealed to me with their sense of idealised loss and nostalgia. Hölderlin and (in the twentieth century) Rilke also left their mark on my imagination. Comparative literature classes on the eighteenth and the twentieth century (European) novel were a pleasure and a revelation as well, though after reading Kafka, Camus, Celine, Malraux and Sartre it was almost too easy—in the wake of the Beats of the 1950s and the first signs of the Sixties Counterculture—to strike alienated and existentialist poses on campus, something also facilitated by a French class on the Theater of the Absurd (chiefly Ionesco and Beckett). My English courses exposed me to a huge range of poetry from Chaucer to Allen Ginsberg (the neo-Whitmanean cacophonies of whose *Howl* seemed to blast open new vistas of poetry). Among my favourites were Wordsworth, Keats, Dickinson, Hopkins, Stevens, T.S. Eliot, Dylan Thomas, and (pre-eminently so) Yeats. The poetry of Eliot (not to mention his concept of the objective correlative) was so well-known in my undergraduate circle that we would spontaneously quote portions of 'The Love Song of J. Alfred Prufrock' or 'The Waste Land' by heart after a few beers. Nothing could be more meditatively exquisite than Wallace Stevens 'Sunday Morning,' and I think my favourite poem at the time was Dylan Thomas 'Fern Hill' which I had first encountered during my senior year in high school. And if the test of great poetry is the poet having a voice of his own, Yeats was the incomparable and unforgettable champion (no matter how bizarre his gyres).

The rich literary culture in which I became immersed as an undergraduate made me feel embarrassed about my lame and amateurish poetic beginnings, but somehow did not propel me much beyond them, though I wrote quantities of verse (both rhymed and free, mostly in English, but also some in German and French). The influence of Eliot in particular seemed inescapable, so that I produced a number of Prufrockian pastiches without intending to. I had decided, however, that I was going to *be a poet*. It was a calling I took seriously—probably and comically so, *too* seriously—though I had enough common sense to know that such a vocation could not be a way of earning a living. Thus the route I ended up taking was conventional enough, especially for someone who found he could excel in academics (I was elected to Phi Beta Kappa in my junior year): I was going to go to graduate school and become an English professor by way of having gainful employment teaching the books and authors I had come to love. And I would have enough time to read and write about literature, as well as to compose poetry. Of course, little did I know in my post-adolescent idealism that far from being able to devote most of my time as an academic to reading and writing about great books, I would spend endless hours—literally years of my life—as a paper-grading grind and attending mind-numbingly boring committee meetings.

The wide range of literature I studied as an undergraduate, both within and beyond the Anglo-American canon, I now consider a necessary kind of field work for becoming a poet. If I have any regrets, it's that I didn't learn more languages than three, and that my little Latin and no Greek debarred me from classical literature (except by way of translation). From the rose-tinted prism of late life wishful thinking, if I had my childhood to do over again and if the adult me could act as the tutor to the boy, I would have him study both Greek and Latin, as well as an Asian language (either Chinese or Japanese). And I would certainly also have him learn, to paraphrase Byron, those sweet bastard offshoots of Latin: Italian and Spanish.

In addition to the many literature courses I took at my university, I also had another important benefit that both helped me become a poet and to develop and hone my critical skills: working on the campus literary magazine, *The Pennsylvania Review*, which had a well-established reputation and was in part funded by the university. I joined its student staff in my freshman year just as the only member of the editorial team to become a famous writer, John Edgar Wideman, rotated off it. The easiest part of the job was going around to local merchants and getting them to buy advertising space in the magazine; the hardest but most rewarding was the long editorial meetings (many hours, usually in the evening) when we discussed in considerable detail, and sometimes with agitated intensity—fueled by strong coffee and enveloped in a blue haze of cigarette smoke—the strengths and weaknesses of the large pile of poetry and short story submissions. What I learned in these animated sessions was to develop my own critical opinions and to defend them before others as we worked as a team to arrive at the contents of each issue. Mostly the submissions were by students at our university and writers from the surrounding area, but occasionally we also got established poets sending us their work. I distinctly remember a poem by Allen Ginsberg in the manuscript pile, but I don't recall whether or not we accepted it for publication.

I also learned how precarious or uncertain a thing expertise is in the judgment of the literary merit of a manuscript by an unknown author. This fact was driven home to me when in my junior year—by which time I had become co-editor of the magazine—we ran a poetry contest. We asked our favourite English professor, Maurice Johnson, a Swift scholar who was something of cult figure among the brightest English majors for his brilliance in analyzing texts and his dry wit and sarcastic digs at underprepared students, to make the final choice of first, second, and third prize from the small group we had winnowed out from the larger submission pile. In discussing with him his rationale for picking the prize-winning poems, I was amazed to see that this man of deep learning and keen intelligence was in fact no better than we the student editors were at the (agonising) process of deciding the relative worth of these poems: in sorting out the question of literary quality, the professor and we students were on a level playing field. This was an eye-opening and strangely liberating experience, because it cast a new light on the issue of expertise in matters of literary or critical judgment. Only many years after Maurice Johnson's death did I learn that he had been one of the founding members of the famous Midwestern literary quarterly, *The Prairie Schooner,* at the University of Nebraska, where he had earned his doctorate. As I discovered when I sent him a copy of one of my published poem in the seventies, and he in turn sent me a couple of (beautifully crafted and witty) sonnets about mortality, he was also a poet.

Another benefit of my being at the university that played a role in my aspirations to become a writer was meeting several contemporary authors. I took a course on the modern novel with a young Philip Roth, who had recently achieved national recognition for *Goodbye, Columbus* and who commuted to campus twice a week from New York City as a guest lecturer for one semester. The only books I recall from the reading list are *Anna Karenina* and *Lolita*. For the latter he shared with the class his writer's appreciation of Nabokov's superb eye for the details of American culture (on Humbert Humbert's cross-country trek with his nymphet). Then there was William Meredith, a poet associated with *The New Yorker,* who also came for a semester (once a week) to teach a poetry writing seminar into which I was accepted after having submitted a writing sample. I don't recall him having much of anything to say about the poetry I wrote for the class, and I found the studied sophistication of his magazine verse boring, and him a most uninspiring–balding, fiftyish, WASP–figure. I'm sure that behind his pose of cool and ironic indifference there were some demons, one of which seems to have afflicted his generation of writers, because at a reception in his honour in the august setting of the rare book room of the university library he got quite drunk and came out of the bathroom with his fly wide open.

The high point of my meeting a famous living author was interviewing William Styron for the campus literary magazine with two fellow editors, one of whom had come up with the idea of interviewing the writer who was recognised as the most important contemporary Southern novelist working in the tradition of Faulkner, and who had won the Prix de Rome in 1952 for the publication of his first novel, *Lie Down in Darkness*. After Styron generously agreed to meet with us, we immersed ourselves in his fiction and also read the contemporary reviews. At his invitation, we drove up (in January 1965) to his estate in Connecticut, and the fortyish author played a very gracious host and interviewee in the large barn that he had converted into his studio. I recall an array of whisky bottles on a shelf, a fact that struck me then, but one that takes on added significance in the light of his late-life and stark memoir about his bout of suicidal depression, *Darkness Visible*. Even though we were only college juniors, he treated us and our questions seriously and offered long and thoughtful answers. He also let us know after the seventeen-page interview appeared that it was the best ever done with him. The three of us had brain-stormed the questions, and Styron, who was impressed by our familiarity with his writings, engaged in extended exchanges with us. I discovered only decades later that this interview ('A Conversation with William Styron') was reprinted in a collection of interviews with Styron published in 1984 by the University of Mississippi Press. The editor of the volume, James L. West III, observes in the Introduction,

> One of the better items in this book ... is the interview conducted by three University of Pennsylvania students and published in their undergraduate literary magazine ... The students ... were well prepared and inquisitive, not only about Styron's writings but about literature and the literary vocation. One sees Styron, in this session, in the unaccustomed role of teacher, explaining novelistic techniques to these young men and revealing to them some of the conditions under which he works (*Conversations with William Styron*, x).

Styron mentioned several times the novel on which he was then working, *The Confessions of Nat Turner,* which went on to win the Pulitzer Prize but also caused a critical controversy in the politicised late 1960s regarding the appropriateness of a white author using the diary and assuming the narrative voice of an African-American slave.

Meeting and talking up close with a famous writer was something of a coming of age experience, because it demystified the process of writing and made the ambition to be a poet seem like something not utterly unrealistic or impossible. So did my encounter with a poet from New York City, Will Inman, who had been invited to our campus for a reading by our magazine. Inman became something of a mentor to our literary circle, and took an interest in me and my poetry, publishing some of it in a mimeograph poetry journal he edited. The campus literary magazine also became an outlet for my poetry, including several poems I published under the pseudonym of C.E. Bracken (I thought my last name sounded too ethnic, so I picked an Anglo name on the model of e.e. cummings and T.S. Eliot). Most of these I've forgotten, barely recognising the titles, except for a piece of automatic writing composed in a somnambulistic trance under the influence of Coleridge's 'Kubla Khan,' but without the aid of artificial stimulants. I also published a poem in a journal at the university put out by the Philomathean Society. And on at least one occasion I read some of my poems in a campus coffee house, teaming up with a friend, Robert Emery, an accomplished folk guitar player who improvised some riffs as I read. I was not surprised that the small audience seemed to enjoy his dobro guitar accompaniment more than my verse.

At some point during my undergraduate years I started sporadically checking out the poetry in leading magazines, including *The New Yorker*, *Poetry*, *The Paris Review* and some of the major university quarterlies such as *The Prairie Schooner*. I soon learned the routine of typing up several of my current poems on separate sheets, enclosing a self-addressed stamped envelope (SASE) in the submission envelope—and waiting eagerly to get a reply. This is where the epic collected edition of my rejection slips had its sad beginnings. Sometimes the poems would come back coffee-stained or the worse for wear (mutilated by an attached paper clip, for instance), so that I could not send them out for another round, but had to retype them. In the days long before word-processing, this was a tedious task. I did manage to have one short poem entitled 'Exodus' appear in the American number (volume 5, March 1964) of *Poet*, a magazine published in Madras, India by the World Poetry Society. This publication in an obscure journal a world away gave a puff of angel's breath to my poetic aspirations, and despite the rejection slips from leading magazines, I was still hoping to make my way in the world of poetry, even though I had no 'name' mentor(s) and no connections with or entrée into that world.

III

My two years of graduate study in England, at King's College, Cambridge, did not significantly change my poetry writing profile. I did publish a playful little piece in a hand-printed collection put out by a Cambridge student whimsically entitled *Captain Moonlight*. Mostly I kept what poetry I was writing (including a long and lachrymose blank-verse narrative poem cum Shelleyan dream-vision about—what else?—love gained and lost) to myself. My second year there a fellow American graduate student at my college, Abbott Small, who was very much the self-proclaimed poet going around campus giving readings, found out I wrote poetry and generously invited me to share the stage with him. Despite his eager encouragement, I stubbornly refused: I wasn't ready to reveal myself as one of the unacknowledged legislators of the Cam. In 2010 I was shocked to come across his obituary in the King's College Annual Report:

> Abbott published mainly in small literary magazines, many pieces ... His family used to tease him that he was the most prolific unknown poet in the country. Abbott's willingness to disseminate the fruits of his work as a poet was evident from the frequent readings he undertook both in the Connecticut area where he lived, and further afield.

The fact that Abbott kept at it all his life without any tangible rewards or recognition signifies the pathos, the beauty, and also the utter futility of a poetic vocation. Abbott, may you rest in peace, *mon semblable, mon frère*. His epitaph, by the way, is marvelous: 'In this place, in the stillness, may the Word be heard.'

The poetic high point of my stint at Cambridge was a reading at my college by Ted Hughes, at the time probably the best-known living English poet. He was friends with one of the English tutors, Tony Tanner, a brilliant and well-known critic with whom I was privileged to work in my second year. Tony had invited him to give an informal reading for the students studying English at King's. Other than Dylan Thomas, who was legendary for his readings, and of which I had heard recordings, Hughes was the most powerful and emotive reader of poetry I have ever listened to. Here's my journal entry of December 2, 1967 describing that reading:

> Hughes was amazingly tense and nervous. He walked up to the reading table stiffly and awkwardly and started in almost without any introductory comments. His remarks between poems were leaner, and more substantial than most of the excursive remarks characteristic of performing poets. He has a tough, rumbling, sea-washing, rock-foaming Northern accent—his vowels come out as from an echo chamber, and some of his consonants are as sharp as spiked fences. He reads under great emotional stress and pressure, as if he were literally battling with himself. His hands, his whole frame, trembled and shook. The rhythm of his speech wasn't patterned, controlled, but rough, coming in surges and swells, tumbling one over the other, in gusts. His words were things being wrenched from him at great cost ... the most emotional, emotive poetry reading I have ever experienced. The destructiveness around which his poetry surges, in human nature and the universe, the animals—wolves, otters, jaguars, snakes—sprang out of his mouth spitting, clawing, tearing, howling and were the embodiment of himself. There seemed to be no difference between Ted Hughes the man and Ted Hughes the Poet ... He spoke his last poem—rather, he lived his last poem—turned, bowed his head, and received an enthusiastic accolade.

After my two years in Cambridge, England, my next four years at the other Cambridge in Massachusetts en route to a Ph.D. kept me too busy to focus much on writing poetry, though I did participate toward the end in an informal creative writing group among the Harvard graduate students in English at which we read and discussed each others' work in an atmosphere of easy collegiality. The only person who later became known as a writer from that group was Marilyn French, at the time a middle-aged divorcee with a teenage daughter who was starting life over after having been dumped by her doctor-husband for his secretary. She read an early draft of a section of *The Women's Room*, and the get-even motive of her confessional fiction was palpable, though none of us had a clue how well it would resonate with the public.

After earning my Ph.D. (in 1972) and gaining a tenure-track position in a small state college in Western New York with a heavy teaching load, I was kept more than busy between preparing new courses, grading endless stacks of semi-literate papers, and the pressure of scholarly publication in order to gain tenure. However, I kept right on writing poetry and sending it out for publication, usually with the same (rejection slip) results. I did manage to get several poems into little magazines, but the doors of the 'name' venues remained closed to me. In this case, persistence certainly did not pay off. One major and at the time almost miraculous exception was *The Literary Review* (published by Fairleigh Dickinson University). I had submitted an autobiographical long poem, 'For the Death of My Mother,' and the editor, Charles Angoff, wrote me a note saying that he liked it and that he would try to get it into an upcoming issue. He was as good as his word, and I will be forever grateful to him for taking a fifteen-page poem by an unknown poet (Fall 1976, XX:1). I thought this piece in a national quarterly might gain some notice and open some doors for me, but such was not the case. In fact I never heard a word about it, except from some colleagues to which I gave reprints (the journal had generously sent me a large number of these). It struck me as something of a revelation when several years later, as I was helping my former department chair pack something into the trunk of his car, I saw a reprint of my poem lying in the back of the trunk, where it had evidently been thrown with casual abandon.

IV

I've been writing poetry now, off and on, for nearly six decades. If I didn't think I had some talent and had produced some poems of merit, I don't think I would have persisted so stubbornly in such an apparently hopeless task. I say hopeless, because a constant stream of rejection slips wears down one's spirits if not one's resolve. Over the years I built up—or had to build up, as a way of keeping on—some thick mental callouses from banging my head against the proverbial wall, but the pain of perpetual rejection never goes away and over time takes its toll by way of wear and tear one's sense of self and purpose. I like the Nietzschean proverb that 'what doesn't kill us, makes us stronger,' and I've tried to keep up writing poetry in that spirit. But the repeated rejection leads to anger and depression—a toxic mixture—and the sense of failure takes on a momentum and a life of its own over the years and decades. However, there have been occasional small beacons of light in that sea of darkness, because over the decades I've had poems appear in over a dozen little magazines (including five poems in *Sou'wester*). But for the rare poem accepted, there has been the blizzard of rejections.

As for my repeated efforts over the decades to get a volume into print, the long odds— until recently— have all been against me. The closest I have come to having a collection put out by a major publisher was in the early 1980s, when I actually had a reading at Norton & Co. After sitting on the manuscript for nearly two years, an associate editor wrote (in February 1983),

> Dear Mr. Stelzig,
>
> This is the letter you have, rightfully, been waiting for with anger. I have finally finished reading—on my own time—all three hundred manuscripts which showed up on my doorstep last year, each one equally and thoroughly. Naturally, I'm sorry to be returning ALCATRAZ OF HOPE after so much time but the option was to send it back unread. Your poems contain a good deal of longing within the pain and the bitterness but I'm afraid they didn't appeal enough to us to make an offer.

If there had been mounting anger at what seemed like the endless waiting, it was largely dissipated and replaced by pity for the editor having to read three hundred manuscripts, and gratitude for her taking the trouble to actually write a personal rejection (so much better than the printed rejection slips by the magazines). If not anger, there was of course the disappointment and the pall of sadness of knowing that I'd had a chance with an important poetry publisher and had come up short.

If I've kept on writing poetry year after year, decade after decade, since adolescence, and despite minimal or no recognition (never mind an audience), so that I often felt like a man silently drowning with no one watching on shore, I suppose I did so because it is simply part of my nature or the fabric of my being. Any aspiring writer wants and needs encouragement and some kind of public or at least peer recognition, without which his or her position is at best problematic. Without such recognition it is difficult to continue to **be** a writer. Self-doubt sets in, and self doubt can be very destructive, the proverbial vulture eating away at one's innards. Even if I was willing to face the possibility that my poetry found no acceptance from publishers because it was not very good, I was willing to keep on working at it and to keep tilting at the windmills standing in my way. Because I hadn't done an MFA in Creative Writing, or attended any writing workshops led by famous writers, I had made no contacts with leading poets, agents and publishers. I was in a literary Outer Mongolia and my chances of ever gaining an award in the poetry volume contests I entered were worse than minimal. The story I've heard about W.H. Auden in his role as judge of the Yale Younger Poets Prize strikes me as telling in this regard. One year, not liking any of the finalist manuscripts given to him by the press to read, he chose none of those, but picked instead the manuscript belatedly put in by one of his protégés (who on the basis of that award went on to establish a reputation as one of the leading contemporary American poets). I know from experience, having met a number of them over the years, that there are so many aspiring and talented but unrecognised writers out there struggling hopelessly against the gatekeepers of the official literary and print culture and the leading magazine coteries. The flourishing and ever-changing small press and magazine world, the explosion of the Internet and the possibilities of online publishing and accessing an audience without the control or censorship of the official gatekeepers are no doubt making some headway against the Auden Factor, and who knows what possibilities the new century holds for aspiring young poets in search of an audience.

It is that small or alternative publishing world, in the form of a regional Western New York poetry publisher whose press, now in its third decade, that finally allowed me to see a volume of my poetry—*Fool's Gold: Selected Poems of a Decade* (Foothills Press, 2008, 70 pages)—into print. Michael Czarnecki, a poet himself who runs Foothills with his family as a labour of love, turning out a number of hand-stitched volumes every year—and managing to do so on a shoe-string, a hope and a prayer— has enabled a number of poets to gain a hearing. Given the fact that I have lived among the rolling hills and farm fields of this scenic part of the state for more than half of my life, and that many of the poems in *Fool's Gold* are rooted in the landscape I have come to love, I find it most appropriate and even poetic that FootHills should be the poetic midwife to have delivered this volume to the small circle of its readers. The opening poem in *Fool's Gold* is in fact the title poem of an earlier collection in manuscript, *A Little Fire in a Wild Field*. I chose it as the lead-in because it captures best my sense of my own poetic identity or vocation. The poem's title is a phrase from *King Lear*, spoken by the Fool in the storm.

V

In the wake of the trashing of my accumulated rejection slips with which I opened this essay, I pretty much gave up on sending poetry out in the snail-mail format. The game of paper submissions no longer seemed worth the candle, not to mention the postage. In recent years, an increasing number of journals have gone to online submissions, and I've tried *The New Yorker* and *Poetry* as well as some university quarterlies a number of times via the 'Submittable' portal. True to form, they have turned me down, but that of course hasn't stopped me from writing poetry, though I notice that now in my later years the impulse to do so is getting less frequent, and the poems shorter, tauter, more ironic. And perhaps that's as it should be. But I don't plan to stop any time soon. The impulse to write, now so long-entrenched and deep-rooted, received a satisfying lift when in the fall of 2015 my college library published *Assorted Selfscriptings 1964–1985* (178 pp.), a selection of poetry from the several manuscript volumes. The library also sponsored a reading which some of my colleagues and students attended. The collection is also available from Amazon.com, and I take a sort of perverse pride in the fact that only a few copies have sold: I'm happy to report that my obscurity as an aspiring poet is still very much intact.

We all live more than one life; indeed, many of us live many different lives, and perhaps more than we are consciously aware of. My career as an obscure but aspiring poet that I have sought to give some account of here is but one of these lives, but it's a life that despite all its failures, frustrations and shortcomings is one I'm glad to have lived—and to be still living. As for the inflammatory impulse with which I opened this autobiographical sketch, I am poetically attracted to and consoled by the ancient myth of the phoenix bird, reborn ever so often from the ashes of its own immolation in fire. That's what I chose to put on the cover of *Assorted Selfscriptings*: a striking pen-and-ink drawing of that legendary fowl that I found on the Internet, its wings spread wide and indistinct from the flames consuming it.

Archive of the (Mostly) Unspoken: A Queer Project of Caring for the Dead

Margot Francis

ABSTRACT

Drawing inspiration from Ann Cvetkovich's (2003. *An Archive of Feeling: Trauma, Sexuality and Lesbian Public Cultures*. Durham, NC: Duke University Press) work on trauma and public affects, I explore contradictions in the public and private stories of my father's life, with a focus on the ways sexual, gendered and colonial power shaped the different narratives he revealed in extremity. My focus is on the development of a condoling methodology to explore this archive. Jack Francis (1918-2019) was a senior public servant in Canadian government during the anti-homosexual purges of the mid-twentieth century and a church archivist. As Cvetkovich (2003) argues, all archives serve as a technology of identity, and contain within them an 'archive of feelings' and narratives of collective life. I attempt to do justice to the intergenerational bond between a parent and child and my own commitments to de-colonial solidarity through reflecting on the connections between anti-homosexual regulation and colonial power. I hope this writing can open up what is often unfathomable in the lives that go before us, on the assumption that we can only reach for future worlds when we take seriously the fragmentary signs from the past.

Prelude

In 1987, I tell my parents I am in a relationship with another woman in a poorly planned disclosure on Christmas Eve. My Dad, in response, stops speaking to me for three months. My Mom, who had been initially accepting, sides with Dad, and the whole conversation falls into an abyss from which it never recovers. For queer people, this experience of familial silence is still incredibly common.

By the mid-1990s I am working as the coordinator for a LGBTQ+ peer education project (Francis 1997), and am involved with a woman who is at risk of losing her kids in a divorce because she now identifies as a lesbian. I am also a graduate student at the University of Toronto completing an MA. Things are tense. There is very little I can share with my parents.

One evening when talking to my folks by phone, I suggest a 'temporary separation'. Consciously, at least, I'm thinking if we can't talk about most things, then let's not talk for a while. The next day, my parents drive to Toronto to initiate a conversation I have remembered for the rest of my life—although, within the next few years they would both deny it ever happened.

When they arrive in town each wants to speak to me on their own. Dad comes first, and his central question is: 'how could I change?' I had an early marriage, so he is asking how my desire could shift. As I start trying to explain (it is not uncomplicated), he interrupts saying: '*One could say that I changed my sexual orientation, but it seemed to me that if I wanted to be loved, I had to have children*'.[1]

This stops me. First of all, it is the first time I have heard him utter the words 'sexual orientation' and they roll out awkwardly, as when you are trying to learn a new language but cannot yet fathom the pronunciation. Yet with this disclosure, it seemed he was reaching beyond what he could bear to acknowledge, in order not to lose our connection.

My Mom arrives back at my apartment shortly after this exchange. When we go out for a walk, my questions to her centre on why she takes Dad's side on this issue, and doesn't hold her own position. To my surprise she says: '*Some things can't be talked about in a family until other people die*'. When I press her, she refuses to say anything further. As we have a very small network of family the question is: who needs to die before she can speak?

That evening we go out for supper at a small Italian restaurant where Dad decides he wants to talk about the research I should undertake for my MA thesis. Needless to say, I am already fully engrossed in my project; however as the dominant intellectual force in our family, he wants to weigh in. His advice is that I should explore '*three generations in a family history and investigate how particular historical circumstances made possible or impossible, notions about sexuality and identity*'. This suggestion, coming so soon after our earlier conversation and Mom's refusal to talk, shocks me. I think, 'Dad! Mom's sitting right here beside us! She's protecting you, and you are talking as if this is just an academic exercise'. It seems clear to me that he is using my research to gesture towards his own family legacy: perhaps starting from the bachelor uncle of '*questionable moral character*'[2] who lived with his family during his youth; to his own (just disclosed) decision to '*change his sexual orientation*,' because he believed having children was the only route '*to be loved*'; to my life which is unfolding in the midst of rapidly accelerating queer movements that are creating safer spaces, but only as the result of intense struggle.

Those conversations permanently alter my relationships with both my parents. I stop being angry and instead experience an intense sense of alliance, permeated with love and grief. They each spoke what they could, and I have now become their witness.

Condolence as an autoethnographic methodology

How does one make sense of an archive of the unspoken, interrupted by rare and traumatic speech? How does one interpret a familial heritage founded on deeply contradictory evidence? This article aims to develop a methodology that can explore the intersection of individual subjectivity and systemic violence in order to engage in a queer project of caring for the dead. My focus is on the life and work of my father, Jack Francis, (1918–2019). Through a series of autoethnographic reflections I explore the traumatic archive left by one man, who amongst many others with queer desires in the early twentieth century, navigated the hetero-patriarchal currents in settler colonial Canada. I draw on the work of Ann Cvetkovich (2003, 2008) to explore the process of witnessing trauma in order to argue for the importance of making public space for very ordinary lives, on the assumption that their very ordinariness could make them historically meaningful.[3]

The public face of Dad's life is as follows: Jack Francis was born in 1918 to parents who ran a corner store in west Toronto, Canada. He was the first in their family to graduate from university and became an accomplished senior federal public servant, working with Lester B. Pearson, Tom Kent and Pierre Elliot Trudeau. In his late thirties he married and had children and in his long retirement (1977–2019), became an archivist and published in the area of Anglican Church history.[4] While this public archive presents a coherent subject, I hope to explore how contradictions in sexual, gendered and colonial power shape the narratives he told about his life in order to engage with what Hegel described as an ethical allegiance to the dead (Ruin 2018, 41). For while the public narrative presents one set of important stories, others remain. Although all stories are interwoven, it is primarily those 'other stories' that are my subject here.

To approach this project as an autoethnographic witness, I develop what I am calling a condoling methodology to listen and reflect on the complex forms of subjectivity that emerge in the context of colonial modernity. Here autoethnography becomes a form of solace which opens up a liminal space to care for the dead and hold them close a little longer. As the practice of condolence as a method emerges to explore traumatic knowledge, I turned to Avery Gordon's work on traumatic memory to reflect on her insight that those who have passed on might continue to haunt us when the stories they leave behind are symptomatic of struggles that can 'no longer be contained or repressed or blocked from view' (Gordon [1997] 2008, 4).

In order to listen to these spectres, and open up space for their consoling relationships with the living, I believe it is important to conceptualise the work of power in shaping my line of view. As Gordon writes, 'Power can be invisible … and it can be dull and routine. It can be obvious … and it can speak the language of your thoughts and desires. It can feel like remote control … It causes dreams to live and dreams to die' (Gordon [1997] 2008, 3). If, as Gordon argues, power reaches inside of us, shaping our desires, as well as the legal, discursive, national and religious structures which provide the scaffolding for social life, then how do we imagine subjectivity in this context? Gordon responds through developing a meditation on what we might aspire to in any academic research: namely the importance of treating the lives of those we write about as complex and worthy of enormous nuance. She continues,

> Complex personhood means that the stories people tell about themselves, about their troubles, about their social worlds, and about their society's problems are entangled and weave between what is immediately available as a story and what their imaginations are reaching toward … Complex personhood means that even those who haunt our dominant institutions and their systems of value are haunted too by things they sometimes have names for and sometimes do not. At the very least, complex personhood is about conferring the respect on others that comes from presuming that … people's lives are simultaneously straightforward and full of enormously subtle meaning. (Gordon [1997] 2008, 4–5)

In what follows I draw on Gordon's meditation on complex forms of subjectivity as foundational to a condoling methodology. Here I combine several different modes to approach my subject. First I honour the traditions of condolence from Haudenosaunee and Anishinaabeg territory, where I live, work and write. Condolence as method and practice was first taught through these epistemological traditions. As a white settler scholar my first responsibilities are to honour and acknowledge these frameworks as they inform my own thinking and practice. Secondly, I draw on the work of Margaret Werry and Roisin O'Gorman to develop an imaginative definition of condolence in order to better flesh out the relationship between analysis and emotion in my methodological practice. Overall, I develop a condoling methodology in order to do justice to the intergenerational bond between a parent and child, and through this to undertake the always unfinished business of reaching for future worlds that can only come into being through bearing witness to the contradictions of the past.

Starting then with Indigenous civilizational traditions, I draw from the work of Mohawk scholar Susan Hill, who argues that the Haudenosaunee condolence ceremony is one of the foundational practices structuring local, intra-community and international diplomacy, including with settlers. First initiated by the Peacemaker and Hiawatha, the ceremony is based on the idea that loss requires a profound and public ceremony of witness, supported by others in community, in order to wipe off the stain of loss, so the 'good mind' can return and allow one to exist in peace in the collective territory of the Confederacy (Hill 2017, 42). The condolence ceremony involves the offering of wampum strings and attention to three processes: wiping away tears so one can see, clearing the ears so one can hear, and clearing the throat so one can speak again. I am in debt to Haudenosaunee and allied scholars and friends who have taught me about this older and still active tradition.[5]

In the prelude to this article, and in what is to follow, I juxtapose autoethnographic excerpts with historical and analytic commentary in order to write as a form of condolence and witness. Drawing from Haudenosaunee theories about the importance of grief being mediated through a profound and public ceremony I place these stories in conversation with a broader intellectual and affective community. This writing presents a fragmentary archive. I present these fragments to clear my ears, so I can hear, my throat so I can speak, and meditate on what it might mean to live collectively and struggle for peace.

Secondly, I draw from the work of Margaret Werry and Roisin O'Gorman on pedagogy and emotion, to flesh out an imaginative etiology for the idea of 'condolence' that might signal its affective role in fuelling this research. Here I riff on the dictionary definition of the term in order to imagine a methodology that can provide a container for this writing:

> con·do·lence, noun: (a) solace, consolation, fellow feeling … [emotion] at work in listening to suffering. (b) a delicate thread drawn between the past and the present; awareness of the past waiting to haunt and animate the present … (c) synonym: empathy, pity, compassion

> Related to doleful (adjective): late 13c, from Middle English dole "sorrow, lamentation" a verb from root *delh- "to chop," "under the assumption that pain was expressed by the feeling of 'being torn apart'."[6]

I develop a condoling methodology to listen and sketch out the complex forms of subjectivity that emerge in the context of colonial modernity. In order to develop this narrative I draw on a range of difficult conversations Dad initiated during moments of extremity. These forms of traumatic speech are juxtaposed with research on the discursive organisation of sexual, legal and state power in order to historicise the contradictions that come into view. Through these reflections I hope to develop a more richly nuanced analysis of the scope, subtlety and meaning of hetero-patriarchal power for those with same sex desires in Canada and the condoling attachments that mediated these contradictions. In the prelude I started with the first haunting exchange that prompted my interest in developing this project and in the remainder of this article I alternate these autoethnographic reflections with historical and theoretical analysis. I conclude with a consideration of the links between anti-homosexual regulation and colonial power in order to reflect on the civilizational context which shaped Canadian modernity. Overall I aim to develop a mode of investigation that reflects on the impacts of modern systems of power on individual subjectivity and the liens, costs, and consolations that ensue.

Three generations in a family history

Here I respond (over thirty years later) to Dad's suggestion to research *'three generations in a family history and investigate how particular historical circumstances made possible or impossible, notions about sexuality and identity'*. My intent is to work through the condoling methodology sketched out above and thus to listen again, and differently, to the suggestion for research my Dad first made many decades ago. The focus will be on the historical context of the late 19th and early-to-mid-twentieth century Canada to trace the circumstances in which my grandparents and my Dad's generation came of age. In my conclusion I'll return to the contemporary era.

Drawing on Gary Kinsman's important work on sexuality and social history in Canada, one key index facing earlier generations of men with same gender desires was the criminalisation of 'sodomy' from confederation in 1867 until 1969.[7] In 1892, during the decade my Dad's parents were born, the Canadian Criminal Code was changed to prohibit acts of 'gross indecency' between men. As sodomy laws required direct evidence of sexual activity, the new wording allowed the law to have greater reach. The prison sentence for gross indecency was a maximum of five years and also included flogging or whipping (Kinsman 1996, 100–101 and 128–134). In addition to law, social purity campaigners were influential and they grouped sex between men together with other discouraged sexual activities (such as prostitution or masturbation) as a 'social evil' or a 'sexual perversion'. Clearly Christian notions of non-heteronormative and non-procreative sex as sinful as well as criminal, dominated this period (Kinsman 1996, 85).

Nevertheless, these discourses had an uneven reach in attempts to name and control sexual behaviour. Most historians now agree that the very definitions of what constituted same gender sex were differently understood, organised and named—or, often left deliberately unnamed, during this period. Contemporary ideas of sexual acts constituting distinct sexual 'identities' were *not* widespread and neither was the assumption that people could be easily defined on the basis of a binary hetero-versus-homo sexual identity (Chauncey 1994, 96–97). For example, George Chauncey's research suggests that some men participated in same-gender sex without fear of being labelled effeminate or 'queer' by asserting the 'masculine' position in the sexual activities they engaged in with other men (Chauncey 1994, 99–127). In addition, prior to WWII, men made sense of their erotic experiences in a context where many lived and worked for long periods in homosocial environments. In this context, Terry Chapman's research on early twentieth century logging and mining communities and railroad gangs suggests that sex between men in these environments was a 'socially tolerated and accepted fact of life'.[8] Thus working class discourse about sex may have looked very different from later middle class assumptions. As Kinsman, summarising a range of research concludes:

154   ESSAYS IN LIFE WRITING

> Working-class cultures, particularly their more 'outcast' or 'rough' sections, were much more
> resistant to linking occasional same-gender sexual acts with an exclusive homosexual iden-
> tity, and had their own practices of same-gender sex that did not revolve around homosexual
> identities. Many working class men did engage in same-gender sex and were involved in the
> emerging homosexual cultures and networks, but they often participated in them differently
> than middle-class men and did not seem to feel as compelled to adopt a particular overall
> homosexual 'identity'. (Kinsman 1996, 67)

It is not clear who my Dad might have been referencing when he asked me to think about 'three generations' in a family history and the impact of historical circumstances on ideas about sexuality and identity. In the early decades of the twentieth century his parent's gen- eration included a bachelor uncle in newspaper distribution, and a spinster Aunt who was a teacher, as well, of course, as many who married. But the uncle who Dad would have known best was his mother's brother, who was employed on the railroad. Like many single wage labourers, he rented a room for accommodation, in this case from his sister and brother-in-law, and consequently he lived in the same household as my father. We can speculate that he would have spent his time in the 'rough' homosocial space of railway work, and when he was on furlough, he could also have participated in the nascent zones of same-gender camaraderie then emerging in rooming houses, hotels, and the YMCA's across Ontario in the early twentieth century (Maynard 1997, 191– 235, 2004, 378–398).

So what can be known about how these ancestors, working on the railway, in teaching or in newspaper work, made sense of their erotic experience? Here, we run into the problem of sources. There are no letters, diaries, cards, photos or other traces which could open a window into the personal and erotic lives of these bachelor and spinster ancestors in the family records, or they have been destroyed. My Dad, the family geneal- ogist, was the guardian of this archive, which I have now inherited. For the uncle in railway work, perhaps the absence of records is not surprising as working class men who engaged in sex with other men were less likely to leave behind a written record of their experiences than those in the bourgeoisie (Kinsman 1996, 65). In general though, without this material we have only court records, of which there are none. And here historians of sexualities are forced to pause, and to read from the mostly unspoken, or deliberately destroyed, about desires which themselves, may not fit within contemporary categories. For any search of archival records cannot look for a 'continuous history of homosexuality … or hetero- sexuality' (Kinsman 1996, 84). Instead we must explore the shifting ways erotic pleasure and danger were imagined, concealed and organised through economies shaped by gender, class, law, religion, forced migration and colonisation. This was a problem Dad and I were likely both puzzling over, albeit differently, in that Italian bistro, so long ago.

So what of the period from the 1930s to the 1950s in which Dad came of age? Here, we find a shifting landscape for desire and one that is starting to be influenced by medical and psychiatric definitions which are vying with older, but still powerful religious, criminal, and popular discourses. Kinsman notes that while sexuality became an object of study by the medical and psychiatric professions in the mid-to-late nineteenth century in Europe, these forms of discourse were unevenly diffused, resisted and taken up in settler colonies like Canada. In the early psychiatric discourse 'homosexuality' was associ- ated with effeminacy and female masculinity with lesbianism, while masculinity began to be seen as inherently 'heterosexual' (Kinsman 1996, 61). In the increasingly dichotomised universe that developed during the middle decades of the twentieth century, though, these practices and definitions began to shift. Kinsman assesses these movements:

> The emergence of capitalist social relations led to increasing urbanization and created the opportunity for men, and later women, to live at least partially outside family relations or on its margins. A new regime of sexual classification and policing took shape, rooted in legal and policing changes, medical and scientific discourse, and state formation. Networks of homosexuals and later, lesbians adopted the category of 'homosexual' to identify their own needs ... The major missing dimensions in this work of historical recovery are the voices of those who themselves engaged in same-gender pleasures ... (Kinsman 1996, 134)

One place where those voices did emerge was in the military deployment during WWII. This war has been described as a 'nationwide coming out experience' for the United States insofar as the mobilisation of troops and industry brought together hundreds of thousands of people in same gender networks that provided a context for erotic liaisons (D'Emilio 1981, 80–81). However, the military also provided a much larger context for mobilising damaging psychiatric labels against recruits, and in Canada thousands were discharged for same gender sex and labelled as 'anti-social psychopaths', 'psychopathic personalities' or as having an 'abnormal sexuality' (Kinsman 1996, 150). Knowledge of these discharges and a vernacular to stigmatise those who were so named also bled into the popular media and can be seen, for example, in an article by Sidney Katz (cited by Kinsman) in *Maclean's Magazine* in 1947, 'Every Canadian serviceman can recall at least a few instances where one of the fellows in his outfit was suddenly sent home for discharge because he was a "queer"'.[9]

Post WWII, the Cold War set the stage for anti-homosexual purges not just in the military, but also in the public service. While my Dad was refused for military service for health reasons, he joined the public service in 1942 and would have certainly been aware that across the mainstream political spectrum homosexuals were seen as an easy target for blackmail and therefore a risk to 'national security' as they were assumed to suffer from 'character weaknesses'.[10] As a result, many were fired, while others were demoted or overlooked for promotions or had security clearances rescinded. Indeed, as the Canadian government itself acknowledged in 2017, thousands of people lost their jobs and careers in the public service in what Prime Minister Justin Trudeau called 'nothing short of a witch hunt' (Canadian Press 2019; Gouliquer, Kinsman, and Roy 2016; Levy 2018).

Some time after that fateful conversation with my parents in 1987, I learn that from the late 1940s till 1955 Dad lived with two friends, both closeted gay men who were ambitious and accomplished members of the federal public service and the military. In 1954 Dad was 36 and it was just before the era of some of the most intensive anti-homosexual purges in the public service began. He decided he wanted to marry and through his friends connected to the local Anglo-Catholic church. He met my mother that spring at a church tea, where Mom was serving tables. They were married the following September. His friends did not marry, but left the public service: Derek Bedson (private secretary to Canadian Prime Minister John Diefenbaker) went to Winnipeg in 1958, to serve as the Clerk of the Executive Council of Manitoba, while Don Clark (Army intelligence) was ordained an Anglican priest. Both men attended my parents wedding and are included in the picture they kept in their living room of the bride and groom and their closest friends just emerging from the church.

Haunting

To become a witness to anyone's sexuality is a difficult task and consequently any conclusions I might draw are necessarily contingent. Nevertheless, to provide a sense of context for Dad's comments made in extremity, some general background seems important.

Dad wrote love letters to my Mom in the first year or two after their marriage and said he had found his purpose in life in their connection. In speaking with his own friends, he attributed his faith to Mom's deep spiritual convictions. While their relationship was not affectionate in the contemporary sense, there was a deep bond between them. While they would not use this language, both would agree that their marriage was organised through a hetero-patriarchal model, where Mom did the care work of raising the children, cooking, and maintaining the home, while Dad was engaged in paid employment which frequently meant he worked long hours and aside from this was often in his study absorbed with his own research. Dad's absence from the family and from the responsibilities of care work was a source of deep frustration for Mom and caused significant conflict. Nevertheless, all of his adult children feel with him a profound bond of love and devotion. Outside the family, Dad retained a network of male friends, particularly with senior members of the Anglican Church, and a small core of close friends who were gay men—these circles, of course, overlapped.

****

In 1976, on the day of my wedding I visit Dad in his study. He has (very reasonably) opposed my marriage on the basis of my youth. That day he tells me, with some bitterness, *'staying married is the most difficult thing I have ever done'*.

None of his daughter's marriages or common law relationships settled well with him.

Dad lives into a vigorous old age and for several decades' works in the Anglican Church Archives. After the age of 95 he slows down, and takes on the burden of care for my Mom, who is slowly being taken away by Alzheimer's. In February, 2019, at the age of 101, Dad is suddenly diagnosed with kidney failure and decides to refuse treatment. He is placed in the same room as Mom, who has been in hospital for month. She is in a precipitous decline and is struggling with delusions. Dad has been the primary support for Mom through eight years and in the past year he has asked for additional support. But throughout this time he has remained determined that he would live independently with Mom (with personal care worker support) and shelter her.

For the first two days after his diagnosis, Dad retains some lucidity (despite the encroaching morphine).

Throughout his dying my sisters and I stay in vigil in the hospital and fill my parent's room with the music of their choosing. Mostly it is classical, with their favourite being the hymn played at their wedding: 'Let all mortal flesh keep silence'. Early in the first day while he still has energy my Dad takes delight in conducting the hymn from his bed. That first afternoon, during an interlude when Mom is sleeping (and my sister is out) he says to me, apropos of nothing in particular: *'I decided to get married. It helped me'*.

Later that evening, he asks me about the dates of birth for his children. After I remind him, he says: *'I knew this would be a problem'*. He seems to be referring to the eight year break between the first two children and the last, but it is not entirely clear. Then: *'I promised myself never to think of it,'* and he begins sobbing, and is absolutely inconsolable. I hold him close in my arms; I have never seen this intense grief from him. Later when he calms down: *'I have to tell your Mother. But I need to find the right time'.*

The next day he is weaker, but at the end of the afternoon is visited by a dear friend, who is a fellow historian, and a gay man. Dad rouses himself for a last conversation that is full of archival in-jokes and deeply affectionate commentary. When the friend leaves, Dad is spent and disoriented. Mom is struggling with another delusion and in distress in the next bed. I am holding Dad in my arms, and he asks about the commotion: *'Who is that?'* he asks a bit irritably. I respond, 'It's okay Dad, it's just Mom'. He responds, with a tone of deeply frustrated disgust, *'Trapped'.*

This is the last coherent thing he says before fading into the morphine and then his death, two days later.

Reflecting on Trauma, History and the Fight for Future Worlds

In the end, we can never really *know* what we owe the dead or what they demand from us. All we can see is that here we are confronted with questions of *justice* and of *obligation* that show how we belong to a polis not only of the living but also of the dead.
Ruin 2018

In this last section I reflect on the 'archive of feelings' referenced above, which unspooled in moments of extremity. As a witness, I want to reflect on the productive power of Dad's speech, for indeed, the narratives recounted here *can* have a role in reaching for future worlds only if we take seriously what they might offer us, as fragmentary signs from the past.

First, as the historical scholarship above suggests, the psychiatric labelling and criminalisation of gay men and lesbians from the 1940s to the early 1970s was at least as devastating in scope—thinking of the numbers of people affected and the pervasive homophobic animus it engendered, as policing from 1869 forward. Hence, in a critique of the narratives of progress that shape popular histories of sexual liberation, my father's generation faced intense anti-gay regulation, particularly in the federal public service, RCMP and military 'witch hunts'. There were also real hazards in pursuing an ambition to rise to the top of the public service if there was any suspicion that you were queer. To return to my Dad's own words: *'particular historical circumstances make possible or impossible'* ideas about sexuality and identity, and consequently perhaps for him, certain life paths.

****

One of Dad's enduring preoccupations from the early 1960s onwards was the research and writing of a *Biographical Dictionary of Anglican Clergy in the Diocese of Ottawa Born before 1900* (2013) as well as several more substantive biographic articles. In this sense, Dad spent a great deal of his own considerable energies in caring for the dead. This life work involved meticulous research and contributed a systematic record of the lives of early missionaries and priests of the Ottawa Diocese, material that is crucial for future generations searching for their ancestors and claiming benefits from the state, as well as providing a primary record for future scholars with their own subjects of inquiry.[11]

In this research, Dad seemed to find a refuge. My sisters and I remember growing up listening to his typewriter clattering away in the basement study, and watching him open the mail with research material arriving by the post. Dad was invested in facts, and described his major work as a project of 'compilation' where the core of his responsibility was to sift through great drifts of material evidence rather than to embark on historiographic analysis.[12] He understood that this biographic dictionary would be the spine for a church archive, the necessary infrastructure providing a record of the men who led in generations past. At the same time, as Ann Cvetkovich argues, all archives also serve as a technology of identity, and contain within them an 'archive of feelings' and narratives of collective life (Cvetkovich 2003). In both the dictionary and in his more substantive articles, Dad's writing contributes to the literature about early missionaries and priests, as, by and large, dedicated to the work of institution building and serving early settlers, along with related projects of poverty alleviation, education and social service. The men he portrays are often exhausted by work in harsh conditions. A few despair and commit suicide, drink, are violent towards their wives, or are dissolute in their labours. But in his preface to the dictionary, Dad describes his own conclusions regarding the overall tenor of the narrative produced by his labour:

> I want to say that it has been a privilege to touch the lives of so many dedicated and committed men. Even a brief scanning of the contents of this volume will make it clear that their service to the Church and to the community at large has played a vital role in the development of Canada as a nation of largely tolerant and at times compassionate people. (Francis and Taylor 2013, Preface, 2)

****

Shortly after John Milloy's book, *A National Crime: The Canadian Government and the Residential School System, 1879–1986* was published in 1999, Dad read it, and we discussed its conclusions. Milloy actually worked with Dad in the public service before departing for graduate school and becoming a historian. Dad was deeply shaken by Milloy's meticulous analysis of the relationship between the government and the churches and reluctantly agreed that the schools seemed to have provided an inferior education for Indigenous students in an atmosphere of neglect, disease, and often abuse. There were no residential schools in the Ottawa Diocese, but many of the missionaries included in his dictionary would have worked in Algonquin communities. While these connections are rarely mentioned there this is likely because most Algonquin people were federally unrecognised, and thus within the terms of Canadian law were not legally 'Indian' (Lawrence 2012, 30). Indeed, one of the primary mechanisms of Indigenous erasure and assimilation by the state has been the withdrawal of recognition of Indigenous status—a process that continues to be enshrined in the Indian Act and Bill C-31 today (Lawrence 2003, 3–31).

While I hoped our initial discussions about Milloy's research could be a breakthrough in attempts to bridge the political divides between us, this didn't last. Instead, Dad seemed to revert to the idea that the abuses of the residential school system were aberrations, and that overall the churches represented the more benevolent aspects of colonisation while the commercial empires (the North West Company and the Hudson's Bay Company) were responsible for the worst of the anti-Indigenous violence. The bigger questions regarding the ways the church colluded with European colonial states in normalising a Christian 'civilizational mission' that legitimised colonial invasion, racial capitalism,

European settlement and imperial governance, and myriad forms of anti-Indigenous violence continued to be fraught territory between us.

Yet, those same Christian values that normalised a hierarchy of people (savage and civilised), and the (unsuccessful) efforts to convert and conquer Indigenous nations, also provided the epistemological framework for deeply homophobic ideas about normal and abnormal sexuality, labelling non-heteronormative sex as sinful and criminal, and legitimating a wide range of violence against gender and sexual minorities, including the anti-homosexual purges in the public service. This colonial and hetero-patriarchal system was stitched together through the power of church and state. The conversations we could *never* have were about the ways the civilizational goals he seemed to hold dear, *injured him*, just as they did so many others.

Concluding

To briefly complete the circle of the '*three generations in a family history*' I return to a moment, earlier in this article, and in my life, during the 1990s, when I worked as a coordinator for a youth LGBT+ peer education project and my partner was about to start proceedings in her divorce, where her ex-husband, an Anglican clergyman, would argue that she was an unfit mother, because she now identified as a lesbian. While Dad decided in the 1950s, to change his sexual orientation in order to have children, in the 1980–90s, LGBT+ people, mostly lesbians, were fighting in divorce courts to keep their children—and sometimes losing them, because it was still a common belief that lesbians and gay men were unfit parents.

There is a triumphal narrative of LGBTQ+ progress which can be used to chronicle legal and social advancements over the past five decades. In Canada this would highlight the changes in criminal regulation in 1969,[13] the furious eruption of Pride Marches in 1981, and the long mass movement to pressure for a host of legal changes including the inclusion of LGBT people in the Canadian Human Rights Act (1996), the legalisation of adoption by same sex couples (1996–2011), the legalisation of gay marriage (2005), the federal apology for the witch hunts against LGBT+ people in the public service, RCMP and the military (2017), and most recently protections from discrimination based on gender identity (2017). Each of these achievements came from the bottom up, and was hard fought.

During the 1990s one of the common arguments made by conservative Christian groups lobbying against establishing a human rights policy at the Toronto School Board was that once sexual minorities became a legitimate subject of conversation in classrooms, these speech acts would be a 'gateway' for mass conversions to homosexuality.[14] While this is clearly not the case, it certainly was true that when I first fell in love with a woman in 1984, this did provide a gateway to parallel movements that have deeply shaped me, including transnational and anti-racist feminism and Indigenous epistemologies and sovereignty. Indeed, acknowledging 'abnormal' sexual desires has been a gateway for questioning the power of the Church and state and this critique of traditional power arrangements might be what most frightens those who control the dominant levers of power. For social movements that foster mutual solidarities can actually become a powerful weapon against hierarchical state and religious power.

And it is precisely these solidarities that must lead to a more circumspect assessment of LGBTQ+ progress. For those who continue to be most vulnerable to anti-queer and anti-trans violence are those who are still excluded from belonging by a white dominant colonial state: namely, Indigenous and racialized people, especially youth, and queer and trans migrants, all of whom face stunningly common everyday violence.

Coda

> I am writing to reach you, even if each word I put down is one word further from where you are.
> Vuong 2019

Immediately after Dad's death, much of my time was spent with Mom who remained in hospital: we were both grieving. As she has Alzheimer's, Mom needed to be told Dad had passed again and again to assimilate this new knowledge. As a kind of condoling practice and in an effort to help us both navigate the loss, I asked what she most loved about Dad. She said, 'He would always do everything in his power to protect you'. This comment is, even now, how I most want to remember Dad, as someone who was there to catch me when I leapt into my life—protective and loving.[15]

Unlike Dad, Mom only occasionally took me into her confidence and her disclosures seemed less inflected with the ragged edge of trauma. I will never really know what she was talking about when she said, '*Some things can't be talked about in a family until other people die*'. Now that she is engulfed in Alzheimer's it seems unlikely that she will ever again tell me that secret or any other. But shortly before the disease took hold she said she sometimes felt like '*the people who knew least about you, were those in your family*'. Her comment hit with a sharp edge of sadness, and perhaps also a warning. And yet, I continue to believe there is productive power in opening up this archive of the (mostly) unspoken. For the narratives recounted here *can* have a role in reaching for future worlds only if we take seriously what they might offer us, as fragmentary signs from the past.

Notes

1. I have placed all Mom and Dads' words in italics throughout.
2. According to Dad, this uncle was an alcoholic. It may be relevant that rates of alcoholism for gay men are disproportionately high. Hughes, Wilsnack, and Wolfgang Kantor (2016, 121–132).
3. With thanks to Cvetkovich (2008, 111–128).
4. https://www.legacy.com/obituaries/theglobeandmail/obituary.aspx?n=jack-peter-francis&pid=191634143. Dad's publications include six entries for the *Dictionary of Canadian Biography*, on Ashton Oxenden, Samuel Massey, Brooke Bridges Stevens, and Edmund Wood. These can be searched by name at: http://www.biographi.ca/en/index.php. In addition, Francis and Peake (1997, 55–76).
5. Here I want to acknowledge my friends and colleagues Sherri Vansickle (Onondaga) and Victoria Freeman who have both been so helpful in my general thinking about Haudenosaunee condolence ceremony and in bringing me back to a place 'of good mind' from grief.
6. I am indebted to Margaret Werry and Roisin O'Gorman for their thinking about imaginative definitions of common terms in their writing on pedagogy and emotion. Werry and O'Gorman (2007, 213–230, 213). See also: https://www.etymonline.com/word/condolence.

7. My focus here will be on legal regulation of male homosexual desire. I have written elsewhere about the construction and regulation of female desire: Francis (2012).
8. Quoted in Kinsman (1996, 101).
9. Quoted in Kinsman (1996, 12). Sidney Katz, 'The Truth about Sex Criminals' in *Maclean's Magazine*, 1 July 1947.
10. Kinsman (1996, 172). See also: Kinsman and Gentile (2010).
11. Ontario has had civil registration since 1869, but Quebec did not until 1994. That meant that all registrations of births, baptism, marriages and deaths were done by the church in its parish registers. In his work at the Ottawa Diocesan Archives, Dad received many requests from people seeking proof of their age, their change of name, etc. in order to claim a pension.
12. For a review of the Dictionary, see: Graves (2014, 33–35).
13. While 1969 did mark a pivotal year in shifting government regulation of same gender sexuality—those changes were much more limited than are commonly assumed. Prime Minister Pierre Trudeau did reform laws against 'gross indecency' and 'buggery' so that no charges would be laid if sex occurred between two people over the age of 21 in private. However, heterosexual sex was legal at age 14: the discrepancy in the age of consent continued on the assumption that gay people preyed on youth, and youth could not make their own decisions regarding their sexual partners; also, gay sex in 'public' continued to be harshly regulated in bathhouses and parks, and the purge campaigns against LGBT+ people in the public service and the military (including large numbers of lesbians), lasted until 1992. https://www.dailyxtra.com/why-these-queer-activists-wont-celebrate-canadas-lgbtq2-decriminalization-story-156466.
14. I was a part of the lobby for human rights and sexual diversity curriculum at the Toronto District School Board and heard those arguments articulated directly by conservative activists. See also: McCaskel (2005).
15. With thanks to Valerie Rohy in her analysis of the final panels in *Fun Home*, (2010, 340–361, 357).

Disclosure statement

No potential conflict of interest was reported by the author(s).

References

Canadian Press. 2019. "Canada to compensate 718 victims of gay purge." *CTV News*, https://www.ctvnews.ca/canada/canada-to-compensate-718-victims-of-gay-purge-1.4506759.

Chauncey, George. 1994. *Gay New York: Gender, Urban Culture, and the Making of the Gay Male World 1890–1940*. New York: Basic Books.

Cvetkovich, Ann. 2003. *An Archive of Feeling: Trauma, Sexuality and Lesbian Public Cultures*. Durham, NC: Duke University Press.

Cvetkovich, Ann. 2008. "Drawing the Archive in Alison Bechdel's *Fun Home*." *WSQ: Women's Studies Quarterly* 36 (1–2): 111–128.

D'Emilio, John. 1981. "Gay Politics, Gay Community: San Francisco's Experience." *Socialist Review* 55 (January/February): 80–81.

Francis, Margot. 1997. "Reflections on the History of TEACH." In *Safely Out: A Collaborative Approach to Anti-Heterosexism Education*, edited by Joanne Bacon, and Vanessa Russell. Toronto: Toronto Board of Education.

Francis, Margot. 2012. "The Myth of Sexual Orientation: 'Field Notes' from the Personal, Pedagogical and Historical Discourses of Identity." In *Queerly Canadian: An Introductory Reader in Sexuality Studies*, edited by Maureen Fitzgerald, and Scott Rayter. Toronto: Canadian Scholars' Press.

Francis, Jack Peter, and Frank A Peake. 1997. "Strengthening the Faithful: The Educational Task of the Church, 1896–1996." In *Anglicanism in the Ottawa Valley: Essays for the Centenary of the Diocese of Ottawa*, edited by Frank A. Peake, 55–76. Ottawa: Carleton University Press.

Francis, Jack Peter, assisted by Elizabeth Taylor. 2013. *Biographical Dictionary of Anglican Clergy in the Diocese of Ottawa Born before 1900*. Ottawa: Anglican Diocese of Ottawa.

Gordon, Avery. [1997] 2008. *Ghostly Matters: Haunting and the Sociological Imagination*. Minneapolis: University of Minnesota Press.

Gouliquer, Lynne, Gary Kinsman, and Martine Roy. 2016. *The We Demand an Apology Network*. https://anti-69.ca/faq/.

Graves, Daniel F. 2014. "Book Reviews." *Journal of the Canadian Church Historical Society* LII: 33–35.

Hill, Susan M. 2017. *The Clay We are Made Of: Haudenosaunee Land Tenure on the Grand River*. Winnipeg: University of Manitoba Press.

Hughes, T. L., S. Wilsnack, and L. Wolfgang Kantor. 2016. "The Influence of Gender and Sexual Orientation on Alcohol Use and Alcohol-Related Problems: Toward a Global Perspective." *Alcohol Research* 16; 38 (1): 121–132.

Kinsman, Gary. 1996. *The Regulation of Desire: Homo and Hetero Sexualities*. 2nd ed. Montreal: Black Rose Books.

Kinsman, Gary, and Patricia Gentile. 2010. *The Canadian War on Queers National Security as Sexual Regulation*. Vancouver: University of British Columbia Press.

Lawrence, Bonita. 2003. "Gender, Race, and the Regulation of Native Identity in Canada and the United States: An Overview." *Hypatia* 18 (2): 3–31.

Lawrence, Bonita. 2012. *Fractured Homeland: Federal Recognition and Algonquin Identity in Ontario*. Vancouver: University of British Columbia Press.

Levy, Ron. 2018. "Canada's Cold War Purge of LGBTQ from Public Service." *Canadian Encyclopedia*, https://www.thecanadianencyclopedia.ca/en/article/lgbtq-purge-in-canada.

Maynard, Steven. 1997. "'Horrible Temptations': Sex, Men, and Working-Class Male Youth in Urban Ontario, 1890–1935." *The Canadian Historical Review* 78 (2): 191–235.

Maynard, Steven. 2004. "'Without working?' Capitalism, Urban Culture, and Gay History." *Journal of Urban History* 30 (3): 378–398.

McCaskel, Tim. 2005. *Race to Equity: Disrupting Educational Inequality*. Toronto: Between the Lines.

Rohy, Valery. 2010. "In the Queer Archive: Fun Home." *GLQ Archive* 16 (3): 340–361.

Ruin, Hans. 2018. *Being with the Dead: Burial, Ancestral Politics, and the Roots of Historical Consciousness*. Stanford: Stanford University Press.

Vuong, Ocean. 2019. *On Earth We're Briefly Gorgeous: A Novel*. New York: Penguin Books.

Werry, Margaret, and Roisin O'Gorman. 2007. "Shamefaced: Performing Pedagogy, Outing Affect." *Text and Performance Quarterly* 27: 213–230.

Index

Note: Endnotes are indicated by the page number followed by 'n' and the endnote number e.g., 57n50 refers to endnote 50 on page 57.

Abdurraqib, Hanif 68–9
abolitionism 41
absolute despondency 25
act of narration 39
A Different Path: Marginality, Resistance and Drusilla Modjeska's Poppy (Rowan) 34
Adorno, Theodor W. 17, 102
Aftermath: Violence and the Remaking of a Self (Brison) 122
A Heartbreaking Work of Staggering Genius (Eggers) 122
Alias Grace (Atwood) 38
A Little Fire in a Wild Field 147
Alvarez, Julia 45
A Million Little Pieces (Frey) 54
An Angel At My Table (Campion) 77–8, 83–4, 86–8, 89n8
A National Crime: The Canadian Government and the Residential School System (Milloy) 158
An Era of Plenty 86
Anishinaabeg territory 151
Anna Karenina 142
Anthropocene 56
anti-social psychopaths 155
Arcades Project 96, 104
archival traces 34, 36
Archives and Manuscripts (Findlay) 31
Arctic Dreams (Lopez) 57
Arendt, Hannah 30
Aridi, Farah 12
Arts and Crafts style 46
A Sand County Almanac (Leopold) 56
Ash, Susan 79, 80
Asmar, Rana 13
Assorted Selfscriptings1964–1985 147–8
Astley, Thea 25, 39
Atwood, Margaret 38, 39
Auden, W. H. 147
Auster, Paul 25
The Australian Love Letters of Raymond Chandler (Close) 53–4
autobiografiction 45

autobiography 2, 5, 25, 26, 28, 35, 36, 45, 56, 77–9, 82, 83, 86, 107, 145, 148
autoethnography 5, 150–3
autofiction 46–7

Backscheider, Paula 52
Baghdadi, Maroun 10
Beck, Zeina Hashem 10
Bedson, Derek 155
Beirut: August 4, 2020 7–8; August 6, 2020 8–9; August 8, 2020 10–14; August 9, 2020 14–17; August 10, 2020 17–19; August 11, 2020 19–20; Kristy's academic and artistic practices 20n2; Post-Traumatic Stress Disorder 20n8
Benjamin, Walter 4, 93, 94, 96, 98–100, 102–5
Ben Lerner fandom 67
bereavement 4–5, 110, 112
biofiction 3, 45, 47
Biographical Dictionary of Anglican Clergy in the Diocese of Ottawa Born before 1900 157
biographical licence 37
biographical subject 52
biography 24, 26, 27–8
Blonde (Oates) 45
Bobinski, George 53
Books that Saved My Life: Reading for Wisdom, Solace and Pleasure (McGirr) 26
Bornean Sun Bear Conservation Centre 52
Bostridge, Mark 25
Bou-Ghannam, Alaa 12
Bracken, C. E. 143
Brecht, Bertolt 14
Brien, Donna Lee 36
Brison, Susan 122
Brookes, Barbara 86
Brown, Ruth 83
Bryant, Katerina 3
Bryson, John 53
Bucher, Matt 3
Buell, Lawrence 55
Burton, Antoinette 33

INDEX

Canada 153, 154
Canadian Criminal Code 153
Canadian Human Rights Act, 1996 159
cancel culture 66, 69, 72
Captain Moonlight 144
Caruth, Cathy 18–19
Carylon, David 40
Chapman, Terry 153
Chauncey, George 153
Chidiac, May 15
Chipperfield, Grace 3
The Chronicle of Higher Education 71
circus history 39
CivilWarLand in Bad Decline 65
Cixous and Khun (1981, 43) 84, 85
Clark, Don 155
Coetzee, J. M. 94
Cold War 155
Collins, Katherine 3
condolence 150–3
The Confessions of Nat Turner 143
conservation 3, 52, 55, 56, 58–60
'contentious' 36
Cook, Terry 31, 32, 40, 41
Coronavirus lockdown 11
The Corrections 65
The Cosby Show 73
COVID-19 12, 14, 106, 124
Critical and Creative Approaches 46
The Crown 72
cultural interpretation 59–60
Cunningham, Michael 45
Cvetkovich, Ann 150
Czarnecki, Michael 147

Dagens Nyheter 132
The Daily Star 12
'danger of oblivion' 30
Darkness Visible 143
David Foster Wallace Conference 64–8, 73
Daybell, James 77
DDR Museum 95
de Certeau, Michel 31
de Gondi, Jean François Paul 103
Depp, Johnny 73
de Retz, Cardinal 103
The Diary of a Nobody 28
Didion, Joan 122
Diefenbaker, John 155
Dillon, Brian 1, 2
Diocese, Ottawa 157
Dutch (Morris) 53

eco-biography 55
economic ruin 97
Eggers, Dave 122
El Ali, Rami 17
environmental interpretation 57–8
The Envoy from Mirror City 79
epistolary 3, 77

Essayism (Dillon) 1
ethnic diversity 52
Evil Angels 53

'false dichotomy' 1
family history 55, 150, 153–5, 159
fandom 65–73
Farge, Arlette 31, 33
Fern Hill (Thomas) 141
fictional biography 34
fictious character 53–4
Fin-de-siècle modernity 97
Findlay, Cassie 31, 32
Flinn, Andrew 38
flummery gossip 27
Fool's Gold: Selected Poems of a Decade 147
Forrest, John 81
Foucault, Michel 83
Fowler, Kathleen 122
Fox, Kerry 84
fragmentation 1, 105
Frame, Janet 76–8
Francis, Jack 150, 151
Frank, A. W. 82, 84, 121, 123
Fraser, Peter 79, 89n3
From Scrapbook to Facebook: A History of Personal Media Assemblage and Archives (Good) 35

Ghanem, Georges 9
Gilbert, Kathleen R. 122
GoFundMe campaigns 19
Goodbye, Columbus (Roth) 142
Good, Katie Day 35
Gornick, Vivian 35
Grand Diwan (Hall) 16
Greenwood, Agnes 34, 35
Grief is the Thing With Feathers (Porter) 122
Guernica 16
Guillette, Suzanne 25
Gurland, Henny 102

Hage, Rawi 15, 16
Hagstrom, Linus 5
Hamasat (Whispers) 10
Hamilton, Ian 26
Hannan, Leonie 81
Hariri, Rafic 10
Haudenosaunee condolence 151–2
Hayes, Tanya 56
hegemony 41
Herring, Philip 37
hetero-patriarchal system 159
Hezbollah-Israel war, 2006 10
hidden grief practices: bereaved parents 117; social world 118
High Fidelity (Hornby) 67
homosexuality 159
Hornby, Nick 67
The Hours (Cunningham) 45

INDEX

Hughes, Jane 4
Hustvedt, Siri 37

The Iliad 140
The Immortal Life of Henrietta Lacks 54, 55
Indigenous erasure 158
Infinite Jest (Wallace) 68, 70–3
In Search of Alias Grace: On Writing Canadian Historical Fiction (Atwood) 38
In Search of J.D. Salinger (Hamilton) 53
International David Foster Wallace Society 69
interpreter 52, 54–6, 58
intersectionality 40–1
In the Time of the Butterflies (Alvarez) 45
Inventing Her Own Weather (Astley) 25, 26, 28
The Island Within (Nelson) 56
Itani, Ziad 18
It's Raining in Mango 26

Janet Frame 4, 76–8, 82, 84, 86
Jensen, Joli 72
The Journal of David Foster Wallace Studies 69
Journal of Women's History's (Burton) 33

Kabili Sepilok Forest Reserve 52
Kahlo, Frida 47
Karavan, Dani 103–4
Katz, Sidney 155
Kent, Tom 151
Khayat, Rola 8–9
Khayat, Yasmine 8–9
King Lear 147
Kuipers, Juliana M. 34

Lamb, Karen 2, 36
Lamerichs, Nicolle 72
Leaving the Atocha Station 65
Lebanese Civil War, 1975–1990 8
Lebanon 2, 8, 10, 12, 14, 17, 18, 20n6
Lerner, Gerda 32
Les émigrés sont pires que les boches (the immigrants are worse than the German soldiers) 97
Lewis, Sinclair 51
LGBT+ peer education project 159–60
LGBTQI organisation 14
LGBTQ+ peer education project 149
Lie Down in Darkness 143
Life Writing 1, 2, 5
liminality 110, 112
The Limits of Critique (Felski) 66
Literary Hub 12
The Literary Review 145
Little Red Riding Hood 85
Lives for Sale: Biographer's Tales (Bostridge) 25
Living, Thinking, Looking (Hustvedt) 37
The Loan 139
'loathsome pariah' 66
lockdown, Coronavirus 11
Lolita 142

Lopez, Barry 57
The Love Song of J. Alfred Prufrock (Eliot) 141

Maclean's Magazine 155
Madness and Civilization 83
Malayan sun bear (*Helarctos malayanus*) 52
Matthews, Brain 36
Matthews, Hannah 4
McDermott, James 38
McGirr, Michael 26
Mearsheimer, John 131
memoir 20n5, 24–6, 31, 35, 36, 54, 56, 110, 122–7
mental unease 60
Meredith, William 142
metaphor 4, 27, 53, 78, 81, 84, 110, 112–18
'Metaphor and Neonatal Death: How Stories Can Help When a Baby Dies at Birth' 4
#MeToo 66, 72–3, 74n5
Middlesex 65
migration 4, 26–7, 93, 95, 101, 105, 106, 154
The Milkshake Café 44
Milloy, John 158
Misha: A Memoire of the Holocaust Years (Defonseca) 54
Modern Languages Association in Seattle 24
Morris, Edmund 53
Mounzer, Lina 10
Mozambique in 2014 8
My Obscure Career as an Aspiring Poet 139–48

Nadel, Ira Bruce 54
Natalie 57
national security 155
natural biography 55–7, 60
Neimeyer, R. A. 121
neonatal death 4, 110–12, 117, 118
Neroni, Hilary 85
Neumann, Iver 131
The New Yorker 142, 144, 147
The New York Review of Books 94
New Zealand 78, 83
Norwood, Tamsin 4
Notestein, Wallace 37

Oates, Joyce Carol 45
The Odyssey 140
O'Gorman, Roisin 152, 160n6
omniscient narrator 53
omniscient voice 53
On Not Writing Biography (Steedmanm) 33
Oregon Historical Society 30
Otago Daily Times 87
Owls Do Cry (Frame) 4, 77–8, 87

palliative narrative therapy 110
The Paris Review 144
passive recipients 2
Pearson, Lester B. 151
The Pennsylvania Review 141
Pepys, Samuel 25

Poetry 144, 147
political destabilisation 97
Porter, Max 122
port explosion 13
postcritique 3, 66
Post Internet culture 97
Post-Traumatic Stress Disorder (PTSD) 18, 20n8
The Prairie Schooner 142, 144
problematic fave 3, 66, 71–3
psychopathic personalities 155
Pye, Sarah 3

The Queen's Gambit 72

Radner, Hilary 87
Reagan, Ronald 53
Relational narratives: Auto/biography and the portrait (Tambakou) 32
resistance 41, 99, 101
Reuben, Elaine 80
re-writing Benjamin's exile 92–107
Rhiel, Mary 52
Ripa, Yannick 79, 80
Roth, Philip 142
Rowan, Leonie 34
Rushdie, Salman 25

Safina, Carl 57
Saint Teresa of Ávila 47
Salinger, J. D. 26
Scarry, Elaine 13
schizophrenic woman 82
Schwartz, Joan M. 31, 32, 40, 41
Schwartz, Susan 79, 80
scientific housework 78
security 10, 14, 131, 133, 136, 155
self-addressed stamped envelope (SASE) 144
self-consciousness 2
self-reflexivity 2
sexuality 37, 38, 40, 153–7, 159
Seymour, Miranda 25
Shapiro, Ester 128
Showalter, Elaine 82
silent witness 52–3
Skloot, Rebecca 54–5
Smith, Sidonie 41
social constructs 31
Spacks, Patricia 88
Spanish Civil War 93
speculative biography 31, 32, 34, 36–8, 40–1
Spivak, Gayatri Chakravorty 95
Steedmanm, Caroline 33
Stelzig, Eugene 5
Stevens, Wallace 141
Strachey, Lytton 51, 52
Styron, William 143
subjective empathy and imaginings 37
Suchoff, David Bruce 52

Summit, Jennifer 81
sun bears 3, 52, 55, 57, 58
Sunday Morning (Stevens) 141
Sursock Museum 16
Swedish NATO membership 131–3, 135

taboo 118
Tambakou, Maria 32
Tamboukou, Maria 41
Thea Astley 25–7, 37, 39
Thomas, Dylan 141
Thomas Report 78
Three Wheels on my Wagon 123
Tilden, Freeman 57, 58
Tompkins, Jane 1
To Those Who Follow in Our Wake 14
traitor 133, 134
traumatic peculiarities 10
Trudeau, Justin 155
Trudeau, Pierre Elliot 151, 161n13
truth telling programme 45
Tueini, Nadia 10

urbicide 12
Uses of Literature (Felski) 74n3

Vandenberg, Kathleen 123
Vanishing Points 27
Velazquez, Diego 47
Vidal, Belén 85

Walden (Thoreau) 56
Wallace, Alfred Russel 58
Wallace, David Foster 3, 37, 58, 64–73, 74n5
Wallace, Miriam 81
The Waste Land (Eliot) 141
Werry, Margaret 152, 160n6
Wilhelm, Kate 78
Winterson, Jeanette 47
Wira Nagaraku (Malaysian Hero) 52
Wolf, Virginia 51
Women of the Future 86
Women's letter writing 77, 81, 82
The Women's Room 145
Woolf, Virginia 112
Worden, J. William 122
World Poetry Society, India 144
The Wounded Storyteller (Frank) 121
WWII 153, 155

xenophobia 97

Yaghi, Zeead 14
The Yale Review (Notestein) 37
The Year of Magical Thinking (Didion) 122

Zeidan, Tarek 14
Zinsser, Judith 40, 41
zoetrope 46